Washington's Western Department

Washington's Western Department

Fort Pitt and the American Revolution

GARY S. WILLIAMS

McFarland & Company, Inc., Publishers
Jefferson, North Carolina

ISBN (print) 978-1-4766-9301-9
ISBN (ebook) 978-1-4766-5417-1

Library of Congress and British Library cataloguing data are available

Library of Congress Control Number 2024038576

© 2024 Gary S. Williams. All rights reserved

No part of this book may be reproduced or transmitted in any form or by any means, electronic or mechanical, including photocopying or recording, or by any information storage and retrieval system, without permission in writing from the publisher.

Front cover: *inset* Monument of Seneca leader Guyasuta and George Washington called "Point of View" on Mt. Washington (photograph © Chris LaBasco/Shutterstock); *background* Fort Pitt and Pittsburgh in 1759, one year after permanent occupation by the English, 1908, Edward White, and De Witt B. Lucas, *150 years of unparalleled thrift: Pittsburgh Sesqui-centennial chronicling a development from a frontier camp to a mighty city; official history and programme*, p. 2. Pittsburgh Photo Engraving Co., unknown artist.

Printed in the United States of America

*McFarland & Company, Inc., Publishers
Box 611, Jefferson, North Carolina 28640
www.mcfarlandpub.com*

Acknowledgments

As with all my books, thanks must go first and foremost to all librarians, who have been universally helpful in all my research. Another group that has been supportive is the fellow researchers and writers I have encountered. It's always comforting to exchange views and 200-year-old gossip.

However, it has been my family, both past and current, that deserves the most thanks. Growing up in Ohio, my family lived with my maternal grandfather, a local historian who was the longstanding editor of our town's daily newspaper. He not only answered all my questions about history but shared his extensive library with me. In addition, my mother was an award-winning journalist, and my father a Revolutionary War re-enactor who served for 50 years on the board of our local historical society, so both writing and history came naturally to me. Our family vacations often led to forts, battlefields, and other historical sites.

Yet it wasn't until years later, after I had retired as a librarian, that I pursued writing about history, and by then I had a different set of family members encouraging me. For this book, my brother Brian Williams provided photos and editing help, while my daughter Meryl Williams Clark helped with editing and formatting. My son Owen Williams served as the art department, editing photos, obtaining permissions, and producing the map.

But it was my wife, Lee Ann Williams, who provided the most support. It has been such a bonus having a partner who shares my enthusiasm for history, as, among other things, it provides me with a solid sounding board for any ideas I might come up with. While doing genealogical research on the same era, she discovered that she was related to a company commander who served at Fort Pitt, which heightened her interest. Traveling and doing research with such an enthusiastic and knowledgeable partner has made a labor of love even more so.

Table of Contents

Acknowledgments v
Preface 1
Introduction: 1753–1774 5

ONE. Lord Dunmore 1774   21

TWO. Connolly 1775   34

THREE. Morgan 1776   47

FOUR. Hand 1777   58

FIVE. McIntosh 1778   74

SIX. Brodhead I 1779   91

SEVEN. Brodhead II 1780   104

EIGHT. Gibson 1781   119

NINE. Irvine 1782   132

Conclusion: 1783–1794 147
Chapter Notes 165
Bibliography 173
Index 179

Above and opposite: The Western Department. Maps created by Owen Williams.

Preface

The focus of this book is the federal war effort in the American Revolution that emanated from Fort Pitt between 1774 and 1783. There are a myriad of books written on the American Revolution, but not many have focused on the war in the west. And, of those that have delved into that subject, none have stressed the federal effort under the auspices of George Washington and Continental Congress. While the American effort in the west lacked the clear heroes and successes found elsewhere, it nonetheless was a colorful story filled with fascinating characters that should be told to fill out the story of the American Revolution.

Almost all research into the pioneer era of the Old Northwest, the area framed by the Ohio and Mississippi Rivers and the Great Lakes, comes from the efforts of Dr. Lyman Draper of the University of Wisconsin. In the 1840s, Draper collected voluminous reminiscences of Revolutionary War veterans. He spent so much time gathering these priceless stories that he was not able to assemble them into a single coherent narrative. But fifty years later, Rueben Gold Thwaites and Louise Phelps Kellogg fashioned these papers into a five-volume primary source collection covering the Revolutionary War years. This work stops in June 1781, however, which leaves the final 21 months of the war uncovered.

Since then, developments have made it easier to study the western federal war effort. Specifically, automation has made it much easier to add and collate relevant material. Many historical works are now available in full text with indices online, and collections such as the American Archives and the papers of Continental Congress have been digitized and made accessible. Most impressive is Founders Online, a website that has printed and annotated every letter written to or from Washington, Jefferson, Franklin, Adams, Hamilton, and Madison, and arranged them chronologically and by correspondent. These changes have made it much easier to complete our picture of this scene.

The American Revolution in the west was a different situation entirely from that of the east. While eastern armies fought European style battles, in the west there were no rules, as all participants were engaged in a brutal struggle for survival. Both the Americans and British had fewer than 1,000 regular troops available to contest an area that covered a quarter million square miles. Both sides required proxy armies to fight their battles, as the Americans turned to the militia raised from the settlers that they were trying to protect, while the British recruited Indian allies to do their fighting. While the rival federal armies never met in battle in the west during the war, that didn't prevent bitter, smaller scale fighting in a harsh environment.

The Native Americans may have been noble, but they were undeniably savage, as they were a people for whom public execution by torture of a hated foe was considered grand public entertainment. But the settlers were just as brutal. They wanted the Indians' land, and for many, the best way to take it was to kill all the Indians. To confuse matters, the struggle for the Old Northwest was international in scope. Each separate tribe considered themselves to be their own nation, and all had their own language, culture, and agenda, while Spain and France still had active interests in the west.

Some key terms need to be explained for the purpose of this book. "George Washington's Western Department" refers to the commander of the Continental Army's relationship with the western front. The amount of control that Washington actually had over these troops varied greatly due to the ebb and flow of Washington's relationship with the Continental Congress, but he was always able to at least select his own departmental commander, and in some cases he was even able to facilitate coordination between his various departments. More importantly, Washington had a personal connection to the area around the forks of the Ohio that punctuated his entire military career.

As a 21-year-old militia officer in 1753, Washington delivered a letter from Virginia's governor to a French fort in western Pennsylvania requesting they vacate the Ohio Valley. The next year, he tried to reinforce this request with troops, and, in doing so, became the first officer to take wagons and artillery across the Appalachian mountains. This effort led to an attack by Washington that launched both his military career as well as an international war. Four times in six years, Washington was involved with efforts to take control of the forks of the Ohio from the French before finally succeeding in 1758. The young officer learned the military trade during this period, but his focus at this time was not just glory but also the acquiring of large amounts of cheap land for himself and his fellow Virginia investors.

Preface

This interest led Washington back to Fort Pitt in 1770 on a land scouting expedition. But by the time he was named commander of the Continental Army, Washington, had matured and was an American first. His decisions concerning the west were now based on what was best for the country, and his familiarity with the western situation left him with a keen interest in developments on this front. Later, while serving as president, Washington was forced to deal with the Whiskey Rebellion, the first great internal threat to the new nation. In 1794, he became the only sitting president to don a uniform and lead troops in the field. Leading 13,000 men towards the forks of the Ohio, he ended his military career in the same area where he started it 40 years earlier. In suppressing this revolt, he established peace and order over a locale that had been a vast wilderness when he first saw it.

Washington's Continental Army was divided into seven different departments. The Western Department, which was the last one created and the only one to remain after the war, was different in several ways. For one thing, the other departments had thousands of troops and were commanded by a major general, while the smaller Western Department was always led by a brigadier general or a colonel. And, while all other departments were mobile forces whose headquarters were wherever the commander took them, the Western Department was static, as the troops were bogged down in garrison duty, with the majority stationed at Fort Pitt. The bulk of the garrison at Fort Pitt left the fort's confines only five times between 1777 and 1783.

Fort Pitt was one of the most expensive and expansive British forts built in North America, and was used for over 30 years. The town that grew around the fort was not incorporated until after the war, so "Fort Pitt" generally refers to the post and accompanying activities in the town that surrounded it. In addition to housing the largest concentration of federal troops on the frontier, Fort Pitt also hosted major Indian treaties and conferences. It was the only post on the frontier that had any significant federal presence at all, conveniently located at the river gateway to all points west.

There were many other Western locales where action dictates the perspective must be shared, but these are discussed mainly in conjunction with their effect on affairs at Fort Pitt. The viewpoints of the British at Detroit, the Spanish at New Orleans, and all affected Northwest tribes have to be considered. And the recently arrived settlers in Kentucky were a special case. Early on, they decided their best hope for protection was to attach themselves as a western county of Virginia. They selected

Preface

George Rogers Clark as their military commander, and his leadership was responsible for the greatest success in the war in the west. But this success came in the name of the Virginia militia. Though Clark worked, with varying levels of success, with the Western Department commanders, no Continental troops were ever sent to Kentucky, so events here are discussed in less detail.

Some distinctions also have to be made about the dates of the American Revolution, since the conflict was well underway before it was determined that it was a revolution involving the creation of a new nation. The First Continental Congress met in 1774, the same year when Virginia based settlers defeated an Indian Army on the Ohio River without British help. Fighting broke out in Massachusetts in 1775, but the war was slower to start, and slower to end, in the west. It wasn't until 1776 that the Continental Congress even sent a federal Indian agent to the west. In June 1777, the Continental Congress officially established the Western Department and sent a general to take command, but no troops were sent until much later. With the exception of one repeater, the Western Department had a different commander every spring until the end of the war.

Each of these qualified commanders came into the job with high hopes, only to meet disappointment at every turn. Their meager forces were too small and poorly supported to take the field and too concentrated in a few posts to adequately defend the vast frontier. Frontier settlers, who hated governmental authority almost as much as they did Indians, made enemies out of tribes that were needed as allies, while the rapidly expanding population struggled just to feed itself. The continental troops on this frontier served under abysmal conditions and had few successes. The Western Department didn't triumph so much as they survived, but their tenacity helped to bring the Old Northwest into the U.S. The story of the leaders and the heroes and the schemers and the scoundrels of this theater of the Revolution is one that needs to be heard.

Introduction: 1753–1774

When considering the Continental Army, most people tend to think of it as a single unit. Even history buffs envision the same troops under George Washington fighting all those battles. But, the truth is, there were seven different departments of the Continental Army spread across the colonies. These other departments covered different regions where separate Continental forces were stationed. While General Washington's Middle Department contained the bulk of all forces, the other departments, all created between 1775 and 1777, had smaller numbers of troops whose leaders had varying degrees of connection to Washington.

There were also varying levels of success in the different departments. Washington's Middle Department fought the British nine different times, but was only victorious three times: with a surprise Christmas attack on Trenton, a follow-up victory over a smaller force at Princeton, and Yorktown, which was possible only due to French help. The French were allied with us due to the victory at Saratoga that had been won by the Northern

The mature George Washington was an American first, but as a young militia officer, he was more interested in obtaining property than liberty (*George Washington* [The Athenaeum Portrait]. Gilbert Stuart, 1796. Oil on canvas. National Portrait Gallery, Smithsonian Institution; owned jointly with Museum of Fine Arts, Boston).

Introduction: 1753–1774

Department. In the Southern Department, the Americans lost two separate armies before having some successes that helped set up the Yorktown Campaign. Other departments played lesser roles. The Canadian Department existed only briefly during the 1775–6 invasion of Canada, the Highlands Department covered only the Catskills region around New York City, and the Eastern Department was the name for the troops left in New England after the evacuation of Boston. And there was the Western Department.

The Western Department was different from all the other departments. It was the last one formed and the only one to remain after the war, and it was different in other ways as well. For one thing, the scope was totally different. Philadelphia was the largest city in the colonies, and in the first U.S. Census in 1790 it had a population of 28,522.[1] But on September 9, 1777, it wasn't even the largest concentration of people in southeastern Pennsylvania, as over 30,000 Continental and Redcoat soldiers fought a European-style battle along nearby Brandywine Creek that determined control of the city. There were nowhere near that many troops, or people, in the West, even though the area being contested was significantly larger, and therefore the style of warfare was also completely different.

There were never any more than 500 Continental soldiers in one place at any time west of the Appalachian Mountains. And, while the other six departments were usually led by a major general, in the Western Department no one higher than a brigadier general ever led, and the commander was often only a colonel. The few British regular troops in the West were scattered at various Great Lakes forts. With the British headquarters in Detroit and the Americans at Fort Pitt, the two forces never fought anything resembling a battle, as the war was fought by proxy by Indians and settlers spread over a vast area. Another difference in the Western Department was the static location of forces. In all but the Highlands Department, which was centered around West Point, separate departments moved around to wherever the commander took his army. But the Western Department consisted mainly of the garrison at Fort Pitt. This garrison did sometimes take the field and small portions were sent to other forts, but there were never any Continental troops stationed in Kentucky, and the Departmental commanding officer was always the commander at Fort Pitt.

Another difference in the West was George Washington's personal connection with the Western Department. Due to the changes over time in the nature of the relationship between the Continental Congress and

Introduction: 1753–1774

the commander-in-chief, there were significant differences in Washington's dealings with various departments. For example, many in the Continental Congress sought to replace Washington with Northern Department commander Horatio Gates after his victory at Saratoga. But Washington was always able to select his own man to head the Western Department, and he maintained a keen interest in events in the West. This interest was a result of Washington's personal experiences in the West and his realization of its importance. In 1754, Washington's first military experience came when he led Virginia militia towards the Forks of the Ohio. Four times during the 1750s he attempted to secure this spot for his country. His last military role came 40 years after his first one, when he led a 13,000 man army towards the same site while serving as President to quell the Whiskey Rebellion.

The Western Department was also unique for its lack of success. The most successful Western campaign, George Rogers Clark's capture of Vincennes, was achieved by Virginia militia with no connection to the Continental Army. In six and a half years, the French cavalry, the Spanish Army, and the Pennsylvania militia all got closer to Detroit than the Continental Army ever did. This also serves as a reminder that a lesser-known aspect of the Western Department was that the conflict was more international than is generally thought. The area between the Great Lakes and the Ohio and Mississippi Rivers is not regarded as a hotbed of international intrigue, but this was the case during the American Revolution.

In addition to the Americans and British, the French were eager to reclaim their hold on North America, and the Spanish based in New Orleans were also hoping to stymie the British. And each Indian tribe of a few thousand members had their own language, culture, and agenda, and saw themselves as independent nations, even though they were nomadic. The first foreign treaty negotiated by the newly named United States of America was with the Delaware nation at Fort Pitt in 1778. Although most of these tribes caught between warring factions of whites wound up supporting the British, their loyalty was sought by both sides.

A final difference is that, while much has been written about all the other departments in the East, the story of the Western Department remains largely untold. And it is a truly interesting story. Among the many intriguing events that occurred in the war in the West were the British attack on St. Louis, the Spanish invasion of Michigan, and the revolt of the Kentucky Navy. Among the colorful characters involved in

Introduction: 1753–1774

the Fort Pitt area were a six foot tall Shawnee princess who secretly met with a French cavalry officer to launch an attack on Detroit; a scion of a wealthy Philadelphia family who arrived in town with a naval commission and wound up becoming a river pirate; and an aide to a general who was actually a Russian nobleman who had fled his country after killing a rival in a duel. The story of these people and the events they shaped needs to be told to fill out the story of a successful revolution.

To understand the action in the Western Department, we first have to step back and look at the geography of the Western Hemisphere. When Columbus first sailed to the New World, it was occupied by hundreds of tribes of primitive natives, and soon a contest was on between European nations to exploit these people and their vast resources. In South America, the Spanish and Portuguese got the pope to peacefully draw a line between their colonial dominion claims, but the struggle for North America led to war.

After minor players like Russia, Sweden, and Holland dropped out, there were three major competitors left. In the south, Spain controlled the rim of the Gulf of Mexico and the American Southwest all the way to California. Despite mismanagement from afar, they managed to retain control of these colonies for over 300 years. In the north, the French colonized Canada and expanded their hold to the Great Lakes. Though few in number, the French lived peacefully among the natives they traded with and posed no threat. And, along the eastern seaboard, the British settled thirteen colonies from New Hampshire to Georgia.

These colonies posed the greatest threat to the French, Spanish, and natives. The British were more interested in permanent settlement and began swarming their way west in increasing numbers. They gradually pushed their settlement lines westward, but were hemmed in by the Appalachian mountain range that ran the length of their colonies. You could cross this range without climbing over 3,000 feet in most places, but there was no water route back, as west of the Appalachians all rivers flowed west to the Ohio and Mississippi Rivers and on to the Gulf of Mexico. Westward settlement beyond these mountains was not yet feasible. In fact, while the French were already sailing on the Ohio and Mississippi Rivers by the 1670s, English speaking explorers never encountered a westward flowing river until 1671.

While the Spanish generally were preoccupied with internal affairs, the French and British colonies fought a series of wars between 1690 and 1760, with the natives playing a large part in these wars. The Algonquin tribes allied with the French, while the Iroquois, a group of

Introduction: 1753–1774

five (later six) tribes who had united into a strong coalition, joined the British. These early wars were fought mainly in the New England area, but gradually the conflict expanded westward. The French could use the St. Lawrence River to bypass the Appalachian Mountains and proceed to the internal Great Lakes after a portage around Niagara Falls. Explorers such as La Salle, Joliet, and Marquette explored the interior of the continent and the French gradually established several trading posts across the midwest. They discovered several places where the distance between the Great Lakes and Mississippi River watersheds was but a short portage, which made it possible to travel by water from Québec to New Orleans with only portages here and at Niagara Falls. By controlling this route, the French hoped to keep the British hemmed in between the Appalachian Mountains and the Atlantic Ocean.

The first such portage spot the French discovered was near present day Erie, Pennsylvania, on Lake Erie. Here, where a long spit of land juts out over the lake, offering a natural harbor, the French built Fort Presque Isle in 1751. The Lake Erie drainage basin is small, and just ten miles below Erie, French Creek starts flowing south, away from the lake. The French built Fort Le Bouef here and then constructed Fort Venango farther downstream where French Creek meets the Allegheny River. From here, the Allegheny flowed south to where it met the Monongahela River at the Forks, where the Ohio begins its thousand mile trip to the Mississippi. The Forks of the Ohio loomed as the final link in a French line of forts that could keep English-speaking people east of the mountains.

This development alarmed some American colonists on the eastern side of the mountains. Pennsylvanians, who wound up owning the Forks of the Ohio, were not overly concerned, as they were still mainly concentrated east of the Susquehanna River. But the Virginia colony had its eye on Western lands. A group called the Ohio Company of Virginia had been formed to explore getting Western land grants, and this move by the French threatened their plans. In 1753, Virginia's royal governor sent a militia officer on a diplomatic mission to the French forts to warn them to cease their operations. The officer selected to deliver this message was 21-year-old Major George Washington. In fulfilling this mission, Washington became "The first officially commissioned representative of his country to cross the mountains."[2]

Washington came from Virginia's landed aristocracy, but he was no spoiled rich child. A rugged outdoorsman who cut a fine figure on horseback, he already had frontier experience working as a surveyor's

Introduction: 1753–1774

assistant while in his teens. An ambitious young man, he was also involved in land speculation with the Ohio Company. Accompanying Washington on his mission were experienced frontier guide Christopher Gist, who had done previous exploring for the Ohio Company, and a handful of Native American guides.

Washington got as far as Fort Le Boeuf, where he delivered his letter to the French commander. He was politely received, but the French had no intention of abandoning their plans. Washington started his return trip December 16 and arrived back in Williamsburg a month later. Along the way, he was fired on by his Indian guides and he nearly drowned when his raft overturned in the frigid Allegheny. He also became the first American to note the military significance of the Forks of the Ohio. He passed all this along to Gov. Dinwiddie, who published Washington's account of his trip. In the spring, the governor dispatched a group under William Trent to build a fort at the forks.

The Virginians arrived at the forks and began construction, but were soon driven off by a larger French force that began construction of Fort Duquesne. While this was going on, the Virginians gathered a force of 165 men, two wagons, and nine swivel guns to follow up. This group was on the Potomac at Cumberland, Maryland, in early May of 1754. They were led by Col. Joshua Fry, but he was seriously injured in a fall from his horse near Cumberland, where he died on May 31.[3] He was replaced by now Lieut. Col. Washington, who, in successfully traversing the Appalachian divide, became the first man to take troops, wagons, and artillery across the mountains.[4]

Washington, who was also assisted by several Indian scouts, discovered a small French party nearby. Even though no state of war existed yet, Washington resolved to attack, and on May 28 he surprised the French party, killing ten, capturing 21, and driving the rest off. This was Washington's first taste of combat and he enjoyed his initiation, saying, "I have heard the whine of bullets, and there is something charming in the sound."[5] This callow disdain for the rigors of war would not remain a part of Washington's persona for long.

As the militia moved on, Washington was informed that a large French force was headed towards them. As he was far from his supply lines, Washington decided it best to retreat towards Cumberland. But the French were closing in on them, and Washington had to make a stand at the Great Meadows near the Youghiogheny River. His Indian allies deserted at the first signs of trouble. Future British officers would later build carefully detailed defense posts in western Pennsylvania, but

Introduction: 1753–1774

the stockade haphazardly thrown up by these militia was built out of necessity, and was named thusly. Set in a broad unshaded meadow, circular Fort Necessity was hard to approach, but had no water supply or natural defense. Worse, as the French surrounded them, a steady rain soaked the defenders and their gunpowder, depriving the commander of the chance to hear the charming whine of the bullets.

With no way out, Washington was forced to surrender on July 4, and for the next 22 years he considered this date a personal day of mourning.[6] The Virginians were permitted to return home and keep their arms, but in signing the capitulation agreement, Washington, who did not read French, admitted to the "assassination" of the French commander. This inadvertent confession outraged the French, and within two years the French were at war with England in Europe, North America, India and the Caribbean. The Seven Years War was a truly international conflict, but it got its start with Washington's impatience.[7]

The following year, the British resolved to attack the French Canadians on several fronts. To lead their westernmost expedition, they sent Maj. Gen. Edward Braddock and 1,000 redcoats. This force was joined by a like number of colonial militia, but Braddock, like many British officers, was not overly impressed by the Americans.[8] His suspicion that the colonials didn't take the French threat seriously enough was compounded when he arrived at Hagerstown, Maryland, to find less than 10 percent of the wagons and horses he needed. Fortunately, his frustration was relieved by Benjamin Franklin, who was present and offered to gather the needed resources. Franklin's success gave Braddock one American that he could praise, as he noted, "He has executed with great punctuality and integrity, and is almost the only instance of ability and honesty that I've known in these provinces."[9]

It's possible that the irascible Braddock just had high standards, since the only other American he had any confidence in was Washington, another colonial of note who had not yet achieved fame. Washington did not have an actual field command, but served as an aide to Braddock, and his experience in the Western country proved useful. As this force worked its way across the mountains, they followed Washington's route, but had to expand the path to allow for heavier traffic. As they slowly approached Fort Duquesne, the outnumbered French feared they would not be able to hold out.

By July 9, Braddock was just a few hours away from the forks when his force crossed the Monongahela River and stumbled into an ambush set up by the French and Indians. The British held to their tightly massed

Introduction: 1753–1774

formations, which made it easier for Indians hiding behind trees to pick them off. The natives also focused their fire on officers, as 48 of 73 British officers were killed or wounded.[10] The British and Americans suffered over 700 casualties before ordering a retreat that turned into a rout. Braddock was mortally wounded, and Washington, who had two horses shot out from under him during the battle, supervised the retreat. When Braddock died, Washington had him buried in the middle of the wagon road so the grave would not be found and disturbed.

While the brunt of the action shifted elsewhere in North America over the next two years, Braddock's defeat gave the French and Indians a free hand on the western frontier. Increased Indian raids in both Pennsylvania and Virginia troubled pioneers and many settlers returned east.

In the spring of 1758, the British resolved to try to take the Forks of the Ohio again, sending General John Forbes to North America. Forbes waited in Philadelphia as an army coalesced that would include 2,000 redcoats in two regiments, supplemented by 4,000 colonial militia, that included three Pennsylvania battalions and two Virginia regiments, one of which was led by Washington. Leading the troops in the field was Col. Henry Bouquet, a Swiss mercenary serving in the British Army in the Royal American Regiment, a regular army unit composed mainly of German immigrants to America. Bouquet was a capable officer who complemented Forbes, and the two cemented their unique relationship by corresponding with each other in French.[11]

The first issue to be decided was the best route to the forks. Forbes and Bouquet agreed that a route across Pennsylvania was shorter, offered more forage for pack animals, and had fewer major stream crossings than the route taken by Washington and Braddock. Washington strenuously objected to this decision, claiming that the road he had already built made more sense. But this "road" was a narrow path that had grown over after three years of not being used, and would have to be rebuilt. Washington's reasoning also contained a strong element of the personal. With his half-brothers involved in the Ohio Company, he knew a government-built road from Virginia to the forks would be a financial windfall for his family. In a ten day period in late summer, Washington hectored Bouquet to the point of insubordination, with four letters and a personal visit urging a change.

To his superior officers, Washington couched his arguments only in terms of how it would affect the mission. But he revealed his true feelings to an associate, informing him, "I have just returned from a

Introduction: 1753–1774

conference with Col. Bouquet. I find him fixed (against us). If Col. Bouquet succeeds in this point with the General, all is lost! All is lost by heavens! Our enterprise ruined."[12] Braddock may have been impressed by Washington, but Forbes was less so, as he told Bouquet that Washington's, "behavior about the roads was in no ways like a soldier."[13]

Once this decision was made, the army became focused on building a road and in protecting it with forts, creating what would serve as an infrastructure for future expansion. The army followed a route that corresponds with the current U.S. Route 30, and by fall they had crossed the divide to where the waters flow to the west. Just 40 miles from Fort Duquesne, they stopped to build a substantial post that they named Fort Ligonier. The British were operating on the theory that the more resources you exhausted in building a fort, the less likely it would be attacked: at Fort Necessity, Washington had already learned that the opposite was also true. While they were here, Bouquet authorized Maj. James Grant to lead 800 men on a raid on Fort Duquesne. This force got within sight of the forks before being discovered, but they were defeated with heavy losses. A French counter raid on Fort Ligonier was also deflected.

Forbes had remained in Philadelphia supervising the considerable logistical details of this expedition. He was also suffering terribly from what was probably stomach cancer, which made it difficult for him to travel. He finally left town on a litter on the road named for him and arrived at Fort Ligonier on November 3. But it was now so late in the year that Forbes feared he would have to wait until spring to finish his campaign. However, on the night of November 12, a patrol that included Washington encountered a French scouting force, and captured troops revealed that the French were low in numbers, supplies, and morale. Many of their Great Lakes Indian allies had gone home for harvest, their supply lines had been ruptured by the capture of key forts, and treaties negotiated had led to some of the local tribes abandoning the French. Forbes resolved to make one last try on November 24. As the troops marched toward the forks, they heard the sound of the French blowing up their own fort with 50 kegs of gunpowder. The French split their garrison, with some going north and the rest heading downstream on the Ohio, and the next day the British and Americans marched in unopposed.

Forbes declared the next day to be a day of Thanksgiving, and then began plans for a more permanent fort. He then returned to Philadelphia, where he died on March 13. As for Washington, he returned home,

Introduction: 1753–1774

left the service, married a widow named Martha Custis and soon became the master of Mount Vernon. He did not wear a uniform for another seventeen years and he stayed away from the Forks of the Ohio for another dozen years. Staying behind were 280 Pennsylvania militiamen under Col. Hugh Mercer. As there was a great fear of French counterattack, the first thing they did was build a temporary fort just a little bit upstream on the Monongahela. During the cold winter, the rivers froze so they couldn't float pickets downstream, and the soldiers were plagued by measles and scurvy.[14]

It wasn't until reinforcements arrived that they were able to finish Fort Mercer. They then began construction of Fort Pitt, the most substantial of the British forts built in North America. This pentagonal post covered eighteen acres and contained five rows of buildings. In addition to the usual log pickets, the fort's defenses also incorporated stone and earthworks. But with the fort being located right at the confluence of two major rivers, it was low-lying, and was seriously damaged by flooding in its first two years.[15] New Western commander Gen. John Stanwix arrived in the summer of 1759 and hosted a large Indian conference while here.

Regulation of commerce with the natives was another main function of the Royal government at Fort Pitt. The government built seven buildings and a store across the Monongahela from Fort Pitt to facilitate trade.[16] The Indian trade had been at the heart of the French and British rivalry. Both sides coveted the cured fur hides of North American mammals that were in such demand in the European clothing industry. To obtain them, they were willing to provide the primitive natives with such otherwise inaccessible luxuries as guns and ammunition, blankets, knives, kettles, shoes, hats, and, of course, alcohol.

Most Indians preferred to deal with the French traders, but the English offered better made and cheaper goods, and began making inroads into the French trade. By the time Fort Pitt was completed, Middle Colonies Indian Agent George Croghan set up a price schedule for how many skins of various animals it took to purchase certain items.[17] Although it was illegal to own land in the area, a town grew up around the fort. A 1761 census conducted by Bouquet revealed a civilian population of 332 people, two thirds of whom were adult males.[18] Almost all residents were connected with the fur trade.

The changing status of the war changed the nature of the fur trade. The French counterattack never materialized, as Québec fell in 1759 and Montréal the next year. Although France did not formally surrender all

Introduction: 1753–1774

North American holdings until the Treaty of Paris in 1763, by the end of 1761 they had abandoned all of their Great Lakes and Midwestern posts. The British now garrisoned these posts with troops from the Royal American Regiment, but promised not to build any more new forts, not to further encroach on Indian land, and to treat Indians fairly. But, without French competition to keep prices down, British traders had a monopoly, and prices rose accordingly. The natives resented this and were also puzzled that the French had given up so easily. When the British broke their word and built a new fort, the tribes were ready to take a stand. An Ottawa chief named Pontiac assembled a nineteen tribe coalition over the winter of 1762–3.

This was no easy feat to accomplish. Although the various tribes were usually at peace with each other and did have a limited common sign language, each tribe of maybe a few thousand members still maintained their own language and identity. In addition, the various tribal attitudes toward whites were predicated by propinquity. Eastern tribes facing immediate encroachment by settlers were more likely to be alarmed than the more distant tribes. But these distant tribes were now faced with Eastern tribes invading their territory as they fled the whites. Pontiac skillfully assembled such a broad coalition and managed to keep whites unaware of stockpiled weapons over the winter.

In the spring of 1763, the tribes struck with great success. Between May 16 and June 21, nine of ten forts west of a line between Fort Pitt and Fort Niagara were captured and destroyed. Detroit, where Pontiac was personally in charge, was the lone holdout. Unlike the settlers who streamed west in ever increasing numbers, Indian population figures were stagnant, and they weren't about to squander their meager numbers by attacking a fortified post. They would usually attack a fort only if they could gain access via subterfuge. In many cases, this was a simple matter of requesting a meeting and concealing weapons. At Fort Michilimackinac, the natives were more creative. They staged an elaborate lacrosse game outside the fort and someone threw the ball over the stockade wall. When the natives were allowed in to retrieve the ball, they were handed weapons and massacred the garrison. All across the frontier, traders were captured, settlers attacked, and families fled back east. Eastern residents showed their support by murdering peaceful Indians who lived among them.

The easternmost posts at Forts Pitt, Niagara, Ligonier and Bedford were also attacked, but they were close enough to supply lines that they were able to hold out. Fort Pitt was under siege from May 9 to August

Introduction: 1753–1774

5. The British considered all sorts of options to relieve the situation, including some unsavory ones. On July 7, Lord Jeffrey Amherst, commander of all British forces in North America, ordered Bouquet to "Try to inoculate the Indians by means of blankets, as well as to try every other method to extirpate this execrable race."[19] This was a written confession of Amherst's genocidal intentions, but, as there was no Geneva Convention yet, and Bouquet was a good soldier, he did not question this order. But he may not have followed through on the level Amherst wanted, as William Trent at Fort Pitt reported, "We gave them two blankets and a handkerchief out of the smallpox hospital. I hope it will have the desired effect."[20] Smallpox did break out among the tribes that year, but this was often the case, so it's difficult to ascertain the success of this early foray into biological warfare.

To lift the siege of Fort Pitt, Bouquet gathered 500 regular British troops and started west. He knew he was being watched, so he was not surprised like Braddock when his forces were ambushed along Bushy Run just 20 miles from the fort on August 5. Bouquet's men adapted and hid behind obstacles as they held off the Indians in a fierce all day battle. Fighting resumed the next day, and with the British running out of water, Bouquet ordered a feigned retreat that lured the Indians into a trap, and he was able to break their ranks. Bouquet's casualties were over 20 percent of his force, but he was able to relieve the garrison at Fort Pitt. At Detroit, the British had been able to resupply the post by ship, and Pontiac finally gave up the siege after six months, an unusually long time for impatient warriors. By the end of the year, there were hardly any whites at all in the West, but Pontiac had to come to realize that the French were not coming back.

The next year, the British sent out a couple of different forces to try to quell this insurrection. Bouquet was ordered to penetrate the Ohio interior, but he felt his force was too small, so he waited until he could gather enough militia to form a 1,500 man army before proceeding in the fall. Following Beaver and Sandy Creeks to the Tuscarawas River, Bouquet's force was too large and well trained to be attacked. He had learned in the Forbes Campaign that a well-supplied and large enough force in the right place at the right time need not risk its troops in battle in order to achieve victory. The key was to put all your resources into becoming too strong to attack.

As Bouquet progressed, the alarmed natives sought to stall him. At present-day Bolivar, Ohio, Bouquet met with Indian leaders and demanded the return of all recently taken captives. He then drove on to present-day

Introduction: 1753–1774

Coshocton where twelve days later they redeemed 206 captives. Bouquet returned to Fort Pitt on November 28, and was finally rewarded for all his work. The British Army overcame their reluctance to advance foreign-born mercenaries and promoted Bouquet to brigadier general. He was sent to command British troops in Florida, where he promptly caught malaria and was dead within a month.[21]

Once the tribes accepted that trading with the British was their only option, matters settled into an uneasy truce. This meant little change for the tribes in the Fort Pitt area who had already been trading there. Among this group were the Shawnee, who had relocated widely and frequently, and who were now living in southern Ohio. Also nearby were the Delaware, who had welcomed William Penn to Philadelphia in 1681 and had been steadily pushed west ever since. They were currently living on the Allegheny and the Upper Ohio and were moving into eastern Ohio. Intermingling with them in eastern Ohio and Western Pennsylvania were the Mingo, who were culturally affiliated with the Iroquois league but were politically independent. Farther away were the Miami, Wyandot, Ottawa, and tribes from Michigan, Indiana, and Illinois who were potential trade partners.

The British at first tried to keep their word to not expand their colonies. In 1763, the king issued a proclamation that confined settlement to east of the mountains. Americans had bled and died fighting over western land, and were outraged to discover that they were not free to settle there. They later became more angry when their taxes were increased to pay for the protection offered by the British Army. This proclamation stopped settlement of the West, but only for a little while.

The 1768 Treaty of Fort Stanwix changed the situation. This treaty was negotiated in upstate New York by Sir William Johnson, superintendent of Indian affairs for North America. Johnson had a good rapport with the Iroquois, who, by their strength, claimed land that they weren't even using. To deflect Americans away from their own turf, the Iroquois allowed settlement of unoccupied Kentucky, even though the Shawnee used this as their hunting ground. The Ohio River was now the border between white and Indian land, and remained so for the next 27 years. Where the Ohio ran north for the first few miles after the forks, the white side was the eastern bank, but after the Ohio leveled off about where Ohio, Pennsylvania, and West Virginia meet, and the river turned south, the eastern and southern shores became open for settlement by whites.

Pennsylvania opened a western land office April 3, 1769, and soon a general land rush was on.[22] Pioneers of different nationalities, religions,

Introduction: 1753–1774

and political persuasions all came seeking land. Those from southern colonies, like Daniel Boone, could now approach Kentucky via the Cumberland Gap, but settlers in the middle colonies traveled west by way of the Ohio River. In the Fort Pitt area, settlement soon went right up to the banks of the Ohio. This boom sparked interest from land speculators, and led to another visit from George Washington. Virginia had authorized land grants for veterans of the Fort Necessity campaign, and Washington was interested in selecting specific tracts along the Ohio. As he headed towards Fort Pitt, he stopped at present-day Connellsville at the home of William Crawford, who had worked with Washington on surveying projects years earlier. Washington hired Crawford to come along to note which properties Washington wanted to have surveyed. With a crew of eight, this group arrived at Pittsburgh on October 17, 1770. In his diary, Washington noted, "We lodged at what is called the town," which he estimated to be about 20 cabins occupied by various traders.[23]

This party left on the 20th and was gone about a month, following the Ohio all the way to the mouth of the Kanawha River at present-day Point Pleasant, West Virginia. Washington made detailed notes on the land he saw and quizzed travelers about land further downstream. He also commented on wildlife, such as the size of the catfish and the exotic sound made by the blue heron, and noted that "This country abounds in Buffalo and wild game of all kinds as also in all kinds of wild fowl."[24]

Washington also ran into an old friend. On October 28, they encountered a large Mingo hunting party led by Guyasuta, who had been one of Washington's guides to Fort LeBouef in 1753. Guyasuta expressed great delight in seeing Washington again, sharing his food and suggesting they camp together. Washington accepted gracefully, but was eager to scout land and impatient with elaborate Indian friendship rituals. In his diary, he complained, "The tedious ceremony with which the Indians observe in their counseling and speeches detained us until 9 o'clock."[25]

Washington and his party eventually managed to get away, and got as far as the Kanawha before turning around on November 1. He selected several parcels for Crawford to survey and picked out some prime acreage for himself. Heavy rains and high water slowed their progress going back upstream, and at Mingo Junction, just below present-day Steubenville, they abandoned their canoes and rode overland to Pittsburgh, arriving on November 21. On their last night in town, they invited some officers in the fort and some other guests to dinner at Samples' Tavern, where they were staying. Among the guests was Dr. John Connolly, a nephew of Croghan, who Washington described as, "A very sensible intelligent man who had traveled over a good deal of this Western country."[26] Connolly spoke of the potential for a vast inland empire in the midwest, and Washington left for Virginia the next day as enthusiastic as ever about western land development.

The settlers coming to the area used both the Braddock and Forbes roads. The British officials at Fort Pitt kept watch over the area, but the fort was evacuated in 1772, which left a vacuum. Without any central governmental authority, the rival colonies of Virginia and Pennsylvania contested for ownership of the forks. This wasn't the easy decision one would think by looking at the current map. The thirteen British colonies had several inconsistent methods of defining their respective western borders. Connecticut, for example, had no fixed western boundary, so that colony claimed a coast-to-coast strip of land that corresponded with their northern and southern borders.

Maryland, on the other hand, had a fixed western border that extended from the Fairfax Stone that marked the beginning of the Potomac River and ran north to the Pennsylvania-Maryland border that British surveyors Mason and Dixon had just surveyed in 1768. Pennsylvania's colonial charter specified its western border as being five degrees of latitude west of the Delaware River, but did not specify from at what point on that winding river. Virginia had no western border stated, and they used their wedge-shape and the fact that the Mason-Dixon line stopped at Maryland's western border to extend their claims to cover the entire midwest.

As settlers moved westward, the usual policy was for the individual colonies to create new counties on the frontier. Pennsylvania acted first here, in February 1773, creating Westmoreland County, with the county seat at Hannahstown. In July of that year, the new royal governor of Virginia, a nobleman named John Murray, but who went by the title of Lord Dunmore, came to Pittsburgh to press Virginia's case. Dunmore found that Western Pennsylvania had "Upwards of 10,000 settlers [but] had neither magistrates to preserve rule and order amongst themselves, nor militia for defense."[27] Knowing he had to act quickly to counter the Pennsylvanians, Dunmore convinced Croghan and Connolly to abandon their support of a Kentucky land scheme and to align with him.

On January 1, 1774, Connolly occupied the abandoned Fort Pitt site, renamed it Fort Dunmore, and called for the militia to assemble for the newly created West Augusta District of Virginia. This led to his being arrested by Pennsylvania magistrate Arthur St. Clair, who ordered Connelly to appear at court in Hannahstown on April 6. Connolly made his appearance, but at the head of 150 armed men, who surrounded the courthouse, and carted off three officials to Staunton, Virginia, 170 miles away.[28] They were held there for a month.

After this, the contest was on, with the residents having to choose which colony they considered themselves to be residents of. Pennsylvania had been slow to militarize, as the Quakers had generally gotten along with the Indians, so they were not as aggressive. The Virginians, who had been the first to approach the forks, continued to push an aggressive policy. They also had lower land prices and permitted slavery, which helped them attract adherents.

But the biggest difference in the colonies' approach was the thuggish behavior of Connolly's Virginia militia. A group of Pennsylvania citizens complained that "Mr. Connolly is constantly surrounded by body of armed men. He boasts the countenance of the Governor of Virginia and forcibly obstructs the execution of legal process," adding that "His militia is composed of men without character and without fortune."[29] Connolly's men threatened Pennsylvania officials, "appropriated" supplies and assaulted men who had the nerve to ask for receipts. Pennsylvania Gov. John Penn complained to Dunmore, but Connolly had Dunmore's support.

One of the concerns expressed about Connolly's conduct was that his aggressiveness was particularly dangerous because of the volatile Indian situation. The Shawnee were objecting to the opening up of Kentucky lands, and Dunmore's aggressiveness was a threat to the peace. Gov. Penn believed, "There is a great reason to fear that his military operations may have a dangerous tendency to involve the colonies in a general Indian war."[30] And that is what happened, as a decade of peace was about to be succeeded by a decade of war.

ONE

Lord Dunmore
1774

There was tension on the frontier in the spring of 1774. The Fort Stanwix Treaty in 1768 had permitted settlement all the way to Kentucky, but it remained uncertain whether the Shawnee and other tribes would accept the Iroquois' giving away of the hunting ground they were using. In the fall of 1773, a group of settlers under Daniel Boone had tried to enter Kentucky via the southern route through Cumberland Gap, but had turned back after an Indian attack killed Boone's son and others. Now, a larger group was attempting to go down the Ohio, as James Harrod was leading a group of surveyors to lay out the first settlement in Kentucky. Among those waiting to learn whether the Shawnee would oppose them was 21-year-old George Rogers Clark. But, in the absence of hard information, rumors flew as everyone waited anxiously.

Virginia officials like Dunmore and Connolly were hoping to exploit this uncertainty. Kentucky was going to be settled by someone, and they wanted to be under the jurisdiction of their

John Murray, Lord Dunmore, was the last Royal governor of Virginia, and the only person involved in Lord Dunmore's War who was not an American ("John Murray, Earl Dunmore, Governor of Va.," The New York Public Library Digital Collections. 1880).

colony. In the absence of militarization by Pennsylvania, the Virginia colony was more aggressive in pursuing expansion, and they felt that an Indian war would force the British government to offer them protection, which would then strengthen their claim. Therefore, they actively pursued provoking conflict. In his own account, Connolly claimed that "every endeavor at pacification was employed by me, but unhappily without effect."[1] But his actual behavior was the opposite of this.

When a group of traders had to be escorted from Indian country to Pittsburgh by friendly Shawnee, Pennsylvania magistrate Arthur St. Clair asked Connolly to reciprocate by sending men to escort the Shawnee back. Not only was he curtly refused, but Connolly dispatched a force to follow the Shawnee and fire upon them to help incite a war. Claiming that an Indian war was part of the Virginia plan, St. Clair claimed, "the distressed inhabitants of this place have just cause to charge their present calamity and dread of an Indian war entirely to the tyrannical and unprecedented conduct of Dr. John Connolly, whose design, as we conceive it, is to better his almost desperate circumstances upon the public and the ruins of our fortunes"[2]

Connolly ultimately found the right match to ignite this tinderbox and end ten years of peace on the frontier. Later in April, he sent a circular letter to all frontier locations advising them that war was all but inevitable and to be prepared for it. This warning served as a self-fulfilling prophecy, as impatient pioneers concluded that if war was inevitable, it made sense to strike first rather than wait to be attacked. In Wheeling, a group of settlers coalesced around the loose leadership of Michael Cresap, an experienced frontiersman, into a quasi-military force looking for Indians to provoke. On April 26, Ebeneezer Zane, a founder of the Wheeling settlement, reported that "a proposition was made by the then captain Michael Cresap to waylay and kill the Indians upon the river. This measure I opposed with much violence, alleging that the killing of these Indians might involve the country in a war. But the opposite party prevailed."[3]

As this group began accosting small parties of Indians along the river, they heard a rumor that a larger body of Indians were encamped on the Ohio side of the river at the mouth of Yellow Creek on today's Jefferson/Columbiana County line. They moved towards this location, but turned back when they heard that this was obviously not a war party, as it included women and children.

The Yellow Creek camp was occupied by the villagers of the Mingo warrior Logan, who were on a spring hunting trip. Logan, who was not with his villagers at this time, was well known as a friend to the whites. The son of a chief, Logan was not a chief himself but was a noted warrior whom one witness called "the most martial figure of an Indian that I had ever seen."[4] But he lived among the English speaking people and remained neutral in the French and Indian war and later told Moravian missionary John Heckewelder of "his friendship to white people."[5] Logan's village was on the Ohio near present-day Beaver, Pennsylvania, but most residents, including several members of Logan's family, had temporarily relocated to the hunting camp.

While Cresap and his party had changed their minds, another group under Daniel Greathouse, picked up where they had left off. There was a settlement called Baker's Bottom across the Ohio from the Indian camp, and Logan's sister Koonay had been crossing over regularly to get milk for her infant daughter. As she was usually accompanied by some braves, the settlers planned a trap. When a group of Indians came across the river for milk on April 30, a number of settlers offered alcohol to the braves as well. This greatly increased the chances of an incident, and, when Logan's brother put on a white man's hat and appeared to mock the whites, a fight broke out. The whites were ready for this and massacred all the Indians and fired upon another party that came across the river to investigate. The only survivor of the Yellow Creek Massacre was Koonay's infant daughter, whose need for milk had led to the tragedy.

It turned out that the girl's father was John Gibson, a prominent Indian trader. Fearing that they might now be in trouble with both the Indian and white worlds, Greathouse's party retreated away from the river to Catfish Camp, at present day Washington, Pennsylvania, taking the girl with them. From there she was given to William Crawford, who was en route to Fort Pitt, for him to save for Gibson. On May 8, Crawford wrote to his business partner George Washington, who hadn't served in the military for more than fifteen years and was still a year away from being named commander-in-chief of the Continental Army. Washington had no direct military interest in western affairs, but still had a strong economic concern. Crawford reported in a letter:

> Expecting a Endien war, Mr. Crisap and som other people fell on som other Endiens at the mouth of Pipe Creek and killed three Endiens and sculped them. Daniel Great House and som others fell on som at the mouth of Yellow Creek and killed and sculped them and took one child about two months which is now at my house.... Our inhabetints is much alarmed.... I am sitting out for Fort Pitt at the head of 100 men, many others is to meet me at Fort Pitt and Wheeling.[6]

This child was probably older than two months. In one of the more gruesome versions of the Yellow Creek Massacre, a pregnant Koonay was killed and her belly was cut open so the murderers could also scalp her fetus. But Koonay could not have been visibly pregnant if she had just given birth two months earlier. However, the child was still an infant, as a witness at Catfish Camp reported seeing his mother "feeding and dressing the baby, chirping to the little innocent, and it smiling."[7] Crawford kept the baby until he could give her to John Neville, a recent arrival who was headed to Fort Pitt, and there she was finally reunited with her father.

The Virginians now had their war, as Logan went on the warpath seeking revenge. For the next several months, he struck terror into settlers' hearts as he led raiding parties against individual families. In one of these raids, he spared a captive's life after getting him to write a letter to Cresap that began, "What did you kill my people on Yellow Creek for?"[8] Logan, like most on the frontier, mistakenly blamed Cresap for the massacre, and some referred to the ensuing conflict as Cresap's War. But Cresap's alibi that he was at that time busy committing other Indian murders was hardly exculpatory. Logan continued his raids until he had personally killed thirteen men, the number of relatives he had lost at Yellow Creek. Afterwards, he took up residence with the Shawnee, as he no longer had a village to return to. The Shawnee were only too happy to have Logan's help in the struggle with the Virginians.

At Pittsburgh, Connolly was discovering that starting a war was easier than winning one. Refugees began streaming to Pittsburgh almost immediately to seek protection. Connolly gathered about 100 militia, but found that many of them lacked proper weapons. To address this, he seized private firearms and ammunition and re-allocated them according to his priorities. In order to recruit men outside the immediate area, he offered captain's commissions in the Virginia militia to local leaders like Crawford and Neville and gave them blank commissions to name their own officers. Cresap's quasi-military band had been useful in starting the war, but now they had to be restrained, lest they turn other tribes against the whites with further attacks. Connolly resolved this issue by co-opting Cresap, offering him a captain's commission and incorporating his men into the Virginia militia.

Another problem facing Connolly was the condition of Fort Pitt, which had been abandoned by the British in 1772 and sold to private interests. Connolly renamed the post Fort Dunmore, but, other than one stone blockhouse, the fort was in complete decay, and had been looted for parts for other construction. Connolly hired John Gibson and Thomas Smallman to conduct an appraisal, and they determined the fort to be worth 1,082 pounds in Virginia currency.[9] Once enough militia had gathered, Connolly put them to work on fort repair.

It was easy enough to convince settlers to shoot Indians, but now Connolly had to stop this behavior so he could recruit Indian allies and isolate the Shawnee. He called for an Indian conference on May 6 that included Guyasuta of the Mingo and White Eyes and Captain Pipe of the Delaware. These chiefs not only agreed to stay neutral, but also journeyed to the Shawnee to try and keep them peaceful. But this tribe was now eager for war, and joined with Logan in launching raids that increased in June, causing settlers to seek shelter in their private community stockades.

This led Governor Dunmore to take an active hand in Williamsburg. He informed the convened House of Burgesses of the situation, but the delegates seemed more interested in expressing sympathy to the citizens of Boston, who had just had their port closed by British authorities. But Dunmore had a lot of latitude in enforcing militia law that required all able-bodied adult free males to participate. On June 10, Dunmore sent a circular letter to all county militia leaders that said, "Hopes of pacification could no more be entertained.... We should have recourse to the only means that are left in our power to extricate ourselves out of so calamitous a situation."[10] He called for all militia to be ready for war and proposed building a fort where the Kanawha River met the Ohio. A month later, Dunmore left Williamsburg to take personal command of his army.

Lord Dunmore was actually a Scottish nobleman named John Murray. His father had supported the Jacobite rebellion to restore Bonnie Prince Charlie, the Stuart claimant to the throne occupied by George II. After the Jacobites were defeated at Culloden in 1746, the elder Murray was sentenced to death, but was spared thanks to the intercession of his more loyal brother, who was the Earl of Dunmore. When this uncle died childless in 1767, Murray's father became the next Earl of Dunmore, and when he died, his son succeeded him. The new Lord Dunmore was a military officer, but was given only noncombatant roles during the Seven Years War, possibly because of his father's disloyalty. He began serving in the House of Lords in 1761, and in 1770 was appointed the royal governor of New York. The following year, he eagerly accepted the governorship of Virginia, which was a larger and more populous colony.[11]

When Dunmore arrived at Winchester in the Shenandoah Valley, he set up a temporary headquarters and began issuing orders to his militia. Despite Connolly's desire for field command, Dunmore ordered him to stay in Pittsburgh and consolidate supplies and support. Dunmore asked Pennsylvania officials for support, but was rebuffed. Connolly then accused St. Clair of timidity in protecting the frontier and proudly stated that his own Indian policy was to "Pursue every measure to offend" them.[12] Sir William Johnson tried to help isolate the Shawnee diplomatically from his home near Fort Stanwix, but died suddenly while hosting a conference. His death on the eve of the revolution left a deep void in British and Indian relations.

Dunmore ordered Captain William Crawford to lead the troops currently at Fort Dunmore. He directed them to proceed downstream to Wheeling and build a fort there. This post was named Fort Fincastle, as that was another one of Dunmore's titles, although it was later renamed for Patrick Henry. When Dunmore had first visited Pittsburgh in 1773, Washington had arranged for Crawford to be his guide, and Crawford had apparently made a good impression, as Dunmore trusted him with many later opportunities.

More than any other frontier campaign, this one would combine troops from both the northern and southern Appalachians. Dunmore now wrote to Andrew Lewis at present day Lewisburg, West Virginia, with orders to organize troops in the area of southwestern Virginia that stretched all the way south to the proximity of the over mountain men on the North Carolina and Tennessee borders. Among the officers who responded to the call were John Sevier and Evan Shelby, both of whom later served at King's Mountain. Officials here had to try to keep the Cherokee out of the war, and also sent out Daniel Boone and another man to warn surveyors to return to the safety of the east. Dunmore's instructions called for Lewis' force to proceed up the Kanawha River towards the Ohio.

Finally, Dunmore directed Major Angus McDonald to take the men he had gathered in the Winchester area and proceed to Wheeling to launch a raid on Shawnee villages along the upper Muskingum River. Like Dunmore's father, McDonald was a veteran of Culloden, and he had fled Scotland for America after the battle. He gathered 400 men at Wheeling in eight separate companies with some noted captains. Among them were not only Cresap and Crawford, but Daniel Morgan and George Rogers Clark both got their first combat commands during this campaign.

On July 26, McDonald's force left Wheeling in canoes with eight days' worth of provisions. They floated down to Captina Creek and then crossed overland towards the Muskingum. As they approach Wakatomica, a cluster of villages near present-day Dresden, Ohio, they were fired on, and in a brief skirmish had two men killed and five wounded. The next day, they entered the now abandoned villages and destroyed them and the surrounding crops. By now, their own provisions were running low, and they returned by the same route. The results of this raid were hardly significant, but it did offer valuable experience for some future leaders of the American Revolution.

The militia on this expedition had to be careful to attack only the Shawnee. Just a few miles above Wakatomica at Coshocton was the principal town of the neutral Delaware, and any attack on them could result in that tribe's going to war alongside the Shawnee. To prevent this, they sent trusted Indian trader John Gibson on a diplomatic mission. As David Zeisberger, a Moravian missionary living among the Delaware, noted in his diary, "Mr. Gibson and another white man arrived here from Fort Pitt…. Came here primarily to be on hand long enough that the Indians here would not be frightened if the Virginians should attack Wakatomica and to stop them if they came into this area."[13]

Zeisberger had established mission towns along the Tuscarawas at Schoenbrunn and Gnadenhutten, and feared that the Virginians would confuse his Christian converts with their enemy. After all, a militiaman could no sooner distinguish between a Shawnee and a Delaware than an Indian brave could tell the difference between a Virginian and a Pennsylvanian. Gibson was chosen for this mission because he had become fluent in the Delaware language while living in White Eyes' village after being captured doing Pontiac's Conspiracy and adopted into the tribe. He remained on the scene until August 8, when Zeisberger reported he "left with some Indians for the fort."[14] White Eyes may have been one of those who accompanied him, as this chief was involved hereafter in peace negotiations as a sort of minister without portfolio.

Dunmore hoped to repeat Bouquet's success in marching an army too large to attack into the heart of Indian country and forcing them to come to terms without a fight. As he was gathering men and supplies, Dunmore wrote to Colonel Andrew Lewis, instructing him to take his wing of the army north up the Kanawha, while he would personally lead the northern wing to meet him for the invasion of Shawnee country. Each wing had just over 1,000 men, while Cornstalk, the principal Shawnee chief, could only marshal about 750 braves, even with help from other tribes. Outnumbered and outgunned, Indians rarely fought whites in open battle unless they had an advantage in terms of numbers, terrain, or surprise. But their current situation made it obvious to the Shawnee that they had to attack before these two wings could meet up.

When Dunmore arrived at his eponymous fort on September 10, one witness commented that "the people of the country seem happy at His Lordship's arrival."[15] After a conference with local Indians he was trying to keep neutral, Dunmore's first military order was to send Captain William Crawford and 500 men further downstream to build a supply post. Taking along 50 pack horses and 200 head of cattle, Crawford headed for the mouth of the Hocking River in present day Athens County, Ohio.[16] Crawford knew this spot, as Washington had made a claim on fertile bottom land near here while on his land exploring expedition with Crawford in 1770. Now, on September 20, Crawford wrote to Washington, "I am this day set out with the First Division for the mouth of the Hockhocking and there to arect a post on your bottom where the troops is to rendezvous."[17] The crude structure they built was little more than a blockhouse with a cattle pen, but Dunmore christened it Fort Gower, after Lord Gower, his brother-in-law. The most significant aspect of the post was that it was the first one built on the Indian side of the Ohio.

Heading downstream with the rest of the northern wing of his army, Dunmore was at Wheeling on September 30 and arrived at Fort Gower on October 4. He sent White Eyes and Captain Pipe to the Shawnee towns on the Pickaway Plains near present-day Circleville to make one last effort to invite them to talk. When this failed, Dunmore focused on his war plans. He wrote to Lewis, changing their meeting point from the mouth of the Kanawha to Fort Gower. To deliver this message through the trackless wilderness, Dunmore entrusted a couple of scouts who shared the same first name.

Simon Kenton was a teenager who had fled to the west after he feared he had killed a love rival in a fight. Despite his youth, he had already established a reputation for his woodland skills. Simon Girty was in his thirties and had been on the frontier all his life. His family was captured by Indians in 1756, and, after burning the Girty boys' stepfather, the Indians sent Simon and his brothers to different tribes. For three years, Simon lived among the Mingo, James, the Shawnee, and George, the Delaware. After being repatriated, all three brothers found they could always find work as scouts and translators. Girty and Kenton left Dunmore's letter in a hollow tree near the confluence of the Ohio and Kanawha, as Lewis had not yet arrived at the site. This is an excellent example of just how difficult it was for eighteenth-century frontier armies to communicate, but the scouts left enough clues on the scene that their message was found.

Lewis' wing had started north on September 6, but found it slow going in the forest. At present day Charleston, West Virginia, they stopped to build boats to float down the Kanawha, and they did not arrive at the Ohio until October 6. They read Dunmore's orders, but were obliged to rest from their journey first. Meanwhile, Dunmore changed his mind again, deciding to enter into the interior of the Ohio country on his own. He sent word for Lewis to proceed and meet him near the Shawnee villages.

These orders were rendered obsolete on the morning of October 10, when Cornstalk attacked Lewis' army. The Shawnee had crossed the Ohio in the night and launched a surprise attack, but the veteran frontiersmen did not panic. Their lines held, and a fierce day of fighting ensued. Late in the afternoon, the Indians fell back, leaving the field to the whites. They carried their casualties with him, so the Indian dead and wounded remain unknown. The Virginians lost 75 dead and 140 wounded, which was an unusually high 20 percent of their force. Officer casualties were particularly high, as among the dead and wounded were three colonels, seven captains, and seven lieutenants.[18] The pioneers were exhausted, but they had held their ground and foiled the last Shawnee attempt that could keep them from uniting with Dunmore.

This spent force required a few days to recover and treat their wounded, but an impatient Dunmore pushed on. His force went upstream on the Hocking before crossing over to the Scioto River watershed towards the Shawnee towns. With one army threatening them and another on the way, Cornstalk realized the grim position his tribe was in. Calling his braves together, he suggested that they kill all their women and children and then fight the whites to the death. When this immodest proposal was met with a stunned silence, Cornstalk responded, "Then, I will go and make peace."[19] The Chief sent word to Dunmore that he was willing to negotiate.

Over in the Virginian camp, Dunmore wanted to make sure this offer was legitimate and not a stalling tactic, so he sent Simon Girty and John Gibson to investigate. Gibson was fluent in Seneca, Shawnee, and Delaware, and as a trader had a reputation for honesty, and he and Girty concluded that Cornstalk's entreaties were legitimate. Dunmore set up a time for talks, but felt that it would mean more if Logan would also attend the peace talks, so he asked Gibson to make another foray into the enemy camp to convince his brother-in-law to give his blessing to the peace process. It has been previously claimed that it was Simon Girty who sought out Logan, but Gibson later made a sworn statement saying that he went alone to seek Logan that day.[20]

As Gibson passed by Cornstalk's town, his sister Nonhelema's town, and the dreaded Shawnee burning ground, a raised plateau in a meadow that offered maximum viewing of captives being tortured, he was surprised to find Logan alongside the trail. He called to him, "My friend Logan, I am glad to see you," to which Logan sullenly replied, "Yes, I suppose you are," before turning into the impenetrable forest.[21] However, a few hours later, as Gibson was conferring with Cornstalk, Logan approached and asked Gibson to come with him. The two men walked to a large elm tree, where a tearful Logan delivered this speech:

> I appeal to any white man to say, if he entered at Logan's cabin hungry, and he gave him not meat; if he ever came cold and naked, and he clothed him not. During the course of the last long and bloody war, Logan remained idle in his cabin, an advocate for peace. Such was my love for the whites, that my countrymen pointed as they passed, and said, "Logan is the friend of white men." I had even thought to have lived with you, but for the injuries of one man. Colonel Cresap, the last spring, in cold blood, and unprovoked, murdered all the relations of Logan, not even sparing my women and children. There runs not a drop of my blood in the veins of any living creature. This called on me for revenge. I have sought it: I have killed many: I have fully glutted my vengeance. For my country, I rejoice at the beams of peace. But do not harbor the thought that mine is the joy of fear. Logan never felt fear. He will not turn on his heel to save his life. Who is there to mourn for Logan?—Not one.[22]

Logan's Lament has been cited as an excellent example of Native American eloquence, and was included in editions of *McGuffey's Readers* for schoolchildren to memorize. Thomas Jefferson said, "I may challenge the whole orations of Demosthenes and Cicero, and of any more prominent orator, if Europe has furnished one more eminent, to produce a single passage superior to the speech of Logan."[23]

The Shawnee negotiated a peace without Logan, but their only option was to agree to all of Dunmore's conditions. They agreed to return all captives, to not molest Ohio river traffic, and to allow the whites to have Kentucky. This treaty was an interim measure, with the final touches to be finalized in Pittsburgh the following spring. Dunmore refrained from any punitive measures, which relieved Cornstalk. He promised friendship and support to the Virginians, and he kept his word right up until the day he was murdered by Virginia militia.

However, the arrival of Lewis' wing on the scene threatened to shatter this peace before it could be implemented. Lewis' now rested troops wanted the chance to finish off the Shawnee. As they approached from the south, the Shawnee became alarmed, and Dunmore sent word for Lewis to come to his camp on October 24 for consultations. But Lewis decided to bring his army with him, and began marching in the general direction of the Shawnee towns. This action threatened to start a battle that would be as bloody as it was unnecessary, so Dunmore selected White Eyes and Gibson to accompany him in a desperate attempt to avoid such a battle. They managed to find Lewis just in time, and one of Lewis' officers reported, "My Lord informed us the Shawnee had agreed to all his terms and that our presence could be of no service, but rather a hindrance to the peace being concluded—he ordered the whole to return."[24] Lewis' men obeyed the order and left the next day, but were so disgruntled that Lewis tripled the guard around the governor's tent that night. The only other military action in the campaign was at the end of October, when Dunmore sent Crawford and 250 men on a raid on a Mingo village at present-day Columbus that had sponsored raids but declined to participate in the peace process.

After Lewis had returned south, the men of Dunmore's wing returned to Fort Gower. Dunmore was impatient to return to Williamsburg, but the rest of his army remained at the fort for a few days to discuss some pressing matters before returning home. During their time in the field, these men had received no news from the east, where the British had closed the port of Boston and Continental Congress was meeting in Philadelphia to discuss a response. While the men were concerned about the situation, they now had a higher level of confidence in their own abilities. Previously, frontier settlers had required British redcoats to help them fight Indians, but the only man involved in Lord Dunmore's War who was not an American was Lord Dunmore.

Led by Colonel Adam Stephen, who had served as an officer alongside Washington at Fort Necessity and Braddock's Defeat, the officers from Dunmore's wing discussed composing a set of resolves stating their position on public issues. On November 5, they approved the Fort Gower Resolves, a document addressed to the king. They begin by politely stating that they would "bear the most faithful allegiance to his Majesty King George the Third, whilst his Majesty delights to reign over a brave and free people."[25] However, they wanted it known that they now believed that "Our men can march and shoot with any of the known world,"[26] implying that their voluntary devotion had its limits. The officers confirmed this by concluding, "as the love of liberty and attachment to the real interest and just rights of America outweighs every other consideration, we resolve that we will exert every power within us for the defense of American liberty."[27]

This warning shot across the bow was not unique, as several other groups of colonists were composing similar documents at this time. For example, on July 11, 1774, George Washington, George Mason, and some neighbors had drafted the Fairfax Resolves at Mount Vernon. What did make the Fort Gower Resolves unique was that they emanated from a crude stockade so far out on the frontier that it was written on the side of the Ohio River where settlement wasn't even legal yet. The hardy men approving this document would go on to help win American freedom and tame the west. Among those who ratified the document, Stephen went on to become a major general in the Continental Army, while Morgan became a brigadier general, Clark a brigadier general of Virginia militia, and Crawford and Gibson became Continental colonels with independent commands. Their statement was issued six months before Lexington and Concord and 20 months before the Declaration of Independence was signed. The Fort Gower Resolves were printed in the *Virginia Gazette* on December 22, 1774, and were later reprinted in several other colonial newspapers as the Americans communicated with each other to coalesce around the idea of independence.

Dunmore returned to Williamsburg, arriving to a hero's welcome on December 4. A Colonial convention resolved that "the most cordial thanks ... are.... Justly due to our worthy governor, Lord Dunmore, for his truly noble, wise, and spirited conduct, on the late expedition against our Indian enemy."[28] Dunmore also retained the respect of the troops who had served under him. The Fort Gower Resolves had made implied threats against the British king, but they made sure to exempt Dunmore from their criticism, saying that he, "we are confident, underwent the fatigue of this singular campaign from no other motive than the true interest of this country."[29] The governor even managed to stay in the good graces of the crown, even though some of his expansionist policies violated both the letter and the spirit of the law. The only time Dunmore got any negative feedback was when he re-opened Fort Pitt after it had been decommissioned.

His continued good fortune led Dunmore to pursue a novel scheme. During the recent campaign, he had some interesting talks with White Eyes, the Delaware chief and diplomat. Unlike most Indians, White Eyes had traveled extensively, and he was a keen observer. He had recently returned from a trip down the Mississippi, and had sailed from New

Orleans to New York and then walked back by way of Philadelphia. White Eyes had noticed that white people who held deeds to the land they lived on never had to vacate their property, and he sought that same security for his tribe. When he proposed to Dunmore that the Delaware purchase their land from Virginia, the governor was intrigued, since it would strengthen Virginia's claim on western land to be the ones selling it to the current occupants.

Specific plans were apparently made, for in February, Zeisberger reported that John Gibson was "Getting ready to travel to Governor Dunmore in Virginia. He was expected to meet White Eyes very soon because the deed for the Delaware Indian land is supposed to be made there and they would take this with them to England."[30] It is not certain whether this plan could have succeeded, but the well-connected governor certainly seemed intent on pursuing it.

But this idea had to be discarded as the outbreak of the American Revolution caused realignments all over the continent. And, in the course of this change, Dunmore lost everything. The governor had already been quarreling with the legislature over funding, but the increase in tension with Patriots who were opposing British policies threatened to drive a much more serious wedge between the governor and the governed. Matters came to a head on April 20, 1775, coincidentally the day after Lexington and Concord. On this day, Dunmore attempted to have the gunpowder in the Williamsburg powder magazine transferred to a British warship. They were caught in the act, and the populace was outraged that their munitions were being stolen by their leader.

The one thing Virginians feared more than oppressive British tax policy was a slave insurrection, and that turned out to be Dunmore's next project. As the war started, Dunmore hoped to recruit troops loyal to the crown, and he offered freedom to any runaway slaves who would join the British Army. He hoped to recruit an "Ethiopian Regiment" of loyalist troops this way. This was the last straw for the Virginians. Not only was their governor trying to steal the people's gunpowder, but he wanted to give it to slaves to use against their masters. Dunmore continued to try and function as governor, but he was too unpopular. On June 8, 1775, he was obliged to flee to a British warship moored in the James River, as he could no longer safely set foot on the soil of the colony he was supposed to be governing.

Two

Connolly
1775

It is not a hyperbolic exaggeration to refer to the first musket fired at the battle of Lexington as the Shot Heard Round the World. For the western world at least, the April 19, 1775, battles between minutemen and redcoats caused everything to shift permanently. This was particularly true on the western frontier, which had already seen considerable conflict in previous years. In the area around Fort Pitt, fighting had first broken out between the English and American forces on one side and the French and Indians on the other. After the French had departed, the Indians fought the English and Americans on their own, and after this ended and the British Army left Fort Pitt, the Virginians quarreled with the Pennsylvanians. Now, it was going to be the Americans versus the British, but it took a while for these realignments to take shape.

There was a fifteen-month gap between the Lexington and Concord battles and the Declaration of Independence, and confusion reigned during this period. Some colonists had taken up arms, but many still supported the crown and others hoped for reform but not necessarily independence. And no one was certain whose side everyone else was on. The idea of a united America was so new that many weren't sure how to approach it. But, as word from Massachusetts reached the west, frontier leaders realized the need for action. On May 16, they got together to discuss colonial unity. Unfortunately for their cause, they gathered in separate locations, as those calling themselves Virginians met at Pittsburgh, while those who considered themselves Pennsylvanians convened in Hannahstown.

While the locals were still conflicted about state identity, calmer heads on a national level were urging all to set aside their differences and unite on behalf of America. On July 25, the Continental Congressional delegates from both Virginia and Pennsylvania addressed a joint letter to the "inhabitants of Pennsylvania and Virginia on the western side of Laurel Hill":

Two. Connolly 1775

It gives us much concern to find that disturbances have arisen and still continue among you concerning the boundaries of our counties.... As representatives of two of the colonies.... We think it is our duty to remove.... Every obstacle that may prevent her sons from cooperating ... towards the settlement of his great and important end.... The period ... will soon arrive when this unfortunate dispute ... will be peacefully and Constitutionally determined.[1]

This wise counsel came from some impressive sources, as the signatories were Thomas Jefferson, Patrick Henry, Richard Henry Lee, and Benjamin Harrison for the Virginians, and Benjamin Franklin, James Wilson, John Dickinson, James Ross, and Charles Humphries representing Pennsylvania. But it would still take a while for their words to be heeded.

Dr. John Connolly, liar, bully, sycophant, and "master of intrigue and artful address," represented a credible threat to Continental efforts in the west (The Filson Historical Society, Louisville, KY; 1913.1.374, R.T. Durrett Collection, late 19th early 20th century).

The confusion over just who was on what side complicated the conclusion of the treaty that had been begun at Camp Charlotte the previous fall. Dunmore had returned to Williamsburg with some Indian hostages, and had left Connolly in command of 75 men at Fort Dunmore. There already was some uneasiness about British policy, as Washington had written to Connolly over the winter, "with us here, things wear a disagreeable aspect, and the minds of men are exceedingly disturbed at the measures of the British government.... A little time must now unfold the mystery, as matters are drawing to a point."[2] But no one was prepared for just how quickly things changed in the spring. The reversal of Dunmore's fortunes made it impossible for him to lead peace treaty talks on the frontier. However, he had conferred with Connolly over the winter and given him instructions on how to proceed.

Since the British Army's abandonment of Fort Pitt in 1772, there had been very little presence of the government in Pittsburgh. The local highest ranking employee of the crown was Deputy Indian Agent Alexander McKee, who was focused on Indian policy, not civil matters. As someone who was dependent on the king for his salary, McKee was openly suspected of Tory sympathy, but somehow Connolly, the assistant to the Royal Governor of Virginia, was able to moderate the spring treaty conferences without arousing suspicion among the Patriots, even though, according to one contemporary, Connolly was known to be "a man of intrigue and artful address."[3]

John Connolly was born at Wrights Ferry (York), Pennsylvania, the only child of his mother's third marriage. His mother died when John was young, and the boy's father arranged for him to study medicine in Philadelphia. John had military ambitions, however, and, after brief service in the West Indies, he wound up on the Fort Pitt frontier.[4] He had connections here, as his uncle was George Croghan, the Royal Indian Agent for the middle colonies. Croghan had been a powerful officer but was semi-retired and under suspicion of being a Tory by 1775. However, he and Connolly both became involved in land speculation schemes. Washington had reported of his first meeting with Connolly in 1770: "Dr. Connolly is so much delighted with the lands and climate on this river that he seems to wish for nothing more than to induce one hundred families to go there to live that he might be among them."[5] Connolly did some river travel, and included in the land he tried to claim for his own were several thousand acres in what is today's downtown Louisville.

The spring treaty conference scheduled for the fort had ostensibly been to finalize the Camp Charlotte agreements. However, the events at Lexington and Concord had exponentially magnified the issues that needed to be addressed. With tribal loyalties at stake, both Tories and Patriots wanted to make their case. Though suspected of being a Tory and even briefly detained, Connolly managed to preside over talks without arousing suspicion, but later claimed he had duped the Patriots and had actively been recruiting the Indians for the British. However, there were still too many issues to address, and it was decided to host more comprehensive treaty talks in the fall.

After concluding talks with local tribes in June, Connolly left for Williamsburg shortly afterwards to consult with Dunmore. The governor's difficulties with the last session of the House of Burgesses had led to Dunmore's ordering the evacuation of the forts at Point Pleasant,

Wheeling, and Pittsburgh. Connolly dismissed his garrison, which left a wartime town bereft of troops. Connolly's visit was allegedly to discuss plans for future treaty talks, but he had a proposal he wanted to lay before Dunmore.

Arriving at Dunmore's shipboard governor's office in early August, Connolly explained his plan to split the colonies in two. His proposal was to recruit a regiment of loyalists near Pittsburgh and take them to Detroit. From there, he would utilize British forces and supplies, and would launch an assault on Fort Pitt with Indian help. After this, he would proceed to the Potomac and head downstream. Dunmore and his troops would move to meet him and the Americans would be cut in half, and more easily defeated. Dunmore was impressed by this plan. Though his power was diminished, he still had influence, as Washington said of him, "if that man is not crushed, he will become the most formidable enemy America has."[6] Dunmore sent Connolly by ship to Boston to consult with General Thomas Gage, the British commander of forces in North America. He sailed away on August 22.

Before he left, Connolly wrote to White Eyes on behalf of Dunmore concerning their plan for the Delaware to obtain deeds for their land. There being no regular mail delivery to Indian villages, Connolly sent his letter to John Gibson, the trader and friend of White Eyes, with instructions to forward it. Because of Gibson's close association with Dunmore, Connolly assumed he was a fellow Tory, and, in his cover letter to Gibson, he revealed too much, as he mocked the Patriot cause and promised Gibson a reward for his loyalty. He urged Gibson to "Avoid the overzealous exertion of what is now ridiculously called patriotic spirit," since that "ill-timed folly must draw upon them inevitable destruction."[7] He advised Gibson to "Be prevailed upon to shun the popular error and judge for yourself; act as a good subject, and expect the rewards due to your services."[8] Although Connolly later claimed "I had reason to suspect Lord Dunmore reposed too much confidence in the gentleman,"[9] he nonetheless sent a letter that revealed his true feelings and plans to a Patriot leader.

While this was going on, the Americans were coming to realize the importance of the west and of the fall Indian conference at Fort Pitt. On July 12, Continental Congress created the American Indian Department, and they followed the British model by dividing the frontier into northern, middle, and southern departments. The middle department was headquartered in Pittsburgh, and had the same goal of keeping the Indians neutral. Virginia also became active, as in their final session, the

House of Burgesses named George Washington, Andrew Lewis, Adam Stephen, and three others to represent Virginia at the fall conference.

Washington, however, could not serve, as he had just been named commander-in-chief of the army by Continental Congress. He arrived in Boston after the Battle of Bunker Hill to lead the troops against Gage's redcoats. For the next few years, he would be too busy fighting the British for Boston, New York, and Philadelphia to pay much attention to the west.

The Virginians also sought to fill a military vacuum by ordering that "John Neville be directed to march his company of 100 men, and take possession of Fort Pitt, and that said company be in the pay of this colony from the time of their marching."[10] Neville was assembling his men in Winchester, Virginia, and did not arrive at Fort Pitt until September. However, at this time, diplomatic efforts were more important than military ones, as the Americans went all out to try and win friends among the Indians. The Virginians sent James Wood, one of their designated agents, on a western tour, and he, accompanied by Simon Girty as scout and translator, set out on an extended trip to personally invite as many chiefs as possible.

Wood left Williamsburg on June 25 and was at Fort Pitt by July 9. Preliminary talks with Indians had just been concluded, and the consensus was that Connolly had done a fair job. Wood quickly found that a part of his diplomatic duties consisted of trying to explain to the Indians why the two English-speaking groups who had previously worked together were now fighting each other. White Eyes approached Wood about his plans to join Dunmore in pursuing deeds for the Delaware, and Wood wrote, "I was under the necessity of acquainting him with the disputes between Lord Dunmore and the people of Virginia."[11] Other visiting tribes had less urgent agendas, as Wood observed, "About fifteen.... Shawnee arrived ... they immediately got drunk and continued in that situation for two days."[12]

Wood and Girty left Fort Pitt on July 18. They were welcomed at the nearby Delaware and Moravian towns on the Tuscarawas and the other tribes on the Muskingum. Wood even attended church in the Moravian mission at Gnadenhutten, noting that the missionaries "prayed in the Delaware language, preached in the English and sang songs in the German," and that "The church is a decent square log building, with plank floors and benches.... A small cupola with a bell, and a very indifferent spinet (piano)."[13] The Shawnee along the lower Scioto were also willing to listen, but at some of the Mingo towns on the upper Scioto, they faced both an undercurrent of warnings and open threats. At Pluggy's Town, a known nest of renegades, Wood found "all the Indians drunk and very troublesome."[14]

The volatility of drunken Indians was a factor in frontier affairs. Alcohol, like firearms and smallpox, was something the Indians had been never exposed to and had no resistance to. A shipment of alcohol could render an entire town too drunk to conduct business for days. A missionary among the Indians explained,

> It is not easy for a white man, used to the warm comfort of civilized life to conceive how delicious and exhilarating rum is to the taste and stomach of an Indian.... Living principally in the shade and damps of the forest and sleeping on the moist ground, exposed to rain and cold with slight covering ... the powerful stimulant of ardent spirits is ... wonderfully exhilarating.[15]

Despite the dangers, Wood and Girty were able to complete their mission. They returned to Fort Pitt on August 11, having traveled 800 miles in 25 days to visit 15 villages.[16] Both the Virginians and the Americans realized what an opportunity the upcoming talks represented. In negotiations, Native Americans usually favored the side that represented the least threat to them, which would often be the French, or the side that offered the best trade goods as gifts, which was usually the British. The Americans normally had little to offer to endear themselves to the Indians.

However, current conditions altered this calculus. The Americans, hoping to get the French Canadians to align with them, had launched an invasion of Canada. But the French stayed loyal to England, and the invasion became the first of many unsuccessful American forays into Canada. However, the Americans had some initial success and were able to capture Montreal. The British supplied all their Great Lakes forts by water—sailing the St. Lawrence River and Lake Ontario to Fort Niagara, where all supplies shipped from Europe were disbursed to the interior. With the Americans holding Montreal, goods could not be shipped to Fort Niagara, so for once the Americans could offer competitive gifts.

Anxious to exploit Two, the Americans sought to maximize turnout for the conference scheduled to begin in late September. On September 12, they impatiently announced that "the Indians not being arrived and the commissioners being informed they were on the road, thought proper to dispatch Mr. John Gibson with the Indian Ellenipsico.... To meet and hasten them."[17] Ellenipsico was the son of the Shawnee chief Cornstalk, and he and Gibson carried a large white wampum belt to all nearby villages.

These wampum belts played a major role in Native American diplomacy. The beads in the belt comprised the message, with predominantly white belts proposing peace and black belts advocating war. A belt would be presented to a village, who then had the choice of either accepting, delaying, or rejecting its message. Gibson and Ellenipsico delivered their peace message and returned to Fort Pitt on September 24. All of the Shawnee had not yet arrived, but Gibson now presented Connolly's letter to the commissioners. This letter exposed Connolly's intentions, and led to orders for his arrest.

The Fort Pitt treaty talks finally opened on September 26, after the arrival of the last of the Shawnee delegation, and Neville's recently arrived garrison participated in the opening ceremonies. The official account of the treaty talks states, "The Shawnee being arrived, the commissioners received them with drum and colors and a salute of small arms from the garrison and ... conducted them to a council house erected for the occasion."[18] The American pre-conference effort led to an unusually large turnout. Among the local tribes, Cornstalk of the Shawnee, White Eyes of the Delaware, and Guyasuta of the Mingo all attended with several other lesser chiefs. Their presence was augmented by Flying Crow of the eastern Iroquois and Shagamba, the son of the great Ottawa chief Pontiac, and Half King of the Wyandot, both of whom came all the way from near British headquarters at Detroit.

The Americans also sent some of their best people. The Virginia delegation was well stocked with experienced frontiersmen who expected to play a major role, since it was Virginia that had originally called for the conference. But the Continental Congress realized the importance of avoiding Indian warfare in the west, and they sent Lewis Morris and James Wilson of Pennsylvania as representatives. Both of these luminaries would go on to sign the Declaration of Independence the following summer.

The finalization of the details of the Camp Charlotte accords was addressed first, but there were many other matters and perspectives to deal with afterwards. White Eyes used this meeting to try to improve the lot of his Delaware tribe. Ever since a treaty in 1744, the Delaware had been forced to accept Iroquois superiority and White Eyes saw this new conflict as a chance to break this hold from the now weakened tribe. He now stated, "I also now acquaint my uncles the Six Nations that ... as we have now acquainted you what lands belong to us, I desire you will not permit any of your foolish people to sit down upon it."[19]

White Eyes had been forced to accept previously that his plans with

Dunmore had been dashed, but the indefatigable diplomat was willing to start all over and cultivate a friendship with the Americans. Immediately after the treaty, White Eyes left for Philadelphia, where he lobbied Continental Congress to send missionaries and teachers to his tribe and sought a Delaware/American alliance with admission as a fourteenth state.

Intensive daily treaty talks ran until October 19. One contentious issue throughout the process was the return of captives and property taken during previous Indian raids. The Shawnee had readily agreed to return captives and property when they were threatened by two armies the previous autumn, but were less willing to do so once the crisis had passed and the Americans wanted favors of them. White children who had grown up among Indians often resisted repatriation. And captured or runaway slaves may have been counted in the "property" column, along with horses, but they were human beings who were loath to be returned to servitude. After much debate, it was finally determined that in the "part of the treaty relating to the delivery of the prisoners, Negroes and horses which remain among the Indians, Mr. John Gibson with one other white man is appointed for the colony of Virginia,"[20] and a handful of representatives of other tribes were named to work with him.

This treaty turned out well for the Americans. They did not convince any tribes to join them, but they managed at least to keep all tribes neutral in exchange for honoring the Ohio River as a permanent boundary. When Thomas Walker, one of the Virginia commissioners, returned to Williamsburg, he reported that "all the different nations who attended the treaty are peacefully disposed, notwithstanding the endeavors of several persons from Fort Detroit to set them against this colony in particular."[21] This result made 1775 one of the most successful years of the Revolution on the frontier, even though the role played by the garrison at Fort Pitt was so small that it was literally just for show.

Keeping the natives neutral bought the West another year of peace. This meant the troops recruited in the West could be sent to join Washington's army in the East, while also encouraging new settlers to head West. At Detroit, newly arrived Lieutenant Governor Henry Hamilton complained to his boss, Guy Carlton, "the Virginians have several emissaries in pay here and have given away in presents and provisions to the amount of three thousand pounds."[22] The American blockade of the St. Lawrence would be temporary, as would be Indian neutrality, but for now, the Americans in the West were off to a good start.

While this was going on, Connolly was making progress with his scheme. He sailed from Virginia on August 22 and arrived in Boston ten days later. He convinced General Gage that not only could he recruit a Loyalist regiment near Pittsburgh, but he could use his influence with the Indians to convince them to join him. Gage endorsed Connolly's campaign and approved a lieutenant colonel's commission in the British Army for him. He issued orders for troops in Illinois to proceed to Detroit and report to Connolly, and gave him access to British artillery and supplies at Detroit. Connolly normally would have sailed directly on to Quebec, but the American blockade of the St. Lawrence meant he had to return to Virginia to plot a land route.

As Connelly was preparing to return to Virginia, his plans were revealed by an aide. William Cowley wrote to Washington, who was already in Boston opposing Gage, and gave him complete details of the expedition, including Connolly's plan to lure convicts and indentured servants to his banner by offering freedom and 300 acres to all recruits.[23] Between this betrayal and Connolly's confession to Gibson, there were enough smoking guns pointed at Connolly that the Americans fully realized how dangerous he was.

Connolly arrived back in Virginia on October 12, and it was here that his officer's commission was sent. After conferring with Dunmore, the two made final plans. After conquering the west, Connolly would head downstream on the Potomac, while Dunmore would lead troops north from Norfolk, and the two would meet in Alexandria on April 20, 1776, to celebrate the splitting of the colonies in two.

But Dunmore never made it to that rendezvous. In December, he gathered what troops he could and tried to fight his way out of Norfolk, but was defeated at the Battle of Great Bridge on December 9. After burning Norfolk, Dunmore retreated to an island at the mouth of the Rappahannock River. In 1776, Dunmore gave up and sailed away. He later served as the governor of Bahamas, then retired to his estate in Scotland, where he died in 1809.

Connolly never made it to Alexandria, either. He originally planned to make his way west by going up the Mississippi River, but ultimately decided on an overland trip across the mountains. He left on November 13 with two aides, but was recognized near Hagerstown, Maryland, six days later. A copy of his letter to Gibson had been circulated, and Connolly was arrested by a group of captors that he deemed "ignorant and stupidly turbulent."[24] Most of his hidden papers were not found, and one of his aides managed to smuggle some letters out, but Connolly was clearly too dangerous to be allowed to remain at large, and he was sent to Philadelphia for imprisonment.

At first, Connolly was visited by his wife, his father-in-law Sam Samples, and his half-brother, who was an officer in the Continental Army. But, after he refused to renounce his allegiance to the king, he was given no more furloughs and received no more visitors. In December 1776, Connolly and some others attempted to escape, but their rope broke and nearly killed one of the would-be escapees. When the Americans were forced to evacuate Philadelphia before the British took it in the fall of 1777, Continental Congress relocated to York, Pennsylvania, and Connolly and other prisoners came along.

At York, Connolly's chief activity was complaining about his treatment. He railed about crowded cells, overzealous guards, and unsanitary conditions that threatened his health, and he demanded to be exchanged for an American prisoner of war of equal rank. In May 1778, he detailed the abuses he had endured in a formal complaint to Continental Congress, where he denounced being "subject to all the indignities and low insults of an illiberal gaoler and turnkey, and placed upon the same footing as horse thieves, deserters, negroes, and the lowest and most despicable of the human race."[25]

Such specific and voluminous charges had to be addressed, and Continental Congress sent a committee to investigate. They concluded that "the account given by the prisoner ... appears to be founded in misrepresentation.... When Mr. Connolly represented himself at the point of death from the severity of his confinement, the board directed Dr. Shippen to visit him, who reported that the situation was directly opposite his representation, his dispositions slight, and merely of an hypochondriac nature."[26] The investigatory board also found conditions uncrowded and adequate and noted that if Connolly had extra security, it was because he had already been caught trying to escape. And, as for the demand to be exchanged, it was pointed out that Connolly was captured as an officer out of uniform behind enemy lines, which made him more eligible for hanging than parole. This should have silenced Connolly, but he continued to complain about his treatment.

Connolly finally was paroled on July 4, 1780, but was not formally exchanged until October 25, after nearly five years' incarceration. He never went near Pittsburgh again, but, like Simon Girty, he was so feared that rumors of his presence abounded. Connolly went to New York City to report for duty. He had been a lieutenant colonel in the British Army for five years, yet he had never worn a uniform or led troops for a single day of that time. It was finally decided to send Connolly south to Virginia to command a regiment of Virginia and North Carolina loyalists in Cornwallis's army.

However, the southern climate proved difficult for Connolly's delicate constitution, as he complained of "putrescent effluvia"[27] that he found incapacitating. He asked Cornwallis for a leave of absence that was granted. But, while heading for a better climate on September 21, 1781, Connolly passed through American lines and was captured again and taken to Washington. He wrote of this meeting:

> I was now to see a man with whom I had formerly been upon a footing of intimacy, I may say of friendship. Politics might induce us to meet as enemies in the field, but should not have made us personally so. I had small time for reflection; we met him coming on horseback to view the camp. I can only say the friendly sentiments he once publicly professed for me no longer existed. He ordered me to be conducted to the Marquis de La Fayette's headquarters.[28]

This time, Connolly was held until March 1782. Upon his release, he went to New York and sailed for London. From there he lobbied for compensation for his sufferings and losses and self-published a pamphlet detailing his travails. When this failed to produce the desired result, Connolly returned to Canada, but continued to engage in intrigue. In 1788, he came down the Maumee and Miami Rivers to Kentucky. The alleged purpose of his trip was to lobby for his Kentucky land claims, but he had a hidden agenda as well. Kentucky was not admitted as a state until 1792, and was considered a part of Virginia until that time. However, the residents felt that Virginia was not doing enough to protect them from Indian attacks, so they were considering other options. Some advocated forming an independent country that might form a protective alliance with Spain or England. Both the Spanish at New Orleans and the British at Detroit had active designs on the west and both feared American expansion.

In a series of meetings with Kentucky officials, Connolly offered 10,000 British troops for protection if Kentucky would agree to wage war on Spain. Unbeknownst to Connolly, one of these men, James Wilkinson, was a Spanish agent. Wilkinson had served as a general in the Revolution and then came to Kentucky after the war. In 1787, he offered his services to the Spanish, promising to convince Kentucky to align with Spain. He continued to be paid in silver as Agent Thirteen of the Spanish government even after becoming commander of the U.S. Army. Wilkinson reported Connolly's activities to Spain, and then

Two. Connolly 1775

advised Connolly to be careful while in Kentucky, lest he be assaulted for being British. Then, to make sure this became a self-fulfilling prophecy, he hired someone to follow Connolly and do just that. Connolly returned to Canada and pursued other unsuccessful schemes before dying in Montreal in 1813.

As 1775 came to a close, there was a tentative peace on the western frontier. The American invasion of Canada had failed, but it would still be a while before the British could get fresh supplies to their Great Lakes posts. One leftover task from the treaty of Fort Pitt was the repatriation of captives. John Gibson, acting as Indian agent for Virginia, was supposed to be in charge of this, but he undertook this delicate mission with less support than had been promised him. On November 11 the Reverend Zeisberger at Schoenbrunn wrote, "Mr. Gibson, the current agent of Indian affairs, arrived here from Pittsburgh with three other white people and some Mingo. They were on a journey to the Shawnee to receive the prisoners and what they had promised them in the treaty."[29]

Like Wood before him, Gibson was impressed by the tranquility of the mission towns. The Moravians were a Christian sect that moved from Central Europe to England to seek religious freedom. Arriving in America in the 18th century, they became involved with missionary work and education among Native Americans. A fellow missionary noticed their success and commented, "The Moravians appear to have adopted the best mode of Christianizing the Indians. They go among them without noise or parade and by their friendly behavior conciliate their good will ... and gradually instill into the minds of individuals the principles of religion."[30] The leader of the Tuscarawas Valley missions, David Zeisberger, spoke seven different languages and had been involved with mission work since 1745, and he and his top assistant, John Heckewelder, had their greatest success here. The streets were laid out in a grid pattern, alcohol was prohibited, and firearms were permissible for hunting only. The mission towns were not only more civilized than other Indian villages, but also in comparison to Pittsburgh. However this peaceful interlude was brief, as Gibson's party now had to go into Shawnee territory to pry reluctant captives from resistant hosts.

Gibson proved to be up to this challenge. On March 29, 1776, Zeisberger noted in his diary, "Mr. Gibson came here from the Shawnee with a party of warriors with about 20 white prisoners. He had spent the winter there and had much trouble and had endured many dangers until he got a party of warriors on his side. They took the prisoners away by force and said if they could not take them to the fort alive, they would take their scalps there."[31] After this bluff, he was able to complete his mission and returned to Fort Pitt on April 8.

Gibson found a changed situation upon his return. He had undertaken his mission as Indian agent for Virginia, but he was also working on behalf of the new federal government, as, on April 24, 1776, the Indian affairs department of Continental Congress authorized the payment of 141 pounds to Gibson, "for sundry services in the middle department."[32] However, Gibson was now informed by Richard Butler that he was being superseded in the federal realm. Butler, who had extensive Indian trading experience himself, would have been a good choice as replacement, but his was only a temporary duty. In April, Continental Congress named George Morgan as Indian Agent for the Middle Colonies. The appointment of the first full-time western representative of the new federal government was a sign that the Americans were now willing to commit personnel to the war effort in the west.

Three

Morgan
1776

Based on experience alone, George Morgan appeared to be a good choice for the job of Indian Agent for the middle colonies. He was born in Philadelphia in 1742 of Welsh immigrant parents and received a good general education. In 1760, Morgan went to work as a clerk for the firm of Baynton and Wharton, a western fur trading company based in Philadelphia. Morgan was intelligent, hard-working, and ambitious, and, in 1764 he also married Baynton's daughter and became a full partner in the firm of Baynton, Wharton, and Morgan.

The following year, Morgan was sent west to Pittsburgh to supervise operations there. In the aftermath of Pontiac's Conspiracy, the fur trade was undergoing great changes, as the French departure from North America and Pontiac's ultimate failure made for an English and American monopoly. An area ripe for exploitation was what was referred to as the Illinois Country. This referred to the entire upper Mississippi Valley, but specifically to a few French towns in southern Illinois along the Mississippi near St. Louis. The departure of the French traders offered new opportunities, and several companies sent representatives to tap this market.

Morgan was in Illinois between 1766 and 1768, fighting for his company's interest in dominating this market. As the area was beyond the control of the law, it was not surprising that the competition was cutthroat. Morgan was more than willing to do his part here, but his firm failed to corner the market, although he did manage to establish good relationships with Indian leaders. In addition, his company also became heavily involved in western land speculation, another popular pursuit for fur moguls.

Morgan became the secretary and agent of the Indiana Company. Also known as the Suffering Traders, this was a group of traders who had incurred inventory losses when Pontiac's Conspiracy broke out. The

George Morgan, a colorful and controversial diplomat, was the first full time federal employee of Continental Congress in the west. He retired to his farm near Pittsburgh, where he continued his agricultural experiments (photographed by Mike Wintermantel. Historical Marker Database, http://www.hmdb.org).

Indiana Company lobbied the British crown for compensation in terms of land grants rather than cash. In the Treaty of Fort Stanwix, many of these traders were awarded land, and Morgan kept the company active in hopes of further grants.

Although he was frequently in the west and a regular presence around Pittsburgh, Morgan kept a home near Philadelphia. During the Revolution, he purchased a farm near Princeton, New Jersey, and began doing agricultural studies and experiments there. When Continental Congress selected him as Indian agent in April, he left immediately for the west, arriving at Fort Pitt on May 16.[1]

Three. Morgan 1776

As the only federal employee of the new American government west of the Appalachians, Morgan's main job was to keep the Indians in the Ohio country from going to war against America. As a diplomat, he already had a favorable view of Native Americans, as well as a disdain for military interference in diplomatic matters. The following winter, Morgan added the duties of commissary general at Fort Pitt to his job duties, and was given the rank of colonel. But, even though he preferred to call himself by that rank, he nonetheless considered the army to be an enemy of peace, and a bully that needed to be reined in. He later told another federal official:

> At what time do a people violate the laws of nations, as the US have done with regards to the Northwest Indians? Only when they think they can do it with impunity. Justice between nations is founded on reciprocal fear. Rome whilst weak was equitable: became more strong than her neighbors, she ceased to be just. The ambitious and powerful are always unjust. To them the laws of nations are mere chimeras.[2]

These lofty sentiments were not shared by the local settlers. Morgan's mere willingness to dialogue with the Indians, let alone his notion of treating them fairly, was enough to arouse suspicion that he was a Tory. But his belief that a peaceful way to settle the west could be found was in conjunction with the goals of Continental Congress, especially now, since no troops could yet be sent westward.

The only American soldiers in the west were a few widely scattered militia at a handful of posts. At Fort Pitt, it was noted that "Captain Neville was occupied with garrison duties and Indian negotiations,"[3] and this was the only account of military activity at this time. Neville was born in Virginia in 1731, and fought at Braddock's Defeat. He settled in the Winchester area and became a county sheriff. After the Treaty of Fort Stanwix, he purchased land near Pittsburgh, and when a call for a Fort Pitt garrison was made, he was selected to lead a 100 man contingent composed mainly of Frederick County (VA) militia. Although he played a role in hosting Indian negotiations, Neville's force was too small to do anything but defend Fort Pitt.

There were smaller militia garrisons posted at a few other nearby forts, such as Kittanning on the Allegheny and Wheeling on the Ohio. The other post they maintained was at the site of the Point Pleasant battle, over 200 miles downstream on the Ohio. The Americans built a fort at this key location in 1775, but it was later abandoned and burned by Indians. In the summer of 1776, it was decided to rebuild that fort, and Captain Matthew Arbuckle passed through Pittsburgh with a company of Virginia militia. Since militia enlistments were short term, most local forts rotated garrisons, but the isolation of this new post made this more difficult, and Arbuckle complained about "My station so remote from advice or counsel."[4]

These were the only Western military forts with standing garrisons, but there were a number of private stockades scattered across the frontier. These posts did not have manned garrisons but were essentially neighborhood safe houses. Settlers who gathered here in times of attack might lose their crops and livestock, but they would be safe, as Indians would rarely attack an armed fort. These forts, or stations, were enclosed stockades, or sometimes just a blockhouse. After Continental troops came west, they were sometimes sent on temporary duty at these community stockades: Lieutenant John Hardin led a 28 man contingent at Holiday's Cove (Weirton, WV), in 1779.[5] This practice of "forting up" was practiced locally all across the frontier, and one author has identified nearly 40 private forts and blockhouses between the Ohio and Monongahela Rivers.[6]

In Kentucky, the first settlers in the new region had also built community stockades, and they initially kept women and children waiting back east. There were just three of these stockades built in 1775, with a total population of about 350 men. By the summer of 1776, Indian threats had left all three posts contemplating evacuation. On June 6, representatives of all towns met and elected George Rogers Clark and one other man to represent them in the Virginia assembly. Clark and his partner made a perilous overland journey, avoiding Indians and bad weather conditions, only to arrive in Williamsburg to find the legislature not in session.

A determined Clark approached Virginia governor Patrick Henry to make his case. Virginia had previously claimed all Virginia lands, and Clark retorted that "if a country was not worth protecting, it was not worth claiming."[7] After meeting with state officials, Clark was able to convince them to assume responsibility for the defense of Kentucky, and they offered 500 pounds of gunpowder to show good faith. Kentucky County was added as a new western county of Virginia and Clark was established as the commanding militia officer. Clark got his gunpowder back to Kentucky by the first of the year. As the population of Kentucky grew exponentially during the war, new counties were created regularly, but Clark remained in charge of Kentucky defenses, and no Continental Army troops were ever sent there. Kentucky remained a Virginia issue and not under control of Washington or his Western

Department, although Clark and various Fort Pitt commanders did try to coordinate their efforts.

For the British at Detroit, their biggest problem was a lack of manpower. They had only a handful of troops assigned to the entire Great Lakes region, and they were widely dispersed in small garrisons. In addition, the Great Lakes and Canadian populations were sparse and mainly composed of French-Canadians whose loyalty to England was tenuous. Hamilton had arrived as Lieutenant Governor at Detroit in November 1775, and was promoted to lieutenant colonel in command of the military the following summer. He had at his immediate disposal just 120 regulars from the 8th Foot under Captain Lernoult, and just about 350 French-Canadian militia, as well as two navy schooners on Lake Erie that each had twelve cannons that fired a six pound ball.[8] With fewer than 500 men at his disposal, Hamilton was going to be dependent on Indian help.

In May, the British hosted a conference at Fort Niagara to try and recruit Indian allies. The invitation was open to all, so Guyasuta attended and reported back to Fort Pitt afterwards. But there were no real secrets here, as the British were trying to buy Indian loyalty and use them as cannon fodder, which the tribes were in a poor position to resist. Not only were the British less of a threat to them than the Americans, but over the years they had become addicted to some of the creature comforts offered by their traders. Every so often, Indian religious leaders would implore their tribes to renounce white products, but the need was too strong, especially in regards to guns. Native Americans were able to obtain rifles easily enough, but they had no ability to repair them or to obtain gunpowder without European help. Gunpowder was such a precious commodity that Indians usually conserved it by using light charges in their rifles.[9]

A lack of gunpowder was also a major problem for the Americans. They had many fine craftsmen who could produce rifles on a small scale, but lacked the infrastructure for the manufacture of gunpowder. It is a measure of just how reckless the Americans were that they declared war on their only source of gunpowder. British rivals like France and Spain were willing to provide the precious powder, but they had to do so in secret to avoid going to war with England. In 1776, the Americans at Fort Pitt tried to make a Spanish connection.

George Gibson was the younger brother of John Gibson by seven years. He came west as John's trading partner and was involved in the Illinois trade. He served in Dunmore's War and, when the Revolution began, he organized a rifle company and became its captain. While his older brother was conscientious and earnest, the 6'5" George was more gregarious. When he found that no one in his company could play the fife, he joined his own company band as a fifer, and it was said that "his lively disposition and fund of anecdote made him universally popular."[10] He was no disciplinarian, and his company got such a reputation for boozing and brawling that they earned the sarcastic nickname "Gibson's Lambs."

However, it was another attribute of Gibson's that now became useful to the colonial cause. The Gibson boys had both learned Spanish from their French Huguenot mother, and now it was determined to send George to Spanish New Orleans to try to purchase gunpowder. He would be accompanied by a handful of his lambs and his second-in-command, Lieutenant William Linn, an experienced woodsman. Linn had been born in New Jersey in 1734, but came west as a young man. He served in the Forbes Campaign in 1758 and was wounded at Wakatomica in Dunmore's War.

Gibson and Linn left Pittsburgh in July. They traveled just under a thousand miles on the Ohio River and then another thousand on the Mississippi to finally arrive in New Orleans. Here, at Gibson's suggestion, he was publicly arrested immediately to throw off the British. The Americans were then housed comfortably while the negotiations progressed. Gibson was aided by the presence of Oliver Pollock, a transplanted merchant who was originally from Gibson's hometown of Lancaster, Pennsylvania. In late summer, the Spanish agreed to sell 10,000 pounds of gunpowder for $1,800.[11] This purchase was made on a draft of the state of Virginia, as the powder would be used by Virginia militia centered around Fort Pitt.

In October, Gibson sailed from New Orleans with a small portion of the powder as a decoy. Meanwhile, Linn and the rest of the troops went north with 98 barrels of gunpowder. They arrived at Arkansas Post, a Spanish fort on the lower Mississippi, on November 26 and spent the winter there. Back on the frontier, there was much concern over the fate of this party and its cargo, and, in January, a militia leader worried, "I have great reason to apprehend danger from the savages."[12] But Linn headed north again in the spring and managed to avoid both British and Indian patrols. They arrived on the Ohio River on March 3, and proceeded to the Falls of the Ohio (Louisville), where they portaged the barrels around the falls by hand. They finally returned safely the first week of May with a sufficient supply of gunpowder to keep the war going.

Three. Morgan 1776

While soldiers were preparing for war, George Morgan was hoping to prolong the peace. He scheduled treaty talks at Fort Pitt for the fall, and decided to repeat the previous plan of sending out an early envoy to help promote turnout. Indian trader William Wilson was chosen to deliver invitations in the same way that Wood and Girty had done the previous summer. He left in June, but it was determined his pleas would be more effective if he had leading white and Indian figures accompany him. Both Morgan and White Eyes came with him to the Shawnee country, and, after Morgan had returned to Fort Pitt, Wilson traveled further with both White Eyes and Cornstalk. Wilson and White Eyes then went on further west into Wyandot territory, and then went all the way to Detroit.

White Eyes had previously been heavily involved with negotiations with Lord Dunmore and other British officials. It was true that he had recently lobbied Continental Congress for teachers for his tribe, but, as a diplomat, he assumed he would always be welcomed for a dialogue with the British. But this turned out to not be the case. Zeisberger reported that Governor Hamilton publicly rejected White Eyes' wampum, "Cut up their belts" and demanded, "they had better leave within the hour.... He told White Eyes he was Virginian."[13]

Despite setbacks such as this, a good turnout was generated at Fort Pitt, and Morgan was able to reaffirm neutrality from the local tribes. On November 8, 1776, Morgan proudly reported to Continental Congress:

> The cloud which has threatened to break over this part of the country has now dispersed. The Six Nations, Delaware, Shawnee, Muncie and Mohican envoys have assembled here to the number of 644, and promised inviolable peace with the US, and neutrality during the war with Great Britain.... Several chiefs have accepted the invitation to visit Congress, which is a further proof of their peaceable disposition.[14]

While it was true that this large contingent confirmed their neutrality and a dozen chiefs did arrive in Philadelphia for a visit on December 7, Morgan's report was clearly made through rose-colored glasses. Though he no doubt wanted to portray his efforts in the best possible light, Morgan left a lot out of his official report. For one thing, among the 644 attendees was not a single representative from the Miami, Wyandot, or Ottawa centered around Detroit, and also none from the farther Illinois or Great Lakes tribes. These tribes were all technically still neutral, but none had cared enough to hear the U.S. overtures. Also, the frontier was hardly at peace. The major tribes might currently be neutral, but smaller bands of raiders roamed freely. The Mingo, a tribe of castoffs with less tribal unity than most, welcomed renegades to their towns on the upper Scioto watershed. From here, raiding parties were launched on individual homesteads in both Kentucky and Pennsylvania. The motive for these raids was more criminal than political, but this offered scant solace to the beleaguered victims.

Even the nominally friendly Shawnee and Delaware had cracks in their ranks. Some younger chiefs from these tribes advocated declaring for the British, and it seemed like treaty conferences often started with leaders on either side having to apologize for the rash behavior of some of their "foolish young men." Cornstalk of the Shawnee remained loyal to the Americans, but others in his tribe were not. And the Delaware were undergoing changes at this time. Their chief spokesman had been Netawatwes, or Newcomer, who had been born near Philadelphia at about the same time that William Penn was landing the first whites on the Delaware. In his long lifetime, Netawatwes had seen his tribe pushed across Pennsylvania and into Ohio, and this would continue. The venerable chief died on October 31, 1776. Just 42 years later, his grandson Anderson would agree that the remains of the once numerous tribe be shipped to a reservation west of the Mississippi. Netawatwes' death left White Eyes as the leading tribal spokesman, and the new chief's principal village was at Coshocton, a few miles downstream from Newcomerstown. White Eyes had an excellent rapport with George Morgan, but he did not share his rosy assessment after his trip to Detroit. Neither did the Reverend Zeisberger, who wrote in his diary, "Everyone now believes there will be a general war."[15] Zeisberger was so alarmed that he started a new mission town near Coshocton to seek Delaware protection. He later consolidated all missions at this site for safety.

Back in the east, 1776 was one year when George Washington gave little thought to western lands, as he was kept busy trying to keep his army intact. After the British had evacuated Boston, their next target was New York, and here the Continental Army was thoroughly defeated and barely escaped from the British. The bedraggled Americans retreated across New Jersey, and it looked like a grim winter ahead until a Christmas night American raid on Trenton and followup victory at Princeton helped revive national morale.

It was now obvious that this would be a long and difficult war. And there was no turning back after the Declaration of Independence had been issued. The Americans had declared war on the country that was the sole source of most of their manufacturing products, so they knew

Three. Morgan 1776

they would need foreign help. But now they also realized that if they were going to defeat the strongest military power in the world, they were going to need a bigger army.

After signing the Declaration of Independence, Continental Congress authorized the expansion of the army. A bill authorizing the creation of sixteen new regiments called for two of these units to be raised on and for the protection of the western frontier. A full-time army in the West would mean permanent garrisons and the possibility of launching offensives. But, in the effort to unite Americans, divisions were still rampant, and these two new regiments recruited in the same area wound up representing different states.

In 1776, Virginia had reorganized the West Augusta District, which had its county seat 170 miles away at Staunton, Virginia, into three counties between the Ohio and Monongahela Rivers. But these new county lines conflicted with existing lines drawn by the Pennsylvanians, which resulted in neighbors claiming to live in different states. This resulted in recruiting men for the Eighth Pennsylvania regiment who considered themselves Pennsylvanians, and then gathering their neighbors who thought they were Virginians to join the 13th Virginia, or West Augusta, Regiment. These regiments were filled in the summer and fall of 1776 with the promise that they would remain on the frontier, but both units wound up being split up.

Even though these new regiments were raised to fight frontier warfare, they were organized along the same lines as European regiments of that era. A regiment consisted of between eight and twelve companies, with each company containing 90 men. A company was commanded by a captain, who was assisted by a first and a second lieutenant, or a lieutenant and an ensign. A regiment was led by a colonel, who was assisted by a lieutenant colonel and a major. Four or five regiments comprised a brigade, which was led by a brigadier general, and two or more brigades constituted a division to be led by a major general.[16] A regiment was supposed to contain between 700 and 1,000 men, but rarely did, and the numbers dropped as the war dragged on. When the Eighth Pennsylvania and West Augusta Regiments were disbanded in 1783, they both had been reduced to just two companies.

The Eighth Pennsylvania was recruited first, starting in summer. Many of the top western Pennsylvania leaders had already joined the army and were serving elsewhere. Richard Butler was commanding a regiment in Washington's army, while Arthur St. Clair was a major general in the Northern Department, on the same frontier where he had served as an officer in the British Army during the French and Indian War. Colonel Aeneas Mackey was named to command the Eighth, but he died of illness early in 1777 and was succeeded by Colonel Daniel Brodhead. While some companies of the regiment were apparently sent to join Washington's Middle Department, others were sent to the Northern Department to join Colonel Daniel Morgan's rifle regiment. Morgan's regiment had already served with distinction in the invasion of Canada, and in 1777 played a major role in the victory at Saratoga.

The 13th Virginia was raised a little bit later. William Crawford was now a colonel in the army who had already enlisted and was serving in the east. He had just been named commander of the Seventh Virginia Regiment, but took time out in the fall to come west to help encourage enlistments.[17] Named to command the newly formed regiment was Colonel William Russell, an experienced frontiersman who had accompanied Daniel Boone on his first attempt to settle in Kentucky. Named as second-in-command was Lieutenant Colonel John Gibson, who would now be a soldier and no longer an Indian agent. Crawford would soon return east to his regiment, and Fort Pitt militia garrison commander John Neville also joined the Continental Army as a full-time soldier, as a militia garrison was no longer needed at Fort Pitt. Neville entered the service as a lieutenant colonel of the 12th Virginia. He later commanded his own regiment in the Southern Department and was captured when Charleston fell to the British.[18]

It took a while to turn this paper regiment into a reality. The creation of the regiment was authorized by Continental Congress on September 16, 1776, but the officers weren't approved and the regiment assigned until December 27. And the unit was not physically assembled at Fort Pitt until February 12, 1777.[19] At this point, the West Augusta Regiment was also split up. Half of the unit was sent to Washington's army, where it was assigned to a Virginia brigade. This unit fought in the battles at Brandywine and Germantown, and suffered heavy casualties in the latter battle.

The remainder of the regiment remained on garrison duty on the frontier. Some of these men were new recruits, while others were former militia men who had decided to join the regular army. This force was still too small to take the field, but at least they gave the major military posts some permanent garrisons. For these troops, the conditions were harsh and the pay abysmal—when they got paid at all. But the soldiers were provided with free food, clothing, and shelter, which was worth a lot on the frontier.

Three. Morgan 1776

After raising some troops in the west, Continental Congress was now finally talking about sending a commander to take charge there. As word got out that Brigadier General Edward Hand would be sent west, the *Maryland Journal* responded to this news by saying, "It is hoped that the arrival of Brigadier General Hand will dissipate all these fears, and add life and vigor to their undertakings. As Brigadier General Hand is universally loved on the Ohio, the people will no doubt flock to his standard and cheerfully go forth to chastise the savage foe."[20]

Four

Hand
1777

On April 10, 1777, Continental Congress "Resolved that Brig. Gen. Hand ... is ordered immediately to repair to Fort Pitt and take measures for the defense of the Western frontier."[1] Edward Hand was a popular choice with more than just Congress. On April 1, George Washington had recommended that Continental Congress promote the balding, 32-year-old Hand to brigadier general.[2] Residents of the Pittsburgh area were also pleased. Not only was Congress addressing their concerns by sending an officer, but it was someone who had previous Western experience as well.

Edward Hand was born in Ireland in 1744. He studied medicine at Dublin's prestigious Trinity College and joined the 18th Royal Irish Regiment as a surgeon's mate. He came with his regiment to America in 1767, and in 1772 he was sent to Fort Pitt, where he purchased an ensign's commission and became an officer. He left the service two years later and began practicing medicine in Lancaster. When the revolution began, he became a colonel commanding the First Pennsylvania Regiment, where Washington noticed his capable handling of the regiment in battle.[3]

Hand was also furnished with a capable assistant. The only Continental troops on the frontier were half of the West Augusta Regiment, most of which comprised the garrison at Fort Pitt. Col. William Russell commanded this portion, while Lieut. Col. John Gibson led the remainder in Washington's army, and it was decided to switch these two officers. This was because when Gibson had lived in the area, he had earned the respect of the tribes the Americans most needed as allies by serving as an honest trader who made the effort to learn their languages. Not only could he assist Hand in Indian matters, but as someone who had been living in the area since 1758, he was familiar with frontier conditions.

Four. Hand 1777

But Hand wasn't given that much else to work with. For one thing, he was a general without an army, as Congress had given him no additional troops with which to complete his mission. The 300 or so men of the West Augusta Regiment were tied up in garrison duty, as they mixed with local militia units in staffing four separate posts: Fort Pitt, Kittanning Blockhouse on the Allegheny, Fort Henry at Wheeling, and distant Fort Randolph on the Kanawha, at the site of the Point Pleasant battle. The British troops at Detroit and other Great Lakes posts were just as few in number. These threadbare forces lacked the numbers to confront each other in battle, especially since the contested area was essentially a vast impenetrable forest.

Brigadier General Edward Hand had high hopes and popular support as the first commander of the Western Department, but was met with disappointment at every turn ("Edw. Hand," The New York Public Library Digital Collections. 1750–1880).

But frontier warfare didn't have to have battles to be savage. In the east, the respective armies massed in tight formations and fired on each other in the European mode. While this led to the usual pain, death, and suffering, there was a sort of gentleman's etiquette about combat. When a British sniper allegedly had George Washington in his sights at the Battle of Brandywine, he refused to pull the trigger when Washington turned his head, because it wasn't proper to shoot a man in the back.[4] A month later, at Germantown, British General Howe's pet terrier somehow fell into American hands. Washington had the dog bathed and returned to Howe along with a polite note.[5]

Such civilized amenities were absent in the west, where the combatants were engaged in a brutal struggle for survival. The pioneers who made up the militia had come west to obtain land, and their biggest obstacle came from the natives who were a constant threat to raid their farmhouses. Being terrorized strengthened their resolve and their hatred of all Indians, including those who might be potential allies. When one settler allegedly was asked why he killed Indian children, he replied simply, "nits make lice."[6]

The natives were also fighting for their way of life. Short lifespans and high infant mortality had kept their population numbers stagnant for centuries, in contrast to the ever increasing hordes of whites streaming across the mountains. They could ill afford to squander their numbers on attacking a fort or engaging in battle. But they excelled at stealthy, small scale raids where individual courage was more valued than military cohesiveness. And, while whites captured by Indians were often adopted into tribes to replace lost members, a special sort of terror was reserved for some captives. The first captives of the season or particularly hated foes were singled out to be burned at the stake. This elaborate ritual was more than just death by fire, it involved fiendish methods designed to prolong the victim's agony. These events were grand public spectacles, and the entertainment was considered a success if the victim was still alive and moaning at dawn.

At Detroit, Lieut. Gov. Henry Hamilton garrisoned the British western headquarters with just 70 redcoats and about 300 French-Canadian militia.[7] Hamilton was no more able to attack Fort Pitt than Hand was capable of moving on Detroit, and he needed the western tribes as cannon fodder. But the Americans' bottling up of the St. Lawrence River had deprived the British of the gifts required to bribe the tribes for much of 1775 and 1776. However, the situation gradually changed and the Americans' early advantage was negated.

As Hamilton convened a tribal gathering at Detroit in June, he got the news he had been waiting for: British authorities would provide the weapons while Hamilton was to encourage the Indians in making war on the Americans settlers. It was easy enough to stir up Indian rage, but Hamilton went a step further and offered a bounty on American scalps. He defended this by claiming he offered a higher bounty for live and unscalped captives, and he gave the natives "The strictest injunctions to discourage and restrain them from their usual barbarities."[8] But the fact that he was paying for scalps outraged Americans and earned Hamilton the nickname Hairbuyer. By July, Hamilton had purchased 73 prisoners and 129 scalps, and Indian raiding parties were so numerous that the year 1777 became known as the year of the bloody sevens.[9]

In addition to the Fort Pitt frontier, the raiders also targeted the new settlements in Kentucky. These isolated posts made such good targets that by 1777, only the stockades at Harrodsburg, Boonsborough, and Logan's Station (or St. Asaph's) were not abandoned. These three towns combined to barely muster 150 able-bodied men for military service.[10] The Kentucky residents had to face the bitter irony that, while they might have come out west seeking wide open spaces, they were now penned up inside stockades. The population of Kentucky would grow exponentially during the revolution, but no continental soldiers would ever be sent there. The citizens were on their own.[11]

Despite being ordered to proceed immediately to Fort Pitt, Hand it did not arrive until June 1. Gibson did not arrive until the end of the month. In his first comments as commander, Hand expressed his confidence in his men and enthusiastically added, "The knowledge I have formed of the country and its inhabitants by a long residence at Fort Pitt, renders my present command highly pleasing to me."[12]

Indian raids on individual families continued throughout the summer, so settlers could not stray far from the numerous private block houses and stockades all along the Ohio River border. In August, the raids increased to almost daily. The usual response was to organize troops to follow the raiders in an often fruitless chase. Some were willing to take their vengeance out on peaceful Indians in their midst. On August 1, Gibson wrote Hand and said, "If White Eyes passes this way, he will be in danger of being killed."[13]

Hand wanted to strike the towns that launched these raids and he tried to round up enough militia for the job. On August 25, he wrote to his wife, "The safety of the country depends on our being able to penetrate the Indian country; but whether I can accomplish it, I don't yet know. Certain it is, that without a proper force (without which it will not be attempted), a measure of that nature be executed without greater danger than this garrison is exposed to."[14]

What finally changed matters was a large-scale strike from a major Indian war party. This 200 man multi-tribal force was large enough to attack the larger frontier settlements, but the Americans were warned of their presence by White Eyes and other friendly Indians. Hand responded by dispatching three additional militia companies to Fort Henry at Wheeling to augment the garrison already there. But this move strained the local food supplies so much that militia leader Col. David Shepard dismissed them, complaining, "They ate too much beef for nothing."[15]

On the morning of September 1, this Indian war party attacked the town, but most settlers were able to make it safely to Fort Henry.

A group of 20 or so militia under Capt. Samuel Mason went out to face the Indians, thinking it to be a typical small strike and run party. But they rushed right into an ambush that killed 15 men immediately. Only Mason, who hid near a falling tree, and a handful of others survived. After scalping and mutilating the dead, the war party killed off all livestock and burned the cabins of the town before leaving the next day.

Samuel Mason performed bravely here as a militia leader, but he is better known for becoming one of the nation's first organized crime bosses. After the revolution, Mason relocated to Redbank (Henderson), Kentucky, and became a respectable justice of the peace. But when his new son-in-law suddenly disappeared from his wedding reception, Mason was suspected of foul play, and soon left town for a life of crime. He joined the notorious robbers then at Cave-in-Rock on the Illinois shore of the Ohio River.

Here Mason advertised "Wilson's Liquor Vault and House of Entertainment" to lure boaters. Not content merely to defraud, Mason soon branched into robbing these boaters of their cargo and killing the crew. The most famous of the other villains who did their preying at Cave-in-Rock were the Harpe Brothers. Among the many murders committed by the Harpes was the killing of a baby for crying, and tying a victim to his horse and stampeding the horse over a cliff.[16]

Eventually, Mason realized it was easier to rob travelers of their cash than their cargo, and he moved his operations to the Natchez Trace, along the route taken north by those who had sold their cargo in New Orleans. He lived on the western (then Spanish) side of the Mississippi to escape U.S. law, but the Spanish eventually arrested him and ordered him extradited. However, Mason staged a daring escape and soon resumed his nefarious activities. But after the reward for him was posted at $1,000 dead or alive, his luck ran out. The story goes that in 1804, two men came to Natchez with a skull they claimed was Mason's. But before they could claim the reward, one of them was recognized as a Harpe brother, and the two were hanged instead of rewarded. The details of this apocryphal story are unverified, but Samuel Mason was never heard from again.

The size and scope of the Wheeling raid raised alarm across the frontier. The small militia garrisons at various posts were rotated regularly, and now some new troops under Capt. William Foreman came in from an Eastern county that had not experienced as much Indian fighting. There were always rumors swirling about potential raids, but Hand soon got reliable information about a party of about 40 Wyandots under chief Half King that were heading for the area.

Four. Hand 1777

This information came from the Moravian mission towns on the Tuscarawas River. The pacifist Moravians had always tried to do their proselytizing away from the corrupting influence of the whites, and with this move to the Tuscarawas they briefly felt safe. But now, with their location on the route between Pittsburgh and Detroit, they were right in the middle of the conflict they had hoped to avoid. And they were living among the Indians that both sides were competing for the loyalty of.

The way of life in the Christian towns of Schoenbrunn and Gnadenhutten was different from typical Indian villages. By stressing family and farming, limiting firearms, and prohibiting alcohol, these people were thriving. The Moravians were known to always have food in their larder, while other tribes lived hand to mouth. Indian protocol dictated that any visiting tribesmen be fed, so raiding parties headed for the Ohio River settlements would stop for a meal at the mission towns. The missionaries had no desire to support such bellicose endeavors, but, as the Rev. John Heckewelder observed, "The quickest way to get rid of all warriors is to give them meals victuals, which is all they want, and to refuse them this would be folly, as then they would shoot cattle, and destroy the corn in the fields."[17]

This particular raiding party availed themselves of Moravian hospitality so thoroughly that Zeisberger complained in his diary, "If they stay much longer they will eat us out of house and home. They do not seem to be in much of a hurry to go to the settlements, much less to have a battle with the white people."[18]

But while they were feeding these combatants, the Moravians sent word of their size and destination to Fort Pitt. On September 22, Zeisberger informed Hand, "We know that 40 of the Wyandots are going it is said to Wheeling."[19] The missionaries continued this policy throughout the war, as Zeisberger and Heckewelder combined to write 43 wartime letters to Fort Pitt, in addition to the letters they wrote at the behest of various chiefs.[20] However, this had to be kept secret to prevent retribution, so a side effect was that the American settlers who were also not aware of this arrangement began to resent the Moravians for providing sustenance to their tormentors.

By late September, things were still in a state of agitation around Wheeling. Someone claimed to have seen smoke south of town towards Grave Creek (Moundsville, WV), so Capt. Foreman took 46 men out to investigate. They found some burned-out cabins, but no people, and spent the night there before trying to return on September 28. Some of the more experienced frontiersmen chose a higher elevated route above the river. This faction was led by Captain William Linn, the same officer who had brought five tons of gunpowder from New Orleans, and who was suspicious of the lower river route. His fears were well founded, as Foreman led the bulk of his men into an ambush at a spot ominously referred to as the Narrows. A total of 21 militia were killed in what is called the Foreman Massacre. Linn later accompanied George Rogers Clark on his Vincennes expedition. It took both skill and luck to survive on the frontier, but Linn's luck ran out when he was killed in an Indian battle in 1781.

These events alarmed frontier residents and many made plans to return east. Hand had other concerns as well. He was in the process of abandoning his post at Kittanning for the newly built Fort Hand, and was trying to conduct diplomacy with the Delaware through Indian Agent George Morgan. Nonetheless, Hand felt a personal inspection at Wheeling was needed, and he left Fort Pitt on October 21 for a ten-day visit. What he saw on this tour was apparently discouraging, because when he returned on November 2, he informed his wife, "I have just returned from a visit to Fort Henry on the Ohio, and am sorry to inform you that I despair of being able to do anything effectual this season. If I can assist the inhabitants to stand their ground, and await the event of our success to the northward, I shall now deem myself worthy of doing a great deal."[21]

Hand was still determined to make one last attempt at a fall offensive, and he called on all county militia leaders to gather their men. His goal was to destroy Pluggy's Town, a nest of Indian raiders based at present-day Delaware, Ohio. Pluggy was a Mingo, which was a tribe without a true sense of identity, and his town attracted similarly disaffected renegades who enjoyed raiding white settlements. Almost all raids were blamed on "Pluggy's Band," but these raiders were not so much a military unit as a loose collection of cutthroats in search of scalps and booty. Pluggy himself had been killed in Kentucky in 1776, but the raids continued, and retribution was desired.

Yet Hand once again met with a setback. Not enough men turned out for an effective campaign, and the leaders who showed up were opposed due to impending cold-weather making for clothing and forage problems. A discouraged Hand had to tell Washington on November 9,

> When I last did myself the honor to write to your Excellency, I fully expected to be able to penetrate the Indian country. But, alas! I was disappointed; the whole force I was able to collect ... did not exceed 800 men. I

am therefore obliged to content myself with stationing small detachments on the frontier to prevent as much as possible the inroads of the savages.... I tomorrow intend to proceed down the Ohio to Forts Henry and Randolph, to establish some order at these posts.[22]

Fort Randolph, the most distant of the posts under Hand's jurisdiction, was manned by rotating militia companies and currently under the leadership of Capt. Matthew Arbuckle. The isolated troops currently here had come from a county far to the east, and now found themselves alone deep in Indian country. However, the Shawnee had remained neutral since being defeated at Point Pleasant in 1774. Cornstalk, their leading chief, was a force for neutrality, even though many Shawnee favored the British.

In November, Cornstalk came to the fort to warn the Americans of increasing Shawnee hostility. Arbuckle informed Hand that, in order to guarantee Shawnee good behavior, "I have here detained Cornstalk and two other Shawnee whom I'm determined to keep confined until I have further instructions from you."[23] When Cornstalk's son, Ellinipsico, came to check on his father, he was also held. Tragically for these detainees, some militiamen had left the fort without permission to go hunting, and one was killed and scalped by Indians that were assumed to have accompanied the Shawnee. In an unfortunate coincidence, the man killed was a relative of someone who had been killed previously by a raiding party allegedly led by Cornstalk. Members of the garrison now demanded immediate retribution. Arbuckle tried to stop them, but the soldiers were in no mood to obey orders. Cornstalk's last words were exhorting his son to die gracefully, as the tribesmen went down in a hail of bullets.

When Hand arrived on November 18, he immediately realized the significance of this act, saying, "If we had anything to expect from that nation it is now vanished."[24] Indeed, the Shawnee now turned on the Americans with a vengeance, and they remained enemies for years to come. They now joined the tribes that were raiding in Kentucky, and in February, they captured Daniel Boone and a party of 28 salt makers. The murder of Cornstalk demanded an investigation, but anti–Indian hysteria was so strong that Hand told Virginia Gov. Patrick Henry, "It would be vain for me to bring the perpetrators of this horrid act to justice at this time."[25] A trial was held the following spring for four soldiers, but the charges were dropped when no one was willing to testify against them.

Back at Fort Pitt, John Gibson held command and sent information on to Hand. He also kept commander-in-chief Washington informed, reporting to him that there were 256 men and 15 officers currently at Fort Pitt.[26] But Gibson was scheduled to leave the Western Department soon due to a reorganization of the Continental Army. Washington's army had fought two major battles that fall, and the Virginia regiments involved had suffered heavy casualties. To fill a vacancy, Gibson had been promoted to colonel and ordered to return to Washington's Middle Department to take command of the Sixth Virginia Regiment. Gibson's promotion was dated October 25, 1777,[27] but his return east was delayed because Hand still needed his expertise for a possible campaign.

Another change resulting from the army reorganization was that William Crawford left Continental service and returned to his home at Connellsville, near Pittsburgh. Crawford was the commander of a Virginia Regiment at Brandywine and Germantown, but at age 55 he now retired from active service. Though no longer a full-time Continental Army officer, his presence offered an experienced military leader of militia who had star recruiting power. He arrived around Christmas, which freed up Gibson to report to his new regiment, now in winter camp at Valley Forge.

After returning by way of Staunton, Virginia, Hand arrived back at Fort Pitt on December 20. He was by now thoroughly discouraged, telling his father-in-law, "I am so heartily tired of this place that I have petitioned Congress to be recalled. Hope it may be granted me."[28] In his official request, Hand told Continental Congress' Secretary of War on Christmas Eve, 1777:

> I assure you that I have fully exerted my poor abilities to accomplish the end for which I was ordered here, yet am sorry to say that little advantage has risen from it; and unless some other measures can be fallen on, I have little reason to promise myself better success for the time to come.
>
> I think that as it is now winter, and Col. Crawford present, my absence for sometime would not be attended with inconvenience. If Congress have no particular objections, would esteem it as a most singular indulgence to be recalled and suffered to join the grand army, with them to share the honors and fatigues of the field. Indeed, unless our affairs will admit of the assistance of a regular force, I had rather resign my office than continue here in command of militia.[29]

Despite this forceful plea, Hand was fated to remain in command at Fort Pitt for another five months.

In the next sentence of this letter, Hand noted the arrival of James Willing, one of many colorful adventurers to appear in town during the Revolution. Willing was the scion of a wealthy Philadelphia family:

his mother was a Shippen from the noted banking family, and his older brother was a business partner of Revolutionary financier Robert Morris. Willing moved to Natchez on the Mississippi River in 1774 and opened a store for the isolated citizens of this former French colony. Through either bad business practices or bad personal habits, he squandered his patrimony and returned home to Philadelphia in 1777.

Willing now managed to convince Continental Congress that he could keep the Mississippi River open and keep the Natchez settlement neutral if given proper resources. He was given a captain's commission in the U.S. Navy and sent to Pittsburgh with instructions for Hand to assist him in outfitting and staffing a proper boat. Willing was able to purchase a boat that he cheerfully renamed the *Rattletrap*. The captain's ship was a galley with long oars and a small sail and a sweep in the stern. The only armaments were two swivel guns. To staff the ship, Hand allowed his men to volunteer, and 20 members of the West Augusta Regiment and 14 other soldiers opted to become sailors as part of the 60 total volunteers. George Girty, brother of Simon, was listed as an officer, although he later deserted. This motley crew left Pittsburgh on January 10, 1778.[30]

The *Rattletrap* made good time and arrived in Natchez on February 19. The surprised and unarmed locals readily agreed to pledge their support, and if Willing had stopped here he might be remembered as a hero. But Willing now began to confiscate the property of anyone he suspected of Tory sympathies, which consisted of all the people he didn't like. Not only was there no organized force to stop him, but his looting attracted new recruits eager to share in the booty, and his ranks swelled to over 100 men.

The British heard about this, and sent a ship up the Mississippi to investigate. The *Rebecca* was a sloop of war with fourteen cannons and six swivel guns. But, on a foggy morning, this ship and crew were surprised and captured in what was the only Revolutionary War naval battle to take place on the Mississippi River. After taking this prize, Willing changed the ship's name to the *Morris*, and later used it to raid other British settlements on the Gulf Coast. Their continued success attracted even more recruits, and as they approached New Orleans they totaled over 200 men.

The Spanish who controlled New Orleans were supposed to be neutral, but they were willing to help the Americans clandestinely. Negotiating on behalf of the U.S. was Oliver Pollock, the American merchant who had previously helped ship gunpowder to Fort Pitt. But Spanish help had to be kept quiet, and Willing's men turned out to be anything but that. Upon landing in port with their prize money, these sailors decided to let the good times roll, and they spent their fortunes in dissipation and debauchery suitable for the pirates they had become.

And they refused to leave, long after they had worn out their welcome. They were still launching raids in July when Pollock complained to a member of Continental Congress, "The small party you sent here under Capt. James Willing without any order or subordination, has only thrown the whole river into confusion and created a number of enemies and a heavy expense ... the only remedy for what has passed is a speedy dispatch."[31] Five weeks later, that speedy dispatch had not yet occurred, as Pollock fumed about Willing in a follow-up letter, "What his next pretense for tarrying here will be God knows.... I'm determined to stop all supplies in order to get him away."[32]

Finally, about 60 men left in August, heading back upstream to join George Rogers Clark's men who were by then at Kaskaskia. Willing himself stayed in New Orleans until October, when he tried to sneak out of town on a ship. But the British captured the ship, and Willing experienced harsh treatment on a British prisoner of war ship off New York before finally being paroled. He was allegedly exchanged for Henry Hamilton.

Back at Fort Pitt, Hand still harbored hopes of mounting a campaign of some sort. He had received reports that the British had a large cache of weapons and supplies at the mouth of the Cuyahoga River, and he now proposed a mid-winter raid. He explained the mission to Crawford and told him that, like privateers and pirates, the militiamen would split the proceeds from the sale of all booty taken in the raid. He concluded, "I therefore expect you will use your influence on this occasion and bring all the volunteers you can raise to Fort Pitt."[33] Nearly 500 men turned out by February 15, and for the first time in the Western Department, the United States sent an army into the field.

Their departure turned out to be the highlight of the campaign. It wasn't exactly a disaster, as the only casualties were one man who was wounded and one who drowned: it was more of an embarrassment. Foul weather usually prevented winter campaigns in this country, but this one began during a rare warm spell. Unfortunately, this was accompanied by heavy rains that melted the snow, left slush and mud everywhere, and raised river levels dangerously. The troops did not get far before having to revise their goal to just looking for Indians to attack.

They were also unlucky in this regard, as the only Indians they saw were two small parties of women and children engaged in salt making. They attacked both. Hand had expected to find warriors present, but found "To my great mortification" that they were attacking non-combatants and "The men were so impetuous I could not prevent their killing."[34] As the soggy troops stumbled home with these few sorry scalps, they knew they had not covered themselves in glory, and the whole affair was derisively referred to as the Squaw Campaign.

Even worse, one of the women they had wounded was the mother of Captain Pipe, a key Delaware chief who now advocated that his tribe join the British side. Hand had arrived as a popular leader with high expectations, but nothing had gone right. Not only had he failed to slow down the Indian raids on the frontier, but the only Indians his men had been able to kill were unarmed members of the tribes that were needed as allies. Indian agent George Morgan was trying to do diplomatic damage control with the Shawnee and Delaware, but the facts kept getting in the way.

Hand's biggest problem was that his army didn't have professional soldiers, and he knew that either he or the next commander had to have them. Writing to Gen. Horatio Gates, head of Continental Congress' Board of War, Hand stressed that unless Continental troops were "Put here immediately to encourage the timorous, though well affected, and overawe the Tory faction, this whole country will be abandoned or overcome."[35]

General Hand was not the only one disappointed so far by the efforts of the Western Department: Simon Girty had also had enough. But for Girty, the problem was he was not given responsibilities commensurate with his ambitions because his loyalty was suspect. As someone who had previously been closely connected to Virginia Royal Governor Lord Dunmore, Girty was suspected of being a Tory and he was never able to earn the Patriots' trust. He did serve as an emissary to the Seneca, but was suspended from this post for drunkenness, and in August 1777, Hand had ordered Gibson to arrest Girty for questioning. However, Girty was cleared and trusted on another mission to the Seneca that Gibson commented on favorably in his report to Washington. Girty went on the Squaw Campaign as a scout with hopes of military glory, but his only prominent role was as an arbiter in a dispute over which militiaman got credit for killing a particular Indian boy. Girty was ripe for a change.

Girty was not alone in being suspected of Tory sympathies. As those loyal to England were forced to leave patriot centers, those in northern colonies could flee to Canada. In the middle and southern colonies, many chose to migrate west for a fresh start amongst the rugged pioneers. The westerners already here were a harsh lot, and a Congressional visitor said of them, "These inhabitants appear to be a wild unmanageable race, little less savage than their tawny neighbors."[36] These pioneers not only hated Indians, but also any Tories who might be among them. A southwestern Virginia judge named Lynch had his name become a verb when he authorized the hanging of suspected Tories without trial. Closer to home, a handcuffed suspected Tory was thrown into the Cheat River. When his death was investigated, a militia leader complained to Hand, "Good heavens that the death of a vile Tory should affect us so nearly and ruin what you have with so much labor, pain and difficulties almost accomplished."[37]

No one was safe from accusation. Indian agent George Morgan came under suspicion because he had formerly been on the royal payroll and because he believed in negotiating with Indians rather than killing them. Former Royal Deputy Indian Agent Alexander McKee was suspected, despite his working hard for U.S. interests. The agitation against him became so great that Hand in August 1777 "Found it necessary, both to appease the popular clamor and for his own security to bring Alexander McKee from his farm and confine him to his own home here."[38] Hand ordered McKee to report to Congress for further questioning, but McKee claimed he was too ill to travel. After Hand returned from his Squaw Campaign, he again ordered McKee back east.

In early March, McKee's good friend and fellow Indian trader Matthew Elliott suddenly returned to Fort Pitt. Missing since 1776, Elliott had been captured by the Mingo and taken to Detroit and then sent on to Québec for further questioning. He was released and returned to Fort Pitt to convince McKee to join him in defecting to the British side. McKee signed on and convinced Girty and a few others to join them, and on March 28, a good portion of the available frontier Indian expertise went over to the enemy. Hand now had to report to Gates and the Board of War, "Sir, I have the mortification to inform you that last Saturday night, Alexander McKee made his escape from this place, as also Matthew Elliott, a person lately from Québec on parole, Simon Girty, Robert Surplus, and one Higgins."[39]

These defectors supplemented their treason by spreading disinformation at every Indian village between Pittsburgh and Detroit. They claimed that Washington was dead, his army defeated, Congress on the run, and that the Americans were coming west to kill them all and take

Four. Hand 1777

their land. In the Shawnee towns, they added Girty's brother James to their ranks, as he had been sent there by the Americans as an emissary. This group finally arrived in Detroit to great fanfare in early June.

At Fort Pitt, everyone was still worried about these defections when Moravian missionary John Heckewelder appeared in town a few days later. He was returning west from an extended stay at church headquarters in Bethlehem, Pennsylvania, but, as they had received no word from the mission towns in six months, Heckewelder didn't even know if they were still standing. Local officials assumed the deserters would spread false news, and Heckewelder now volunteered to take the truth to the towns. Leaving immediately, the 36-year-old missionary rode nearly nonstop for three days, arriving at Gnadenhutten around 11 in the evening.

Here he was told that the Delaware at Coshocton had believed what they had been told and were preparing to go to war against the Americans. Heckewelder took a four hour nap and then rode a fresh horse onto Coshocton, narrowly avoiding a Wyandot war party encamped nearby. When he arrived around 10 a.m., he found former friends eyeing him suspiciously, and even White Eyes was reluctant to be seen shaking his hand. When he was accused of not being a friend to the Delaware, Heckewelder responded by telling them that if he was not their friend they would not see him there. White Eyes now took charge and related the stories that they had been told and asked Heckewelder if they were true. Heckewelder was not only able to rebut these tales with specifics, but in his saddlebags he had newspapers with published accounts of the British surrender at Saratoga. White Eyes displayed this for all to see, and all talk of going to war was forgotten. Not content with just his own tribe knowing the truth, White Eyes then sent a message onto the Shawnee, telling them, "Some days ago a flock of birds, that had come on from the east, lit at Coshocton, imposing a song of theirs upon us ... should these birds ... endeavor to impose a song on you likewise, do not listen to them, for they lie!"[40]

While all federal efforts at Fort Pitt had stalled, there was one campaign in the works involving Virginia militia. Kentucky militia commander George Rogers Clark journeyed to Williamsburg in the fall of 1777 to seek help. He got Virginia Gov. Patrick Henry to back his plan to weaken Detroit by attacking the former French posts at Kaskaskia, Cahokia, and Vincennes, from where many tribes launched their raids. Clark arrived at Redstone (present-day Brownsville, Pennsylvania) on the Monongahela in February 1778, and began his preparations. Hand supported Clark in gathering supplies, but Clark had to recruit his own soldiers. This proved to be difficult, since the war effort in the West was going poorly, and Clark was also keeping his ultimate destination a secret. He was only able to gather 150 men by the time he started down the Ohio in May.

The Americans were gradually realizing that they needed more troops in the west. In February, Washington, tried to combine the split contingents of the West Augusta Regiment. He informed Henry Laurens, President of Continental Congress, "I am under some embarrassments respecting the 13th Virginia Regiment. It was raised on the west side of the Allegheny and towards Pittsburgh with assurances from the officers, it is said, that the men would not be drawn from that quarter.... I think the whole should be united, either here or there, and wish Congress to direct me on the subject."[41] The only change made at the time was that Col. William Russell, who commanded the portion at Valley Forge, was transferred to lead the Fort Pitt portion.

Part of the reason for the slow progress in addressing Western Department needs was due to confusion over Washington's role. In the winter of 1777–78, a cabal of officers and Continental Congressmen concluded that Washington was not up to his job and should be replaced by Gen. Horatio Gates. Washington had failed to keep the British from taking New York in 1776, and now he had done the same in Philadelphia, while Gates had won a major victory at Saratoga, capturing an entire British Army. Gates was adept at intrigue, and he had friends in Congress who installed him as the head of the Northern Department. Now, his congressional cronies reorganized the Board of War to give it more authority, and then named Gates as board president. This generated confusion, as Hand was not sure who he reported to, and the situation threatened to make Washington's position untenable.

Over the winter, this cabal began to unravel and its adherents were discredited, which strengthened Washington's control over his army. Gates was eventually offered command of the Southern Department (over Washington's objections), where he led his troops into a career ending disastrous defeat at Camden. With Washington in firm control again, Congress began addressing Western needs, and on May 2, 1778, they made these resolutions:

> Resolved—That two regiments to be raised in Virginia and Pennsylvania ... for the protection and operation on the Western Frontier.... That Brig. Gen. Hand be recalled from his command on the Western Frontier, agreeable to this request.... That a superior officer be immediately sent to take command

Four. Hand 1777

on the Western Frontier.... That Gen. Washington be desired to appoint the officer to take command at Fort Pitt.[42]

The two regiments to be assigned to Fort Pitt, were the 8th Pennsylvania and the 13th Virginia, both of which had been raised on the frontier and then split up. Part of the 8th Pennsylvania was with Washington's army, while a few companies had been sent to serve under Daniel Morgan at Saratoga. The two portions were now reunited under the command of Col. Daniel Brodhead. The 13th Virginia/West Augusta Regiment was also to be reunited, as the Valley Forge contingent was transferred to Fort Pitt. But they would not be under Russell's command, as Washington now ordered Russell and Gibson switch regiments. There was a need for Gibson's unique linguistic and Indian skills at Fort Pitt. When Spanish officials in New Orleans had sent a letter to Fort Pitt over the winter, it had to be forwarded to Philadelphia because no one in Pittsburgh could read Spanish. Gibson was not only fluent in Spanish and French, but also spoke the languages of the three "near tribes" that lived closest to the fort. His reappearance would help make up for the loss of Elliot, McKee, and Girty.

Free to pick his own departmental commander, Washington's first choice was Lieut. Col. Richard Butler of the 9th Pennsylvania Regiment, who had Indian experience similar to Gibson. Butler has served as an officer under Bouquet during Pontiac's Conspiracy and later was an Indian trader who lived among the Shawnee, where he fathered a son with Nonhelema. But Butler was only a lieutenant colonel, which meant he was outranked by both regimental commanders who would report to him. An even bigger problem, according to Washington, was "He does not seem to wish to go upon the expedition, as he says his influence is not so great among the inhabitants of the backcountry as the board imagine."[43] It's also possible Butler did not want to become involved in the contentious Virginia-Pennsylvania feud.

Washington now limited his search to general officers and looked for an outsider free of local factions. After careful consideration, on May 26 he announced the selection of Brig. Gen. Lachlan McIntosh of Georgia as the new commander of the Western Department. With a new general, and some soldiers to follow him, the Americans could now launch an offensive in the west.

Five

McIntosh
1778

General Lachlan McIntosh seemed to be a good choice to command the Western Department. Like Washington himself, he had a strong sense of duty and cut a fine figure on horseback and he was also noted for his good looks. A perceived bonus was that, as a Georgian, he was free from the Virginia-Pennsylvania controversy that plagued other possible candidates for the job. Washington parted with his general with some reluctance, telling McIntosh, "I am induced, but not without reluctance, from the sense I entertain of your merit, to nominate you as an officer well-qualified from a variety of considerations, to answer the objects they may have in view."[1] Adding to Washington's sense of loss was the fact that he was also losing control over McIntosh's service. The collapse of

the Conway Cabal in January 1778 had restored Washington's control over his own troops, but Continental Congress' Board of War, although they did allow Washington to select the commanders of the various other departments, still maintained control over day-to-day operations of them.

McIntosh was born in Scotland in 1725, and came to the

Brigadier General Lachlan McIntosh came west as an objective outsider, but his lack of awareness of frontier ways severely limited his effectiveness (Lachlan McIntosh, 1806, bust portrait, facing right. Library of Congress).

newly established Georgia colony with his family when he was just 11. This colony found itself in conflict with the Spanish in Florida that was a part of a worldwide conflict. In Europe, it was known as the War of Austrian Succession, but in the southern Atlantic, it was referred to as the War of Jenkins' Ear, because of an incident where a Spanish Coast Guard captain sliced off the ear of a British captain. McIntosh's father was captured by the Spanish in this war, and died not long after being returned. Young Lachlan served at Fort Frederika on St. Simons Island, which means that his own military career began when George Washington was still a 10-year-old.[2]

As an adult, McIntosh moved to Charleston, and got a job clerking for prominent businessman Henry Laurens, with whom he maintained a lifelong friendship. He married and returned to Georgia and prospered. When the revolution began, he was able to raise a regiment and became its commander. The McIntosh family was among the leaders in the revolutionary movement in Georgia, but were embroiled in a fierce rivalry with a contingent led by Continental Congressman Button Gwinnett. When Gwinnett ordered the arrest of McIntosh's brother, the general challenged him to a duel and killed him just eleven months after Gwinnett had signed the Declaration of Independence, which is why Gwinnett's rare autograph is the most prized of all the Founding Fathers. McIntosh was acquitted of murder charges, but the controversy necessitated a transfer, so he was sent north. At Valley Forge, he commanded a brigade of southern troops and made a good impression on Washington.

However, merely changing generals in the Western Department was not enough. Whoever was in charge needed regular soldiers. General Hand had agreed to remain until he could greet and brief McIntosh, and he now wrote to Gates and the Board of War complaining of "The disordered state this country is in," stressing that, "it is my sincere belief, but if a few men are not put here immediately ... this whole country will be abandoned or overrun by the enemy in a short time."[3] Continental Congress was well aware of this, as Timothy Pickering informed Washington, "To repel the incursions of the Indians, nothing, in our opinion, will be effectual but a regular force, under the direction of good officers."[4]

McIntosh left immediately for York, Pennsylvania, where Continental Congress had been meeting since the British captured Philadelphia. He hoped to get final orders and get started, but was frustrated by the slow congressional pace. He wrote to Washington, "These circumstances, sir, afford me but a poor prospect of being serviceable to my country this season, already so far advanced without Your Excellency's assistance."[5] However, Washington at this point lacked direct authority over the whole of his army, and he had to tell McIntosh, "I am sorry to find that your vigorous measures have not been pursued.... I would willingly give aid, (but) at present, the situation of affairs will not permit me."[6] Fortunately, the log jam broke soon afterward, as on June 11, Continental Congress authorized an expedition on Detroit, and allocated the unusually specific amount of $932,743.33 to pay for it.[7]

McIntosh also had two regiments released to his command, but he still had to gather them at Fort Pitt. The portion of the 13th Virginia that was at Valley Forge was soon reunited with the troops already on garrison duty in the west, but the 8th Pennsylvania had a more circuitous journey. This regiment was in Lancaster, Pennsylvania, for most of June, and had only gotten as far as Carlisle by July 8. Here they received word of a massacre by Indians and Tories of patriot settlers in the Wyoming Valley near present-day Wilkes-Barre, Pennsylvania. The regiment was dispatched there in the aftermath to assist and did not return to Carlisle for another month, and did not arrive at Fort Pitt until September 9.[8] By this time, it was so late in the year that Continental Congress had "deferred" the attack on Detroit in favor of a general campaign against the Indians.[9]

While all of this was going on, those already in the west remained active. Indian raids on individual homes continued, and larger parties of Wyandot and Shawnee attacked Forts Randolph and Donnelly in West Virginia and Fort Hand near Pittsburgh. To help defend the frontier, a Virginia militia expedition under Colonel George Rogers Clark launched an ambitious campaign. After Clark recruited about 180 men in western Pennsylvania and Kentucky, he started his campaign from the Falls of the Ohio at Louisville on June 26, 1778. They put their boats out on the Ohio during a solar eclipse without being informed of their destination, and it wasn't until later that Clark announced that they were headed not towards Detroit, but rather Kaskaskia on the Mississippi River, one of a handful of French trading posts founded in southern Indiana and Illinois.

The others were Cahokia, located north on the Mississippi opposite St. Louis, and Vincennes on the Wabash River on the current border of Indiana and Illinois. These towns were heavily involved in the Indian fur trade. The French inhabitants had been transferred to English control after the Treaty of Paris in 1763. They did not like this, but accepted it when the British allowed them to continue to practice their Catholic faith.

Five. McIntosh 1778

Clark's force managed to approach Kaskaskia undetected, and was surprised to find the French residents were aware of the new American/French alliance and eager to join them. Kaskaskia fell without a shot and a contingent of locals went with Clark's men to convince Cahokia to do the same. A small force was then sent on to Vincennes to complete the conquest. Not only did this campaign put pressure on the British at Detroit, but Clark's military occupation gave the Americans a legitimate claim to the land north and west of the Ohio River. This was a major victory for the Americans, but it was achieved by the Virginia militia without any federal support. The Continental Army could have been used to help this campaign, but they were never made aware of it, as Clark and Virginia Governor Patrick Henry kept the mission a secret.

Meanwhile, McIntosh arrived at Fort Pitt on August 6, and Hand returned east a few days later, where he continued to serve as a brigade commander and later served a term in Congress.[10] The new commander still didn't have his brigade assembled yet, but he still had plenty of work to do. The biggest task he faced was an upcoming treaty with the Delaware tribe. This treaty, the first ever negotiated and signed by the newly named United States of America, was required to obtain American forces' permission to pass through Delaware land on their way to Detroit. The Americans also hoped for the Delaware to join them on their campaign.

Continental Congress had directed Pennsylvania and Virginia to send negotiators to Fort Pitt, but Pennsylvania never made any nominations, while Virginia sent the brothers Andrew and Thomas Lewis. This pair, who were about 60, had extensive frontier experience. Andrew Lewis had served as an officer in Washington's, Braddock's and Forbes' Campaigns, and was taken prisoner in that last expedition. In 1774, he commanded the victorious American forces at the battle of Point Pleasant. When the Revolution began, he was named a brigadier general in the Continental Army, but he resigned in protest after being passed over for promotion to major general. He then became an Indian agent, which he had some experience with as he had helped negotiate the Treaty of Fort Stanwix. But the Lewis brothers were better known as warriors than diplomats.[11] Andrew Lewis had arrived at Fort Pitt on August 1, but so far had only complained of a lack of instructions from Continental Congress.[12]

The Pennsylvania delegation was not the only ones absent from these important treaty negotiations. Also missing was George Morgan, Indian agent for the middle colonies. Morgan had been involved in the Indian trade since before Pontiac's Conspiracy, and he enjoyed a good reputation among the Indians, particularly the Delaware. Morgan held the rank of colonel in the Continental Army, but, as a diplomat, he tried to maintain frontier peace, which made him suspect to his Indian hating neighbors. Morgan had extensive business interests back east in Princeton, New Jersey, and also served as a deputy quartermaster for the Western Department. Confusion over these accounts led him to Philadelphia to straighten things out, and he was not able to return to Fort Pitt until well after the treaty had been signed. In his absence, American officials took a much harsher stance with the Delaware.

The Delaware tribe had undergone a change of leadership when the venerable Netawatwes had died in 1776 at about the age of 90. The three chiefs that the Delaware now sent to Fort Pitt for the treaty were Gelelemend, or John Killbuck, Junior, the grandson of Netawatwes, Captain Pipe, a pro–British war chief, and White Eyes, who had succeeded Netawatwes as the principal chief. White Eyes was a unique native in terms of his understanding of white ways. He was married to a white woman and also had traveled extensively in the white world. Most illiterate Native Americans had no sense of the past and the precarious nature of their daily existence rendered planning for the future a frivolous luxury. But Baptist missionary David Jones said of White Eyes, "He was the only Indian I met with in all of my travels that seemed to have a design of accomplishing something future."[13] Moravian missionary Christian Frederick Post called him "one of the cleverest Indians" he had ever met.[14]

Between 1772 and 1778, White Eyes journeyed down the Ohio and Mississippi Rivers to New Orleans and then took passage on a ship back to New York. He also addressed Continental Congress on April 10, 1776, and remained in town for a while afterwards to lobby on behalf of his tribe. While other great Native American leaders like Pontiac and Tecumseh tried to align diverse tribes into a coalition to resist the whites, White Eyes rejected this notion. He realized that a coalition of tribes, each with their own language and culture, could not hold together for long, and he also saw that the technological advantages the whites held and the exponentially increasing number of white settlers streaming westward every year doomed the Indian way of life. He concluded that he could best save the Delaware by getting them to assimilate into white society, and he had some ingenious ways of pursuing this goal.

During Lord Dunmore's War in 1774, White Eyes traveled with the Americans as a sort of diplomat without portfolio. He proposed to

Five. McIntosh 1778

Dunmore that the Delaware obtain deeds to the land they occupied, correctly reasoning that the Anglo legal system would make it harder for any whites to evict them. Dunmore liked this idea, because if the Delaware bought their land from the Virginia colony, it would strengthen their claim to all Western lands. The two men made tentative plans to travel to London to present this scheme, but the start of the American Revolution canceled those plans.[15]

When White Eyes later went to Detroit, British commander Henry Hamilton cut up his wampum belt and ordered him out, saying he was no better than the Virginians. So White Eyes now had to start his diplomacy all over again with the Americans, but he was willing and able to do this. He and Netawatwes had already encouraged the Moravian missionaries to bring Christianity and literacy to their tribe, and now he went even farther by offering to have the Delaware align with the Americans in exchange for becoming the 14th colony. This radical proposal might have had a chance of coming to fruition had Morgan been present or had the Americans negotiated in better faith.

On September 8, the 8th Pennsylvania finally arrived at Fort Pitt. With this event, the reunited 13th Virginia regiment, which was now re-designated the 9th Virginia, and a small contingent of North Carolina dragoons, McIntosh finally had his brigade fully assembled. Although an artillery battery and a small group of Maryland troops would be sent later, this current configuration represented the largest concentration of Continental troops ever assembled west of the Alleghenies. And they arrived just in time to open treaty talks, as the opening ceremonies included parade drill, a small arms demonstration, and fife and drum music.

Treaty talks lasted from September 12 through 19, but the final treaty contained only six articles. In Article 3, the Delaware not only agreed to let the Americans cross their land, but also promised to join them as guides and soldiers if the Americans would build a fort in Delaware country to protect them while their warriors were away. That's the way the Americans interpreted it: the Delaware felt they had merely agreed to serve as guides rather than combatants. In response to this article, the Americans agreed in Article 6 to consider a statehood application from the Delaware. To seal the deal, the Americans offered White Eyes an officer's commission that, "confers upon White Eyes the title of Lieutenant Colonel of all the Indian nations between the rivers of Ohio and Mississippi and the lakes."[16] All of this was in bad faith by the Americans. They pressured the Delaware into joining them with an empty promise of statehood that Congress would likely never take into serious consideration. Even the rank awarded to White Eyes was just a hollow title with no real authority or responsibility conveyed.

McIntosh now had his army and his treaty, but there was still another major item he had to address: he wanted to launch his expedition further downstream, and needed to build a new fort and a road to it. After the Monongahela and Allegheny Rivers meet in Pittsburgh to form the Ohio, this river flows roughly north for a few miles before turning south at about the point where Pennsylvania, Ohio, and West Virginia meet. Here the river turns to the south before eventually heading west for another 700 miles. McIntosh sent Colonel Daniel Brodhead and his Eighth Pennsylvania regiment to build a road that ran from Fort Pitt on the western side of the Ohio. Where this road crossed the Ohio, at its northernmost point, Gibson's Virginia regiment was sent to construct Fort McIntosh at present day Beaver, Pennsylvania. This was the first U.S. fort built on the Indian side of the Ohio. The man who designed this fort was Louis Antoine John Baptiste, Chevalier de Cambray Digny, a French officer who had been trained as a military engineer. Like Lafayette and others, Cambray Digny crossed the Atlantic to offer his services, and, after serving in the Monmouth campaign he was temporarily loaned out to the McIntosh expedition.[17] The construction projects at Brodhead Road and Fort McIntosh took up most of October, but McIntosh was finally getting ready to take the field. He made final supply arrangements and put out a call for a militia rendezvous that resulted in 700 militia turning out under Crawford's leadership. When added to the 500 continental soldiers McIntosh was able to gather for this trip, this force of 1,200 men would be the largest concentration of troops collected at any one spot in the West during the Revolution, and on November 4, McIntosh finally put his new army into the field.

In the fall of 1764, Colonel Henry Bouquet had led a similar sized army from the same spot, following Beaver Creek on the Ohio-Pennsylvania line to the headwaters of Sandy Creek that flowed to the Tuscarawas. Bouquet's force was well supplied, disciplined, and too large to attack, whereas McIntosh's force only filled the last category. Consequently, his trip did not go nearly as well. Part of the problem was the quality and quantity of the pack horses used to haul the army's scant supplies. McIntosh complains that his horse procurers "have used me exceedingly ill in sending such horses on the journey, they detain me unaccountably. They are tiring every day and cannot travel above four or five miles a day."[18] The lateness of the season also made forage scarce, forcing the livestock to wander farther at night, which made it difficult to reassemble them the next day. The army frequently didn't start moving until 1 p.m., which gave them only a few hours of daylight to travel. Another problem was the November weather: the army was obliged to remain in camp all day on November 14 because of a snowstorm, and three days later they were detained by an all-day rain.[19] The undisciplined militia were also a problem. Two men who disobeyed orders and went out hunting were killed and scalped by the Indians that the troops now realized were watching their every move. This slow moving, ill supplied, and undisciplined force took two weeks to traverse the 70 miles between the Ohio and the Tuscarawas—a pitiful average of just five miles per day.

They finally arrived at the Tuscarawas River on November 18. From here, the Great Trail they had been following branched off towards Lake Erie and Detroit, while the Tuscarawas flowed south towards the Moravian and Delaware towns. It was decided to build a fort here both to protect the downstream Indians and to use as a launching pad for an invasion on Detroit in the spring. McIntosh's men crossed the river and went downstream a few miles to a plain just below present day Bolivar where Bouquet had once camped. Here they found a contingent of Delaware waiting for them. The combined crew spent the first day clearing out a 60 acre area to build a fort upon.

On November 20, McIntosh gathered everyone together to announce the sad news that White Eyes had died of smallpox back at Fort Pitt. Dying along with him was his vision of a Delaware state. Heckewelder observed that "the death of this great and wonderful man was severely lamented by, and a great loss to, the (Delaware) nation; and although his ambitious and political opponent, Captain Pipe, with an air of prophecy, uttered: 'that the great spirit had probably put him out of the way that the nation might be saved': it was not so considered by the faithful part."[20] White Eyes was replaced by Gelelemend, who tried to keep Delaware neutrality, but had difficulty restraining braves as the Delaware began drifting towards British support.

It would have been much worse had the Delaware found out that White Eyes had actually been murdered by American militia. No one spoke of this until George Morgan returned to the west, and there is no dramatic account of the killing like there is of Cornstalk, so White Eyes has even been denied a martyr's death. If White Eyes had actually held a legitimate colonel's commission in the Continental Army, his killers would have been arrested and likely hung. Instead, officials concealed the crime with a hasty cover-up that was so successful that the perpetrators of the vile deed remain unknown to us to this day. All that remained of White Eyes' vision was contained in a sad list of his meager personal effects compiled by officials at Fort Pitt.[21]

McIntosh likely knew the real cause of White Eyes' death, but was able to pull off his deception. However, in a speech on November 22, he squandered his ill-gotten advantage. Addressing the assembled Delaware, McIntosh blustered about American might and how he would crush anyone who tried to oppose him. But then he had the nerve to ask them for supplies. The Delaware contrasted McIntosh's bellicose tone with the appearance of the poorly shod and clad troops before them, whose rations had already been cut in half even though winter hadn't even started yet, and were said to have "set up a general laugh."[22] The Delaware then returned to their villages with an impression of the Americans as aggressive panhandlers, alternately begging and threatening.

Work on the fort progressed over the next ten days, despite grumbling from troops, who referred to the post as Fort Nonsense. By November 29, most supplies had been moved to inside the perimeter of the fort, and on December 1, McIntosh held a Council of War for all of his officers. He proposed moving on to Detroit, but was opposed by every officer, all of whom noted the poor conditions they had encountered so far that were only going to get worse. McIntosh then decided to leave Gibson and 180 men of his regiment to spend the winter in the fort, which he now named after his old friend Henry Laurens, currently President of Continental Congress. At the treaty of Fort Pitt, White Eyes had requested "that Col. John Gibson may be appointed to have charge of all matters between you and us. We esteem him as one of ourselves, and he has always acted an honest part by us, and we are convinced he will make our common good his chief study, and not only think how he may get rich."[23] McIntosh honored this request by naming Gibson in command of the fort that was built to protect the Delaware.

Fort Laurens was rectangular and covered about an acre of ground. There was no artillery, but they did build raised bastions at each corner. The log pickets were fifteen feet long and sunk three feet into the ground, with a six foot ditch surrounding the stockade. The curtains between bastions were 180 feet long and the only blockhouse was near the gate at the center of the western curtain. Several buildings were constructed inside the fort, and the hospital was built just outside the gate. As with Fort McIntosh, the fort was designed by Cambray Digny.[24]

Five. McIntosh 1778

In preparing for the return trip with the rest of his force, McIntosh issued two days' worth of food and whiskey rations and then left his men to their own devices. No longer bothering to try to even be an army, some men returned to Fort McIntosh in two days, after taking two weeks to get to the Tuscarawas, while others burned through their rations and had a longer and hungrier return trip. But they were not attacked along the way, and the militia was able to return home for Christmas, before their enlistments expired.[25]

Unbeknownst to McIntosh, this would have been an excellent time to attack Detroit. Alarmed by Clark's capture of Kaskaskia, Cahokia, and Vincennes, Hamilton had left Detroit in October with 175 men, including 60 redcoats, to retake Vincennes. They succeeded in this on December 17, capturing the token American garrison left behind there. Hamilton decided to spend the winter in Vincennes and pursue Clark in the spring, since he now stood between Clark and any possible reinforcements and supplies. Hamilton left Captain Lernoult in command of Detroit, but the British could barely summon 150 regulars and militia to defend the place.[26]

However, McIntosh instead returned to Fort Pitt and considered his expedition to be a success, telling a Pennsylvania colonial official that, despite considerable obstacles, "I erected a good strong fort.... Which I expect will keep the savages in awe, and secure the peace of the frontier."[27] Others in the West did not share his confidence. Brodhead, the senior regimental commander at Fort Pitt, bypassed the chain of command and wrote to Washington directly on January 16, to "inform your Excellency that General McIntosh is unfortunate enough to be almost universally hated by every man in this department.... There is not an officer who does not appear to be exceedingly disgusted."[28] Washington had to remind Brodhead that military command was not a popularity contest, and that his complaints were "by no means a foundation for any measure on my part respecting him, that will either convey or imply censure."[29]

McIntosh's personnel problems were compounded when George Morgan returned to Fort Pitt in January. McIntosh had been selected for command partly because he was an outsider free of the divisive local factions. But he was also ignorant in all local matters, and not using Morgan's years of experience with the Delaware made for a different treaty. Morgan was outraged by the result of the treaty, saying, "There never was a conference with the Indians so improperly or villainously conducted as the last one in Pittsburgh."[30] The treaty was a *fait accompli*, but Morgan sought to undermine it by writing to the Delaware that they had been deceived into war and they should renegotiate. He also heaped personal opprobrium on McIntosh, complaining of "the blunders and absurdities already committed"[31] and "the ignorant, absurd and contradictory conduct and orders of General McIntosh throughout the whole campaign."[32] McIntosh returned these feelings of disdain, complaining to Washington that Morgan "keeps almost all his public business in this department a profound secret from me among his other schemes."[33] The two men continued their feud until Morgan returned again to his eastern home in Princeton, New Jersey.

Back at Fort Laurens, Gibson was putting final touches on the fort. On December 10, his first day in command, he was visited by John Heckewelder, who had paddled upstream from the Moravian missions. The fact that it had taken Heckewelder six days to make the trip showed that, while the fort was located along the route to Detroit, it was still a long way from the Indians it was supposed to be protecting. One of the reasons the Moravian converts had prospered was that, as Christian pacifists, they didn't expend any of their valuable resources on their own defense. This might have made them prey for other tribes, but most of the converts were Delaware who had family living nearby. The non–Christian Delaware considered the converts to be like wayward siblings who had joined a cult: they might be an embarrassment, but they were still family and entitled to protection. When the Delaware chief town was at Newcomerstown, the Moravian villages of Gnadenhutten and Schoenbrunn were just 20 and 30 miles, respectively, from the site of Fort Laurens, while the Delaware capital was just fifteen miles below Gnadenhutten. After Netawatwes' death in 1776, the principal Delaware town was moved to the Coshocton, another 15 miles downstream. The Moravians then decided to move their missions to just three miles from Coshocton in order to take advantage of Delaware protection. So, by the time Fort Laurens was built, it was 70 miles from any Delaware town—the same distance it was back to Fort McIntosh.[34] Gibson was well aware of this, and offered to help move the Moravians closer to the fort, but Zeisberger rejected this offer, reasoning that "the war will go wherever there is a fort, and we are safest far away from there."[35] The other major problem Gibson faced was keeping his isolated force supplied over the winter. To address this, he dispatched Deputy Assistant Quartermaster Sam Samples to Coshocton to trade with the Delaware.

In their current precarious situation, the British at Detroit were duly alarmed by the construction of Fort Laurens. Captain Lernoult sent Simon

Five. McIntosh 1778

Girty and about 17 Mingo braves to reconnoiter. When Girty found out that Gibson, an officer who had previously ordered him arrested, was in command of the fort, he vowed to personally take his scalp. Zeisberger wrote to Gibson warning him of Girty's presence, and Gibson changed the password sign used by friendly Delaware to gain access to the fort.

On January 21, Ensign John Clark of the 8th Pennsylvania arrived at the fort with valuable supplies of shoes, clothing, and whiskey. Before Clark started his return trip the next day, Gibson wrote to McIntosh, Brodhead, and Morgan and included a letter of warning from Zeisberger which concluded with his saying, "I am exceedingly glad and much obliged to you for having our safety at heart."[36] Concerning the warning about Girty, Gibson cavalierly told McIntosh, "I hope if Mr. Girty comes to pay a visit I shall be able to trepan him."[37]

The next morning, Clark and his fourteen men had only gotten a few miles from the fort when they were attacked by Girty's party. This was as close to battle as Continental soldiers got in the West, and on this occasion the troops acquitted themselves well. Refusing to panic, they dispersed the Indians with a bayonet charge and fought their way back to the fort with casualties of two men killed, four wounded, and one captured. Unfortunately, the captured man was a courier who carried letters revealing American weaknesses and Moravian complicity.

Since none of the party could read these dispatches, Girty did not realize what was in them until after he returned to Detroit on February 3. Since deserting the American cause the previous March, Girty had been suffering from traitor's remorse, as he wondered if he had done the right thing. In September, he was sent to interrogate a Kentuckian who had been captured trying to steal Indian horses. The prisoner had been marked for death by being painted black and had already run the gauntlet in several villages, so it was well into the interview before Girty recognized his old friend Simon Kenton, who he had served with on scouting missions during Dunmore's War. Girty expressed some regrets to Kenton about his choice and also went to some lengths to help get his friend sent to Detroit, where he escaped.

But Girty's attitude hardened once he heard what Gibson had thought of him. According to Girty's biographer, "the letter of Colonel Gibson revealed to Girty that he was particularly pointed out as one who, if captured, could expect little mercy. A feeling of despondency was succeeded by vindictiveness against his countrymen such as before not possessed him.... His hatred of Gibson thenceforth was intense."[38] At a conference in Detroit, Girty now advocated an all-out attack on

Fort Laurens, and claimed that he had over 800 braves assembled in the Sandusky River region who were eager for such a campaign.

The British responded by sending Captain Henry Bird of the 8th Foot to investigate and also asked for volunteers to go along, and about ten soldiers did so. Bird, a recent transfer from Fort Niagara, was a decent man sent into a savage world. He discovered that Girty had greatly misrepresented the situation, as they were only about 200 braves assembled, and they were focused "to the exclusion ... of all else" on the torture of the captured American messenger.[39] Many tribes would often take the first captive of a new campaign and burn him at the stake in a sort of macabre opening day ceremony. Bird was horrified by this practice and sought to purchase the freedom of the poor wretch, but was rebuffed. He at least tried to give the victim a decent burial afterwards, but the body was dug up and the skull put on display. Bird then denounced the Indians in no uncertain terms which confused them more than angered them. It's possible that Bird did not even accompany Girty's raiding party to Fort Laurens but it didn't matter. It was clear that Girty, who held no military rank or authority, was the real leader of this Indian raiding party.

While this was going on, the troops at Fort Laurens were still struggling to keep themselves fed. Gibson again sent Samples and seven men to Coshocton to purchase supplies. They set up a camp near the Delaware village, and the next day the guard posted there was killed and scalped. Gelelemend apologized but could not seem to restrain his younger braves, as a few days later another soldier was wounded and horses were stolen. After this, the Americans stayed at the nearby Mission town, as Zeisberger noted, "Mr. Samples spent most of his time here with us, because he did not believe he was safe in Coshocton."[40] Samples was so uneasy that he requested an escort back to the fort, which was provided by a combination of Gelelemend's Delaware warriors and Moravian Indian converts. This led Zeisberger to complain of the Americans, "They made many promises about how they would protect us, but we did not receive any protection from them. On the contrary they bring the war into our town, and then we have to protect them."[41]

At Fort Pitt, McIntosh was also trying to address ways to get supplies to Fort Laurens. At a Council of War on February 7, it was decided to send Major Richard Taylor and 100 men to escort 200 kegs of flour, 50 barrels of beef and pork, and quantities of whiskey and medicine.[42] However, the continued lack of packhorses and the fact that the last overland supply convoy has been attacked led the Americans to try a water route this time. The plan called for two boats to go 200 miles down the Ohio, then upstream on the Muskingum for 110 miles to Coshocton, and then upstream for another 70 miles on the Tuscarawas. It showed just how unsafe the American Army felt on Ohio soil that they preferred a water route that was five times longer.

Taylor left the next day and made good time going downstream on the Ohio. But when he tried to ascend the swollen Muskingum he ran into trouble. After having two men killed by Indians and only traveling twenty miles in six days, Taylor got a letter from Heckewelder warning of more Indian troubles ahead. Realizing the futility of his mission, Taylor returned to Fort Pitt, arriving March 8.[43] Taylor at least made an effort to help Gibson, and, 33 years later, Gibson repaid the debt, when, as Governor of Indiana Territory in 1812, he sent a relief column and supplies to a surrounded fort being held by Taylor's son, a young Captain Zachary Taylor. But for now, it was becoming increasingly obvious that the only acre of ground in the Ohio country that the Americans had any control over was the one inside the stockade at Fort Laurens. And it was in jeopardy.

As Girty's war party of around 200 Mingo and Wyandots headed east, word got out, and the Moravians warned Gibson that he was threatened. Gibson wrote to McIntosh, "you may depend on ... my care to prevent surprise,"[44] but the attackers managed to get to the fort undetected. On the morning of February 23, a wood cutting detail of nineteen men was ambushed within sight of the horrified garrison. In a single volley, Gibson's garrison was literally decimated, as seventeen of his 172 available troops were killed and two captured. If there were any British redcoats that came along on this mission, this volley would also mark the only time that American Continentals faced British regulars in combat west of the Appalachian mountains. Afterwards, the attackers scalped their victims, and both sides settled in for a siege.

In a strange coincidence, on the very day that Gibson was attacked by Girty, Clark attacked Hamilton at Vincennes. When Hamilton had left Detroit to retake Vincennes in October, he was accompanied by 175 Regulars and militia and about 60 Indians, but he picked up several hundred more Indian allies along the way. It took them 71 arduous days to travel 600 miles, but they were easily able to retake the post from the American skeleton crew. Hamilton then released all but about 80 of his men until spring, as he was convinced Clark would not act until then, and meanwhile, Hamilton had him trapped against the Mississippi, far from his Kentucky supply lines and reinforcements.[45]

Both Hamilton and McIntosh had looked at winter frontier conditions and resolved to stay out of action, but Clark looked at the same factors and decided to go full speed ahead with an attack. With 180 of his men and some French volunteers, Clark set off across southern Illinois on February 5. They made good time at first, but conditions worsened as they approached Vincennes. An early thaw had caused extensive flooding that made their final approach a nightmare. The troops had to wade through chest high water and then were not permitted to build fires, lest they be spotted by the enemy. But on February 23, Clark established contact with sympathetic French settlers. Later that day, they startled Hamilton by attacking his fort.

After the two sides had exchanged fire overnight, Hamilton the next day requested a parlay. A dramatic moment then occurred when an Indian raiding party returned from Kentucky. This group employed the familiar dreaded "scalp halloo," a unique cry that served as an invitation for all to turn out to marvel at the raiding party's collection of booty and scalps. But their cry died in their throats when they suddenly realized that their town was now under the control of the relatives of the people whose scalps they had dangling from their belts. Clark immediately ordered the public tomahawking of four of the raiding party. This conspicuous and capricious cruelty was the kind of behavior that Indians used to terrify whites, and seeing it used against them had an effect. Between Clark's sudden appearance and his brutal behavior, he became the one white man who could inspire fear in Indians.

Not long after this, Hamilton agreed to surrender. This was the biggest victory on the western front and had major repercussions for the future. Clark and McIntosh both had inadvertently helped each other's campaigns, but if they had cooperated, rather than kept secrets from each other, the Americans might have had a chance to take Detroit at this time.

Back at Fort Laurens, Gibson was not overly worried about being surrounded by hostile Indians at first. As an old Indian hand, he knew the natives rarely had the patience for a protracted siege, and game was almost as scarce outside the fort's gates as it was inside. Also, he had managed to send a message to McIntosh informing him of his plight. So, for the first two weeks of the siege Gibson left his men on full rations.[46] But the attackers also had an advantage. Once the Americans were hemmed up in their fort, it wasn't necessary to keep all the attackers present; they just needed a presence at certain key junctions to keep the defenders feeling trapped. Zeisberger began to notice braves milling around Coshocton, and their numbers increased as the siege wore on.[47]

Five. McIntosh 1778

After two weeks, Gibson became sufficiently alarmed at the besiegers' persistence that he reduced rations to a quarter pound of flour and beef daily. By the end of this week, the garrison was subsisting on a half a biscuit a day, and they were getting desperate. During the next week, two men died and four became ill from eating poisonous roots. When one soldier managed to kill a deer and bring it in, it was devoured immediately without even being cooked. Others boiled their own moccasins or beef hides in an effort to make a nourishing broth.[48]

At Fort Pitt, a discouraged McIntosh had already requested a transfer from the Western Department, but he responded when informed of Gibson's predicament. By March 19, McIntosh had gathered 300 Continentals and 200 militia, as well as a large quantity of supplies. Making much better time on this trip, they arrived at Fort Laurens in just four days. The invaders, who were aware of the presence and size of McIntosh's force, abandoned their siege and melted away undetected. At dusk on March 23, the starving and dispirited garrison heard the sound of an approaching army. When they discovered this column was there to rescue rather than attack them, they fired their guns in a joyous celebration. Unfortunately, this had the effect of stampeding the pack horses into the woods. They spent all the next day trying to gather wagons and supplies, but most was never recovered.[49]

A furious McIntosh held a Council of War where his officers were unanimous in opposing an attack on Detroit. Some accounts claim he was upset by their choice, but McIntosh informed Washington, "I returned.... And was happy I did."[50] Before returning, the garrison retrieved the bones of their butchered brethren from the wood cutting detail and put them in a pit dug outside the fort. The next day, they found a pack of wolves trapped in the pit who were gnawing on those bones, and they took their revenge out on these wolves before filling in the pit. McIntosh then relieved Gibson and his garrison and replaced them with Major Frederick Vernon and 106 men from the 8th Pennsylvania. The rest of the army then left and was back at Fort Pitt by March 30.

This was McIntosh's last act as commander of the Western Department. Washington had some strong ideas for a western campaign, but it would have to be under a different leader. Back in January, Continental Congress had expanded Washington's authority so that "the Commander in Chief be authorized and directed to superintend the operations from Fort Pitt.... And from time to time give such orders respecting the same as he shall judge expedient."[51] With the newfound authority to coordinate his departments, Washington immediately wrote McIntosh proposing a campaign either on Detroit or upstream on the Allegheny from where Indian raids had been launched. Washington requested information on distances and travel times, forage and river crossings, and best possible routes, and told McIntosh, "I would recommend to you immediately to discharge every useless mouth, that your magazines be spared as much as possible."[52]

But McIntosh would not be a part of this campaign. He had formally petitioned Continental Congress to be recalled, and, in response to Washington's queries, he told him that he could not get professional estimates because the experts were gone, mostly to Kentucky, and that "I would not be surprised and expect to hear soon of the application for a Continental Army for the protection of these new and remote settlements, although we have every corner of our country already to defend and struggle for."[53] McIntosh also had personal concerns to deal with. Not only was his command becoming "increasingly disagreeable,"[54] but, as he informed Henry Laurens, "I am lately informed my own country, all my family, and everything of property I have in the world, are now in the hands of the enemy. I am extremely unhappy not to hear anything from them. Desire to be there."[55] So, after returning from his Fort Laurens rescue mission, on April 4, McIntosh turned over his command to senior regimental commander Colonel Daniel Brodhead.

Six

Brodhead I
1779

Brodhead's selection to head the Western Department was hardly the result of a detailed search. Washington was impatient for a campaign to be launched from Fort Pitt, and he didn't have time to bring a new commander up to speed. The commander-in-chief had originally intended to bring McIntosh east for consultation on this proposed offensive, but McIntosh's request to be relieved had changed that. Washington now needed an insider familiar with the local situation, and on March 5, he offered the position to Daniel Brodhead, saying, "from my opinion of your abilities, your former acquaintance with the back country, and the knowledge you must have acquired upon that last tour of duty, I have appointed you to the command in preference to a stranger."[1]

Although born in New York in 1736, Daniel Brodhead had grown up in Pennsylvania. He became a surveyor and was the Deputy Surveyor General of Pennsylvania when the Revolution began. He became a lieutenant colonel of a rifle battalion and saw action in

Colonel Daniel Brodhead was energetic and ambitious, and had some early success, but his overreaching eventually led to his downfall ("Daniel Brodhead," The New York Public Library Digital Collections. 1886).

the New York campaign. He was promoted to colonel and given command of the Eighth Pennsylvania regiment, and his commission as colonel was six months senior to that of John Gibson, the other colonel on the western front.[2] Brodhead was energetic and ambitious, and he yearned to be the one to take Detroit, which he considered to be "the source of all the calamities the inhabitants suffer."[3] But it appears that by the time Washington offered the job to Brodhead, the commander had already determined that his proposed expedition would be launched up the Allegheny River.

Although Brodhead may have had a different destination in mind, he agreed with Washington that the troops needed to be freed from garrison duty if they were to be effective. He told Washington, "it appears to me that small garrisons are not of half the benefit in protecting inhabitants that light parties will be if employed to scout on the Indian side up and down the river."[4] But his first duty was to give his commander a return on just how many men he had available. In the same letter, Brodhead reported that he had 722 Continental troops available for duty— 392 from the Eighth Pennsylvania, 258 from the 13th/9th Virginia, and 72 men from an independent company. However, this force was spread out over several distant locations. The largest concentration of troops was the 337 men at Fort Pitt, but there were also garrisons of 123 men at Fort McIntosh, 106 at Fort Laurens, and 28 each at Wheeling and Holiday Cove (Weirton, West Virginia).[5] Brodhead had already planned to abandon smaller posts at Forts Randolph and Hand, and he complained of the difficulties in supplying Forts Laurens and McIntosh, derisively referring to them as "hobby horses."[6] However, Washington, knew that these two newer posts caused alarm among the British, and he ordered them held for as long as possible.

Another matter that Brodhead needed to address was Indian relations, and here he showed a marked improvement over McIntosh's policies. In addition to trying to placate the nearer Delaware and Shawnee tribes, Brodhead also invited the more distant and hostile Wyandot and Ottawa tribes to treaty talks. These tribes were generally pro–British, but might be lured away if the Americans experienced success in this campaign. Brodhead even got a Cherokee delegation to head north for a treaty of friendship. He got along so well with the Delaware that they gave him the name Great Moon, and Washington complimented him on his efforts to "cultivate" the Delaware.[7]

However, George Morgan's complaints about the previous treaty had alarmed the Delaware. Morgan, who the Delaware gave the name Taimenand, or wise councilor, had suggested that the Delaware petition

Continental Congress for a meeting, and they had requested one. Just as Sam Samples had required an Indian escort from the Coshocton, a delegation of fourteen Delaware traveling across Pennsylvania was going to need a military escort for their protection. There were rumors that a group of Tories planned to murder the Delaware to embarrass the Americans, but it was more likely that the Americans would embarrass themselves without any outside help. Indeed, Brodhead had to report that a soldier from the Ninth Virginia had recently "maliciously killed one of the best men of the Delaware" and had to be arrested.[8]

Brodhead selected Gibson to lead a large military escort to Philadelphia. Gibson, who had been given the Delaware name Horsehead when he lived among them during Pontiac's Conspiracy, could serve as a translator as well as an officer of sufficient rank for this diplomatic mission. Gelelemend and two other chiefs were the main members of the Delaware delegation, but there were others of note. Traveling with them were three young Delaware boys heading east for education. These were the teen son and half-brother of Gelelemend and a six-year-old son of White Eyes. They were part of a plan by Morgan to compensate the Delaware for White Eyes' death and to consolidate the tribal connection to the Americans. These boys were to be deposited at Morgan's home in Princeton to begin preparation to enter the university there. But the cultural differences were too much for the youth, and the experiment did not go well. The two older boys were dismissed: one for drunkenness and the other for impregnating a maid. The youngest child, whose full name was George Morgan White Eyes, did matriculate at Princeton, but did not graduate.[9]

This delegation crossed Pennsylvania without incident, arriving at Morgan's home on May 9, and from there they wrote to George Washington at army headquarters at nearby Middlebrook, New Jersey, to request a meeting. This meeting occurred on May 12. Although Washington was not able to address their political concerns, he did the courtesy of meeting with them, and he also invited them to attend a review of the troops of General Maxwell's New Jersey brigade scheduled for May 14. Native Americans were great fans of pump and military displays like this. They eagerly watched the Americans go through their marching routines and small arms demonstration, unaware that they were not making such a great impression of their own. A surgeon for Maxwell's brigade described the scene of George Washington leading the procession, saying,

> his Excellency, with his usual dignity, followed by his mulatto servant Bill, writing a beautiful gray steed, passed in front.... He was accompanied by a

singular group of savages, whose appearance was beyond description ludicrous. Their horses were the meanest kind, some of them destitute of saddles.... Their personal decorations were equally farcical, having their faces painted of various colors, jewels suspended from their ears and nose, their heads without covering, except for tufts of hair on the crown, and some of them wore dirty blankets over their shoulders.... In short, they exhibited a novel and truly disgusting spectacle.[10]

On the same day as the military review, Washington received a letter from McIntosh requesting a court martial to clear his name of accusations Morgan had levied against him. This letter was answered by Washington's top aide, Lieutenant Colonel Alexander Hamilton, who responded that, while McIntosh was entitled to pursue his case, it would be impractical to do so. Hamilton stressed the "Delay, expense, and trouble" it would involve, and concluded, "the General thinks it best the matter should rest where it is."[11] After thinking the matter over, McIntosh concurred, and returned to the south. He was reunited with his family, and he continued to serve in the southern campaigns, but he was never able to recoup his prewar wealth. But when Washington visited Savannah on his presidential tour of the country in 1791, he stayed with McIntosh.

The Delaware delegation now turned their attention to Continental Congress, the group they had come to see. While they were waiting for a reply to their request, they were treated to a meeting with the newly arrived French envoy. The Delaware had been allied with the French years earlier, and were pleased to know that France had now joined the war on the American side. On May 29, the tribesmen finally got their chance to address their concerns with a Congressional committee. They noted that "The putting the tomahawk in our hands last summer threw us into great confusion and has been attended with very disagreeable consequences to you and us. Yet when we see that we can be of service, we shall not be backward."[12] It wasn't like the Delaware could be drafted, so the differences were talked out without any need for any formal signings. However, a result of this encounter was the immediate resignation of George Morgan as Indian agent. In his letter, Morgan maintained, "An agent for Indian affairs is at present unnecessary" since the army was going to do whatever they wanted to, and, "a perseverance in the late adopted policies will terminate in a general Indian war."[13] Meanwhile, Gibson escorted the Delaware back to Fort Pitt, where they arrived around June 20. Like McIntosh, Morgan was now out of the local scene, but his career was not through yet.

Six. Brodhead I 1779

Morgan continued his experimental farming at Princeton. He joined the American Philosophical Society, and the Philadelphia Society for the Promotion of Agriculture gave him an award for his research. After the Revolution, Morgan became involved with the settlement of Missouri. At this time, the Spanish controlled land west of the Mississippi, but they lacked the manpower to colonize the area. Spanish officials approached Morgan for help in setting up a community of Americans looking for cheap land. In 1789, Morgan went west and established the town of New Madrid, but he only stayed six months and did not remain involved with this project.

In 1796, Morgan relocated to the Pittsburgh area, where he continued his research on a farm he called Morganza. He was living here in 1805 when Aaron Burr paid him a visit. Burr had just recently left the Vice Presidency after killing Alexander Hamilton in a duel, and was now headed west for reasons undetermined. But his plans did involve consultations with many major frontier leaders. In addition to Morgan, Burr also met with Henry Clay in Kentucky, Thomas Worthington in Ohio, William Henry Harrison in Indiana, and Andrew Jackson in Tennessee. To each, Burr told them only what he thought they wanted to hear, and he attracted a lot of interest. Morgan, however, was suspicious from the start, and almost immediately wrote to President Thomas Jefferson to warn him about Burr. After Burr was arrested and charged with treason, Morgan testified against him at his trial in Richmond. Morgan then returned to Morganza, where he died in 1810. The following year, the town he had founded at New Madrid was at the epicenter of a major earthquake.

While the Delaware traveled east, George Rogers Clark still had hopes of taking Detroit. He sent word for additional Kentucky militia to join him at Vincennes for a final push, but was not able to coordinate with his own militia, as the Kentuckians instead launched an unsuccessful raid on the Shawnee in southwestern Ohio. This left them less likely to turn out in numbers at Vincennes, and Clark was forced to return to the Falls of the Ohio after spending over a year in enemy territory.

Washington was hoping to address the same issue of coordinating various forces in his proposed campaign. He was hoping to use the various departments of his Continental Army in a coordinated assault on the mighty Iroquois confederacy in upstate New York. This six tribe coalition had unified to become a dominant force among natives, and they were closely allied with Sir William Johnson, the most powerful white man in the Indian world. As he enjoyed the loyal support of the Iroquois, Johnson served as commander of combined British and Indian forces during the French and Indian War. In peacetime, as the Royal Indian Agent for North America, Johnson amassed wealth and power that continued unabated until his sudden death on the eve of the Revolution.

The large hole he left was largely filled by Joseph Brant, a Mohawk who was the younger brother of Johnson's mistress. Young Brant had gained military experience as a teen fighting in his brother-in-law's army, and in peacetime he was given every opportunity to advance himself in the white world. He converted to Christianity, was educated by the founder of Dartmouth, and became a Mason. He traveled to London on diplomatic business, where he was feted and was profiled by James Boswell for London's *Gentleman's Magazine*. When diplomacy failed and the Revolution began, Brant joined with the hated father and son Tory duo of John and Walter Butler to launch a series of terrifying raids on Americans. Brant was heavily involved in the Saratoga campaign of 1777, and the massacres in the Wyoming and Cherry Valleys in subsequent years. Continental Congress now resolved to address these raids by sending a large force directly into the Iroquois stronghold around the Finger Lakes of New York.

The plan called for a division under Major General John Sullivan to head north from Easton, Pennsylvania. This force, which contained the brigades of Generals Hand, Poor, and Maxwell, would proceed north on the Susquehanna. Meanwhile, another brigade under General James Clinton would leave from upstate New York. The two armies were to meet on the Pennsylvania/New York line and march in to destroy Iroquois villages. Brodhead's much smaller force would launch a diversionary attack on the Mingo and Seneca towns on the Allegheny to keep them from coming to the aid of the Iroquois. If things went well, Brodhead was to join Sullivan for an assault on Fort Niagara.

Washington contacted Brodhead and encouraged him to write to Sullivan directly but didn't require it,[14] which shows that Washington was the real commander of the mission. He peppered Brodhead with all sorts of preparation orders as the two men exchanged 20 letters between March and July to plan the expedition.[15] Washington was familiar with Brodhead's proposed route, as he had traveled it as a 21-year-old on his way to Fort LeBoeuf. Insisting on a water route, Washington issued specific instructions to build 60 boats to haul supplies upstream and stipulated that Fort Laurens be occupied until the last minute when the garrison would join the expedition.

The success of the mission would depend largely on how many militia would turn out to join Brodhead's army. On July 17, Brodhead issued a request for militia to rendezvous at Fort Pitt on August 5. He announced that "his Excellency the commander-in-chief has at length given me latitude and I am determined to strike a blow against one of the most hostile nations that in all probability will effectively secure the tranquility of these frontiers for years to come," and promising good treatment and bounty, "which I apprehend will be considerable."[16]

The militia that were needed to complement Continental Army troops were temporary citizen soldiers defending their homes by responding to a government call out. But they also wanted a cut of the action. Like the naval privateers who made a legal living committing piracy on foreign ships in wartime, the militia shared in the sale of the proceeds of any items looted during their campaign. This was a better recruitment incentive than fighting hostile Indians, although the outnumbered natives usually refused to engage in battle without a decided advantage in terms of numbers, terrain, or surprise. A normal outcome of a raid like this was the looting of abandoned villages and destruction of crops.

Brodhead could also count on the help of a contingent of Delaware braves who served as armed guides. Back in January, McIntosh wrote to Gelelemend proposing the Delaware raise a 60-man fighting force and choose captains so "that I may appoint them and desire our beloved man, Colonel Gibson, to tell them what they are to do."[17] This part of the treaty agreement survived the discussions in Philadelphia, and Gibson's fluency in Delaware made him a logical commander of the force. However, in practice, these Delaware scouts worked in the field with Captain Sam Brady and Lieutenant John Hardin of the Eighth Pennsylvania, the two American officers most skilled in Indian style tracking and fighting.

Brady was a renowned woodsman whose exploits have been mythologized like those of Lewis Wetzel or Simon Kenton. But these stories had a background of truth, as in June 1779, Brady led a party that successfully recaptured three children who had been taken in an Indian raid.[18] But John Hardin has never gotten his due from history. Brodhead described Hardin as a man who was "well calculated for frontier service,"[19] and he had an interesting career on the frontier. Hardin served as an officer in Dunmore's War at the age of 20, and became a lieutenant in the Eighth Pennsylvania when the Revolution began. He served with Morgan's riflemen at Saratoga, where he was wounded. After the war, he moved to Kentucky and became a brigadier general of militia.

In 1790, he commanded a force that was defeated by Little Turtle near present-day Fort Wayne. Three years later, he volunteered to go into Indian country to try to discuss a peace treaty. While traveling through the Ohio county now named for him (Kentucky and Illinois have also named counties for him), he was murdered by his Indian guides, joining a mostly Indian list of martyred peacekeepers that included Cornstalk, Ellinipsico, and White Eyes.

After making his final preparation and pleas for troops, Brodhead was rewarded by a combined federal and militia turn out of 605 men, and this force started north from Fort Pitt on August 11. Brodhead had his supplies shipped up the Allegheny to the head of navigation, where Mahoning Creek joins the river. From there, the supplies were transferred to pack horses. Meanwhile, the troops advanced upstream along the banks. They were delayed for four days by heavy rains, and encountered more difficulties afterwards. The riverbanks were often high and winding ridges so overgrown that the troops had to pass in single file. But the men pressed on towards the upstream towns of Buckaloon and Conewego.

On August 19, they encountered an Indian raiding party headed down the river. Lieutenant Hardin was leading an advance party of about fifteen Pennsylvania troops and eight Delaware scouts when they made contact with the enemy. Hardin led a charge that scattered the Indians, who had already abandoned their canoes as well as five dead comrades by the time the rest of the army arrived on the scene. These were the only Indians sighted on the expedition, as the survivors returned upstream to warn the others. The Americans thereafter encountered only abandoned villages, which they burned along with several hundred acres of ripening corn. Brodhead got as far on the Allegheny as the New York line, but they were now far from their supply source and lacked a local guide, so an assault on Fort Niagara was ruled out. On his return route, Brodhead crossed overland east to French Creek and returned along Washington's old route down to present-day Franklin and the Allegheny. They returned to Fort Pitt on September 14, and Brodhead was able to report that his force had covered 400 miles in 33 days, destroyed ten Indian villages and seized $30,000 worth of bounty, without losing a man.[20]

The eastern portion of this joint campaign was also successful. The Tories and Iroquois tried to slow down the American advance with raids, but the trained Continentals plowed ahead and Sullivan and Clinton met up on the New York/Pennsylvania line on the Susquehanna on August 22. They refused to be lulled into a surprise attack, and on August 29, John Butler and Joseph Brant put up a stand at Newtown, near present day Elmira. After a brisk fight, with the Americans using their artillery effectively, the vastly outnumbered Tories and Indians were forced from the field, and the Americans met no more resistance. For the next four weeks, this 3,200 man forced tore right through the heart of Iroquois country. After they had destroyed the Six Nations principal towns along the Genesee River, they returned home by a different route so they could destroy a different set of towns. They returned in triumph, having destroyed 41 villages while only losing 41 men.[21]

This raid did serious damage to the Iroquois confederacy, as that winter thousands of starving natives appealed for help at Fort Niagara, straining the already scarce British resources. Just as importantly, the expedition showed that Washington could coordinate his various departments into becoming an effective fighting force. Continental Congress concurred and passed accolades all around. Brodhead was voted the body's official thanks, and Washington informed him, "I am extremely happy in your success."[22] This was the most successful expedition launched from Fort Pitt during the war, although there wasn't much other competition. Brodhead's success in his initial campaign gave him incentive to propose new efforts in his quest to take Detroit.

Another factor working in Brodhead's favor was that his triumphant return was made in front of several tribes who were already gathered for a prearranged conference at Fort Pitt. All tribes preferred to support a front runner, and they got to see Brodhead at his apex. The Wyandots and the formerly hostile Mekoche clan of the Shawnee now expressed interest in neutrality and friendship with the Americans. This might have been a good time to make a run at Detroit. The fort there was in decay, and morale was low after Hamilton's capture until Major Arendt De Peyster was sent from Fort Mackinac to take command. The British needed a victory to lift their spirits, and Simon Girty gave them one.

Late in September, Simon Girty, his brother George, and Matthew Elliott led a raiding party of about 100 braves south towards Kentucky. Just after crossing the Ohio on the morning of October 4, they spotted five boats heading upstream near the site of present day Cincinnati. It was just luck that they had stumbled across this flotilla that was transporting valuable gunpowder and supplies to the Americans. Under the command of Colonel David Rogers of the Virginia militia, this group had been gone for over a year after having traveled all the way to New Orleans to procure supplies.

The Spanish in New Orleans had not officially joined the United States' side in the war, but they were still willing to clandestinely help them. Virginia governor Patrick Henry sent Rogers and 30 men on a perilous trip in June 1778. When Rogers arrived at a Spanish post in Arkansas, he was informed that the gunpowder had been shipped to St. Louis, but he still needed to go to New Orleans to obtain a release for the goods. Traveling in a canoe with a handful of men, Rogers completed his dangerous journey, working with merchant Oliver Pollock and Governor Bernardo de Galvez. Rogers left New Orleans in December and managed to avoid the British on his upstream trip. He departed from St. Louis in August and arrived at the Falls of the Ohio in late September. Clark was thrilled to take much of the supplies and sent Rogers upstream to deliver the rest, along with an escort of 65 men and five boats.

Girty's men now set a trap for them at the spot where the Licking flows into the Ohio. They lured the men ashore and attacked them with their full force. The Americans fought back, but were outnumbered and tried to shove off in their boats. Although one boat did manage to get away, 40 men were killed, including Rogers, a dozen were captured, and only thirteen escaped.[23]

This incident also illustrated the importance of boats on the frontier. Before moving on Vincennes, Clark had outfitted and armed a boat that he named for James Willing, but this craft did not arrive until after Hamilton had surrendered. Faced with the problem of defending such a vast area with so few troops, Clark later toyed with the idea of loading artillery onto boats that would patrol the river as floating forts. However his plans for a Kentucky navy had to be abandoned when his men balked at rowing cannon laden boats upstream. A series of forts at key junctions on major rivers was an expensive alternative, but Clark was ordered by Virginia to build a fort just below the confluence of the Ohio and Mississippi Rivers. This post, named for Jefferson, was not only over 800 miles as the crow flies from Williamsburg, but was also 981 Ohio River miles below Pittsburgh, so the logistics of supplying such an isolated spot hampered its questionable value.

Back at Fort Pitt, Brodhead was eager to follow up on his success. He had another advantage in that the Virginia/Pennsylvania border dispute was finally being resolved. The two states had each sent representatives who approved the border in late August. Pennsylvania ratified the agreement in November, but Virginia delayed ratification until the following June, so they could sell more land to buyers who expected

Six. Brodhead I 1779

Pennsylvania to honor their titles. The final survey was not conducted until 1784, but at least now militia recruiters could finally be sure in what state they were recruiting.

Brodhead wasted no time lobbying Washington for a proposed winter assault on Detroit. The two exchanged eight letters between October and December before Washington canceled the operation. On January 4, 1780, he informed Brodhead, "I regret the situation of affairs does not permit us to undertake it. We cannot furnish either the men or supplies necessary for it."[24] The commander-in-chief was apologetic and encouraged Brodhead's initiative, but felt any assault had to be deferred for now. Washington also turned down Brodhead's secondary proposal, a raid down the Mississippi to Natchez that would have left Fort Pitt undefended. However, Washington, did promise to try to send an artillery detachment to Fort Pitt.

It was just as well that neither of Brodhead's proposed campaigns were attempted. For one thing, the Spanish made the Natchez assault unnecessary. Word had reached New Orleans in August that Spain was officially at war with Great Britain, and Governor Galvez wasted no time. In September, he took a large force on the lower Mississippi and captured three British posts between Baton Rouge and a re-occupied Natchez. After this, there was no longer any British presence on the Mississippi between New Orleans and St. Louis. As for a Detroit campaign, the factor against a winter attack was that the winter of 1779–80 was one of the harshest in memory in all quarters. At Fort Pitt, Brodhead reported boats "carried away by ice: such a deep snow and ice never known there before."[25] A correspondent in Kentucky called it "the severest winter that was ever known."[26] Along the Tuscarawas, John Heckewelder wrote of "the snow being so deep and the weather so continually cold."[27] These harsh conditions began in November and lasted through February, so almost all winter plans had to be put on hold.

However, as soon as any thawing occurred, the natives began their raids on settlers even earlier than usual. Early in March, raiding parties struck individual families in the Fort Pitt area. Although it turned out that the Wyandots were responsible, there were some who blamed the nearby Delaware tribe. Many Delaware were now more openly favoring the British, and some had even moved to the Sandusky River region closer to Detroit to be with other pro–British tribes. Gelelemend was also having difficulty restraining his local braves who remained. But on this occasion, he denied all involvement and Zeisberger backed him up. Indians in other areas also took up arms early this year, as in upstate

New York Joseph Brant led his braves on a series of vengeful raids that proved the Iroquois were not finished as a fighting force. The raiding around Fort Pitt was so extensive that, on April 24, Brodhead reported to Washington, "Since the first of March, the Indians have killed and taken 43 men women and children."[28] Brodhead called out the militia, but feared that, "disputed jurisdiction will probably interfere with their coming."[29]

Washington could offer little encouragement for Brodhead. Although he did report, "I have directed General Knox to detach an officer of artillery with a proper number of men for the duty of the garrison at Fort Pitt," he had to conclude, "There is little or no prospect of any offensive operations."[30] Continental Congress did not even have the funds to repair the boats that had been damaged over the winter.

These setbacks were frustrating for Brodhead, who was anxious to repeat his early success. His aggressiveness sometimes led him to overstep his bounds. Almost immediately after taking command Brodhead had proposed to the president of Continental Congress that he be allowed to offer a bounty on scalps. Since this was the same practice that had made Henry Hamilton the most hated man in the west, the Americas were not eager to repeat it, so President Joseph Reed replied to Brodhead, "We have sounded Congress and the government about giving a reward for scalps, but there is so evident a reluctance on the subject that at present we cannot venture to make any authoritative offers."[31]

Brodhead also interfered with the delicate balance between local militia and the federal army. In recruiting for the Continental Army, he tried to lure local rangers to join before their militia enlistments had expired, which earned him another rebuke from Reed. Still eager to assert his authority, on April 4, Brodhead issued orders for the seizure of all public watercraft in private hands on the Ohio and Mississippi Rivers, an edict that was as unenforceable as it was illegal. The colonel's impatience was causing him to make enemies who would later cause problems for him.

Brodhead was also losing friends among his own officers. In a letter to Captain Joseph Irwin of the Eighth Pennsylvania, Brodhead said Irwin's disobedience would be reported to authorities, and he castigated him and his men for "wasting their time at the public expense."[32] When his second-in-command John Gibson failed to satisfy an order, Brodhead informed him, "It always creates in my breast a great share of uneasiness when I find a gentleman with whom I have a contracted an intimacy under pretention of friendship, aiming to destroy my peace of mind. But more particularly where an officer travails so far out of the line of duty as to disobey my orders."[33]

Major Frederick Vernon, who was second-in-command of Brodhead's former regiment, lodged formal and specific charges against his commander. In December, he accused Brodhead of letting a certain Nancy McCauley, who was apparently Brodhead's mistress, sell furniture that was made by others, and of "sporting away" public money designated for recruiting expenses, and of allowing the same Nancy McCauley to take "unbecoming liberties" with some of the officers in Brodhead's presence. Vernon announced that he would no longer dine nor associate with Brodhead, a serious step since the handful of officers at Fort Pitt regularly ate together.[34]

Despite these ominous signs, there was hope as spring finally arrived. Major Isaac Craig and the company of Continental artillery had left for the west on April 15 and should soon be at Fort Pitt. With better weather, artillery, and a chance to raise sufficient numbers of militia, Brodhead still might be able to mount the offensive he desired.

Unbeknownst to Brodhead, the British also had major plans for a 1780 campaign. After years of having their western troops holed up in small garrisons spread across the Great Lakes region, they were finally ready to throw all their men into a western offensive that would range from Mackinac to Pensacola. Unfortunately for them, the Florida part had to be scrapped when the aggressive Galvez captured the nearby British port in Mobile in March. However, the British still planned to send large forces to attack both Kentucky and the Spanish post at St. Louis. The next six months or so would illustrate the truly international nature of the American Revolution in the west.

Seven

Brodhead II
1780

As Colonel Daniel Brodhead began his second year in command of the Western Department, he was most anxious to return to action after a long winter. He wanted to mount an offensive campaign, but was waiting for the arrival of the artillery company he had requested. He was still waiting in early May, when some visiting dignitaries passed through Fort Pitt.

The first contingent was a delegation of Moravians on their way from church headquarters in Bethlehem, Pennsylvania, to the Tuscarawas Valley. This group included Heckewelder's fiancée Sarah Ohneberg, who was en route to her wedding. Over the winter, the Moravians had become so alarmed by the Delaware gradually abandoning their neutrality that they decided they were safer back at their previous villages. So, in the spring they reoccupied Gnadenhutten and built New Schoenbrunn across the river from the old one. They also started a new mission called Salem at present-day Port Washington, Ohio, and it was here that the Heckewelder nuptials were to take place. The Moravians were treated well by Brodhead and Gibson, who had just returned from furlough, and it was reported that "The governor of Pittsburgh, Colonel Brodhead, and Colonel Gibson treated these travelers with great kindness. The latter gave them a traveling tent, and assisted them in everything requisite for their safe conveyance."[1] So, while top American brass did not attend the first white wedding in what is now Ohio, they did at least send a gift.

The other visitor of note was Daniel Linctot, a former French officer with considerable experience among the Indians of North America. Linctot, along with his father and brother, had served with French forces in the midwest before France was forced to forgo these claims in 1763. Linctot remained as a fur trader and allied with Clark when Cahokia was captured. He had influence with the Indians and he took

Seven. Brodhead II 1780

some of them east to meet with the Virginia officials in 1779. He was commissioned as a major and Indian agent for the Ohio tribes by that state. From Fort Pitt, Linctot traveled on to Vincennes in the hopes of aligning western tribes with the U.S.[2]

After these visitors had departed for the west, Brodhead was more eager than ever to take the field. He had promised the Moravians and his militia officers an aggressive campaign, but a lack of provisions and the tardiness of his artillery's arrival meant more delay. He finally had to cancel his proposed expedition on May 20. This proved to be wise, as Craig and his 28 man artillery company did not arrive for another month.

George Rogers Clark not only had success in the west, but was the one white man the Indians feared. But his victories were on behalf of the Virginia militia, not the Continental Army (National Portrait Gallery, Smithsonian Institution).

While Brodhead was experiencing forced inactivity, the British were on the move. As early as February, Patrick Sinclair, the Commandant at Fort Mackinac in northern Michigan, began making plans for a spring offensive. His targets were the tiny Spanish outpost at St. Louis, and the French settlement right across the Mississippi at Cahokia, where Clark had left a token occupying garrison. But Sinclair was not planning to risk the few troops he had at his disposal. Instead, he recruited Indian traders to lead his raids. These men often had military experience and the trust of the natives that would comprise the army. Leading the assault on St. Louis would be Emanuel Hesse, a trader who had previously served in Bouquet's regiment. The attack on Cahokia would be led by Charles Langlade, a half breed renegade with a military career that went back 30 years. In 1751, while working for the French, Langlade had led a raid on a village in Piqua, Ohio, where they boiled and ate a Miami chief who had welcomed British traders into his village. Hesse came down the Mississippi, recruiting more braves from more tribes until he had amassed 950 warriors, while Langlade came down the Illinois River towards Cahokia with a smaller force.

It was impossible to gather that large a force without word getting out, and the citizens of St. Louis soon found out that they were threatened. The French had transferred their western claims to the Spanish so they wouldn't have to surrender them to the British after Canada fell, so the Spanish now claimed the land west of the Mississippi, and they had established St. Louis in 1764. But it was now defended by just a single company of 29 men under the command of Captain Fernando de Leyba. Even with the addition of all the inexperienced militia he could muster, de Leyba still had only about 200 men to defend St. Louis. His original defense plan called for the construction of four separate tower platforms, but they only had time and supplies to complete one of them. At the corner of Fourth and Walnut Streets in today's downtown St. Louis, they built a stone tower 30 feet in diameter and 30 feet tall, and mounted their artillery on top of it.

On May 15, the American commander at Cahokia, Lieutenant Colonel John Montgomery, crossed the river for a consultation with de Leyba. The two tried to coordinate plans, but they were still on their own on opposite sides of the river. However, the Americans did get a boost from the ubiquitous Clark, who just happened to be in the "neighborhood" supervising construction of Fort Jefferson, just 150 miles downstream. When told of the impending attack, Clark hurried north with all the men he could gather, arriving on May 25.

The next day, the British led Indians attacked on both sides of the river. On the St. Louis side, the Spanish artillery did their job and threw the Indians back in confusion. The frustrated attackers took many civilian prisoners and did extensive crop damage, but never seriously threatened to take the town. The Spanish reported casualties of 22 killed, seven wounded, and 70 taken prisoner.[3] Across the river at Cahokia, the attack was even more easily repulsed, and it was alleged that the natives had no desire to press the attack once they found out that Clark was on the scene.

This venture had ended in disappointment, but the British at Detroit had plans for an even bigger campaign to be launched against Kentucky. Major De Peyster over the winter had made plans for a spring assault, and he was putting all available resources into it. The expedition under

Seven. Brodhead II 1780

Captain Bird would include regular troops, Canadian militia, over 100 Indians, and the entire staff of the Indian department, which included Alexander McKee, Matthew Elliot, and all three Girty brothers. And they also had a new weapon to unveil: two cannons, one of which fired a three pound ball, and a six pounder. Along with these wheeled pieces was a company of artillery to man them.[4]

However, Bird's efforts to keep his advance a surprise were ruined by Lieutenant Abraham Chapline, a man with Kentucky pioneer credentials as strong as those of Daniel Boone and Simon Kenton. Chapline had arrived on the frontier while still a teenager and he was one of the original settlers of Harrodsburg, the first town in Kentucky. Later that same year, he fought in the Battle of Point Pleasant. In 1778, he was one of 28 salt makers captured by the Shawnee when Boone surrendered them in a successful attempt to divert an attack from Boonsboro. Like Boone himself, Chapline escaped and returned to Kentucky, where he joined Clark's expedition. Here he participated in the heroic and harrowing trip to retake Vincennes. When David Rogers deposited supplies at Louisville in the fall of 1779, Chapline led the military escort that joined them, and he was re-captured when Girty's party attacked them.[5] After spending the winter as a captive near Lake Erie, Chapline now escaped again on April 28, and three weeks later he was at the Falls of the Ohio warning of the raid.[6]

It proved to be a major operation hauling artillery from Detroit to Kentucky. The Spanish had sent their cannon up the Mississippi on large boats, and the Americans could follow the future U.S. Route 30 to Pittsburgh, but Bird was denied these advantages in the trackless wilds. He had to take his field pieces upstream on the Maumee River, then unload them for an overland trip to the Great Miami watershed to be floated downstream. But the British were up to the difficult task and arrived on the banks of the Ohio on June 12.

Bird had more difficulty with his Indian allies. Indian warriors were brave and courageous fighters who excelled in individual and low level tactics, but unit cohesion, discipline, and long-term planning were alien concepts to them. As Bird progressed south, he was joined by more men until he had gathered around 700, which proved to be an unwieldy force too large to handle. After a lengthy conference, the natives, many of whom had traveled a great distance in pursuit of scalps and plunder, announced that they were no longer interested in attacking the original target at the Falls at the Ohio, an important military target. They may have been afraid of Clark's being there, or maybe they just wanted an easier target, and they chose instead to attack smaller posts on the Licking River, and Bird had no choice but to go along.

On June 26, this force managed to approach the 350 person settlement Ruddell's Station undetected, but a premature shot alerted the fort. As the two sides squared off firing at each other, Bird wheeled up his three pounder and fired two shots against the stockade that failed to do any major damage, and the Kentuckians were hoping that they had dodged a very large bullet. But when Bird pulled out his six pounder, the settlers realized that they were powerless to prevent a breach of their walls and the ensuing massacre. They asked for surrender terms and Simon Girty came to the fort under a flag of truce to negotiate. They were promised safe passage in exchange for their surrender, but the natives refused to honor this. Bird, who was ultimately responsible for controlling the situation, had to admit, "They rushed in, tore the children from their mother's breasts, killed and wounded many."[7] It's not certain just how many were murdered before Bird was able to reestablish control. And the natives still found it necessary to slake their blood thirst by slaughtering the settlement's entire herd of cattle, which proved to be exceedingly unwise.

The British Indians next moved on to Martin's Station, where the 50 defenders surrendered before a shot could be fired. There were only minor post truce murders this time, but Bird now had several hundred captives to transport and feed. When the Indians heard a rumor that Clark had returned, they were anxious to retreat across the Ohio, and Bird was again forced to comply. He got to the Ohio by July 1, but still had difficulties on the return trip. For one thing, he had to provide supper for 1,000 people every night while a herd of cattle lay rotting in a Kentucky field. In addition, low-water made it hard to take his artillery upstream, so he had to hide his field pieces and leave them behind. The expedition did not return to Detroit until August 4.[8]

While the British were launching attacks all over the midwest, the Continental Army remained holed up in their respective forts. Brodhead faced several major obstacles related to the increase in population. Many of the immigrants streaming westward were just passing through en route to Kentucky, but some of them were suspected of Tory sympathies. Hostility against them was strong, particularly in Southwestern Virginia where Judge Lynch's summary justice prevailed. The influx of new settlers also strained local resources to the point where the population's ability to feed itself was in doubt.

Brodhead yearned to take the field despite these conditions. He sent

Seven. Brodhead II 1780

out another circular asking for a militia rendezvous, but again had to cancel due to a lack of supplies. His own garrison was too small to accomplish anything without militia support, which was so unreliable that Washington conceded, "Militia, besides being very expensive, are so exceedingly capricious, that I should be loath to attempt anything with them which depended upon more than a very short time to accomplish the object."[9]

Brodhead seemed to take out his frustration on his own full-time troops, as he spent his summer court-martialing them. Many soldiers were charged with lesser offenses, such as theft, drunkenness, or sleeping on guard duty, but at least a dozen deserters received between 100 and 500 lashes. These prosecutions became so frequent that in the seventeen weeks between June 5 and October 2, second-in-command John Gibson spent fifteen days presiding over courts martial.[10] And this still wasn't enough for Brodhead: he petitioned Washington for permission for a standing court martial to always be in session, so he could more efficiently prosecute more men from his own army. Washington had to rein his subordinate in by informing him, "I cannot conceive that I have a right to delegate a general power to hold court marshal. There must be an application for a court whenever objects present themselves. This may, it is true in some measure delay the course of justice, but it cannot, from the necessity of the case, be avoided."[11]

There was some activity at Fort Pitt that summer, but it did not directly involve the Continental Army. Late in June, Colonel Mottin de la Balme arrived at the fort. La Balme was a French officer who had offered his services to the Americans, like many other Europeans had done. Some of these came out of a love of liberty, while others came also to advance stalled military careers, and they didn't hesitate to embellish their resumes. For example, Baron von Steuben came to America with a letter from Benjamin Franklin claiming he had served as a general in the Prussian Army, when he really was only a captain.

La Balme, however, had legitimate credentials. He had served as a cavalry officer in the Seven Years' War, and afterwards wrote guidebooks on cavalry training and tactics. He came to America in 1777 and was given the rank of colonel and the title of Inspector General of Cavalry, but he resigned this post when Casimir Pulaski, another foreign officer offering his services, was given the job of Chief of Calvary. This left him a colonel without an assignment, and, after some work in Maine, he wound up at Fort Pitt.[12] La Balme claimed to be working under secret orders from Washington, but this has never been confirmed.

His plan was to go to the French settlements at Vincennes, Kaskaskia, and Cahokia to gather a force of French and Indians to mount an assault on Detroit. To assist him, Nonhelema now came to Fort Pitt for clandestine consultations. Many knew Cornstalk's sister as Grenadier Squaw due to her stature, but she had been baptized under the name Catherine, and was also called Kate. Years earlier, she had had liaisons with several white traders, many of them were several years younger than she, and she had children with both Alexander McKee and Richard Butler. Nonhelema had remained pro–American even after they had murdered her brother and nephew. She served as a translator and had even helped messengers disguise themselves as Indians so they could warn of impending attacks. What made her particularly useful to de La Balme was her fluency in French, English, and several Indian languages. As these two conferred, Daniel Linctot returned to town with several chiefs. Although Brodhead had played no part in these plans, this French contingent made their plans in his fort before leaving for the Illinois country in July.

Back in Kentucky, Bird's raid caused the residents to yearn for revenge. Clark had hurried east towards the Falls of the Ohio as soon as he heard of Bird's movements, but had to travel in disguise to avoid Chickasaw war parties seeking to disrupt the building of Fort Jefferson. Upon arriving, he was criticized for building an isolated fort while letting the population be attacked. Brodhead had recently written to him that he had no troops or supplies to spare and the Kentuckians were on their own, so Clark decided an immediate counterattack was called for. On August 1, at present day Covington, Kentucky, he assembled nearly 1,000 mounted men, including Boone, Kenton, and many of the leading figures of early Kentucky history. Also included was artillery shipped upstream from the fort at Louisville.

This force, the largest Clark ever led, proceeded upstream on the Little Miami River. The first Shawnee town they came to had been warned and was abandoned, but, on August 8, they encountered resistance at the town of Piqua near present-day Springfield, Ohio. The outnumbered Shawnee put up a fight, but the American numbers and cannon were too much for them. This was the home village of a 12-year-old Tecumseh, who already had reason to hate the Americans after they had killed his father at Point Pleasant. Now the Kentuckians destroyed his village and all of its crops. They also killed 73 Shawnee, while Clark's casualties numbered 20 dead and 40 wounded.[13] Among the dead was a cousin of Clark's who had been captured months earlier who was shot by his own men while trying to escape dressed as an Indian.

Clark now had artillery and more men than they had to oppose him in Detroit. But he still had the same problem of how to feed that many men in enemy country, and he regretfully had to turn back yet again short of his goal.

While the Spanish cannon roared in Missouri, the British cannon blazed in Kentucky, and the Kentuckians fired their cannon in Ohio, United States Army's guns at Fort Pitt remained silent. Brodhead still desperately wanted to mount a campaign, but was frustrated at every turn. On September 4, he announced a scheduled militia rendezvous for October 15, but had to cancel again at the last minute, as Washington advised him to "Confine yourself to partisan strokes."[14] A disconsolate Brodhead told a militia leader, "I cannot but lament the repeated disappointments we have met with for want of resources to enable us to retaliate upon the Hell-hounds of the forest, but I must console myself with a conscientiousness that the blame lies not at my door."[15]

The biggest problem, as usual, was a lack of supplies. The local situation was so acute that Washington did appeal to Continental Congress for relief, but the shortages were universal. In August, Washington, informed Brodhead, "The distress on the score of provisions has not been confined to you alone but has been severely experienced in every quarter, and I think you will be happy if you can adopt any expedient to supply yourself without depending wholly upon the commissary."[16] Brodhead did show creativity in some ways, such as requesting Zeisberger to provide fifteen to twenty of his converts to do hunting for the garrison. However, in trying to deal with the problem of farmers refusing to accept hyper inflated Continental currency for their goods, Brodhead seriously overstepped his bounds.

On September 14, Brodhead directed Captain Sam Brady to impress provisions from area residents to feed his garrison. Brady, who had recently used his special skills to rescue yet another captive, was now reduced to taking crops and livestock from the very people he had been rescuing. Brodhead cautioned Brady not to pilfer from poor families or those who had already sacrificed loved ones to the war, but he saw no other alternative. He informed Washington, "I have sent out parties to take cattle and grain from the inhabitants, ... But the inhabitants disappoint us getting beef by driving their cattle into the mountains, and we have at present neither bread nor meat."[17]

Local residents were uniformly outraged by this policy. Frontiers were already conducive to anarchy, and the earlier Pennsylvania/Virginia controversy had made the situation even more so. The citizens thus far had gotten little from government and therefore had little respect for it. All they were asking for was protection from Indian raids and they weren't getting it. And now, the same people who were failing to protect them were actively engaged in trying to steal their crops and livestock. Captain Uriah Springer of the 9th Virginia reported to Brodhead that farmers in the Redstone area intended to rise up in arms to oppose the impounding of their stores. Brodhead had to concede of his officers' efforts, "the success has been so small…. I have now ordered them in."[18] After many complaints, and a formal protest from the troops themselves, Brodhead appointed Gibson to chair a committee to smooth over differences and work on price controls.[19] This helped the situation somewhat, but on December 10, Brodhead still reported that "troops have not tasted meat at this post for six days."[20]

While this was going on, Colonel de La Balme was recruiting volunteers in the Illinois country. While at Fort Pitt, de La Balme felt that all but the top brass was virulently anti–Indian, but he found the French residents of the interior towns to be more receptive to him and his plans. He traveled between the three major towns and was able to raise 100 men willing to march on Detroit. De La Balme was a colonel in the Continental Army, but he was also cooperating with the French Minister, so it was not entirely clear whether he was attacking on behalf of the U.S. or France. Either way, he left Vincennes in October for Detroit. They got as far as the Miami stronghold near present-day Fort Wayne, and stopped to enjoy a cache of supplies they had come across. It was here they were attacked by a Miami war party, and the entire force was killed or captured. The leader of his attack was a hitherto unknown war chief named Little Turtle. A decade later, Little Turtle and Blue Jacket of the Shawnee would lead a formidable coalition of tribes that would defeat American armies under Generals Josiah Harmar and Arthur St. Clair before being defeated by General Anthony Wayne at Fallen Timbers in 1794. After this, Little Turtle became a great friend to the Americans. He traveled to meet with Presidents Washington, Adams, and Jefferson, and even had his portrait painted by Gilbert Stuart.

This was not the end of international activity in the Old Northwest for the season. The Spanish wanted revenge for the British attack on St. Louis, and they made their move in January 1781. De Leyba had been promoted to colonel as a reward for his defense of St. Louis, but he died of illness before word of this got across the Atlantic. His replacement, Captain Eugenio Pourre, led 60 militia and a similar number of Indians towards Fort St. Joseph in the southwestern corner of Michigan. There they surprised the British, who surrendered immediately. The Spanish invasion of Michigan was a brief win, as they left the next day, but it did mark the only Spanish occupation of a Great Lakes fort.

In the campaign for the West that year, the British had attacked the Spanish in Missouri, the Spanish attacked the British in Michigan, the British used artillery in Kentucky, the Kentuckians used artillery on the Indians in Ohio, and the French launched an attack on Detroit from Indiana. But while soldiers marching on behalf of England, France, Spain, and Kentucky were all over the region, the American Army at Fort Pitt remained dormant. The Spanish Army, Kentucky militia, and French cavalry had all gotten as close to Detroit as the American Army ever would. But a chance to change all this came from Virginia governor Thomas Jefferson, who proposed a uniquely American experiment: a joint state/federal operation involving George Rogers Clark and the garrison at Fort Pitt.

This type of cooperation is common today, but was a new concept at the time. At this tenuous stage of the fledgling cooperation among the former colonies, it was not even certain if Virginia and the U.S. would wind up on the same side. As Washington pointed out to Brodhead in 1779, "Colonel Clark is not an officer in the Continental line—Nor does he act under my instruction. He is in the service of the state of Virginia."[21] Clark was claiming the Illinois country not for the United States, but for Virginia, and they did not surrender these claims until 1784.

Still, they were on the same side right now, fighting for independence from Great Britain, and Clark and Brodhead regularly corresponded. Early on, they agreed on general goals, as Brodhead told Clark, "I think it is probable that before next winter I shall have the pleasure of taking you by the hand somewhere upon the waters of Lake Erie."[22] However, these two men had separate problems and agendas, and were never able to work things out together. Brodhead rarely offered any support, and in each letter to Clark he was more focused on Clark's apprehending deserters from the Continental Army who were fleeing to Kentucky.[23] When Jefferson wrote to Washington in February 1780, to ask that the Continental Army cooperate with him on a plan, he did not think that a joint venture was feasible, as he informed Washington, "The enterprising and energetic genius of Clark is not altogether unknown to you. You also know (what I am a stranger to) the abilities of Brodhead.... It may be necessary, perhaps to inform you, that these two officers cannot act together, which excludes the hopes of assuring success by a joint expedition."[24]

But Jefferson decided to try again around Christmas, and he now wrote to Washington to propose just such a joint expedition. The biggest problem with the federal garrison at Fort Pitt was that it was too small to take action, but the state of Virginia could solve this with a star militia recruiting draw like Clark, who had gathered nearly 1,000 Kentuckians in less than two weeks the previous summer. But Jefferson had to concede that "our treasury is utterly without money."[25] Here the federal government could provide help. The army may have been low on food at Fort Pitt, but they did have artillery, weapons, ammunition, gunpowder, boats, and tools like shovels and axes, as well as a regular source of federal funding. Jefferson asked these items be made available for Clark, as well as a contingent of federal troops from the garrison. Washington approved, and told Jefferson on December 28, "I do not hesitate a moment in giving direction to the commander at Fort Pitt, to deliver to Colonel Clark the articles which you request."[26] It is not certain that this was the first attempt at a joint state/ federal project, but it did bode well for the new nation that the founding father most associated with states' rights and the founding father most known for advocating a strong federal government were able to set aside their ideological differences and work for the common good.

Washington and Jefferson didn't get around to discussing personnel issues in this exchange, but Jefferson got an idea soon afterwards when John Gibson came to Richmond. As a colonel in the Continental Army, Gibson served under Brodhead and Washington, but as commander of a Virginia regiment, he also had some obligations to state government. In January, Gibson came to Richmond to discuss payroll and supply issues, but arrived just as Benedict Arnold was sacking the city. Arnold, now a brigadier general in the British Army, had sailed up the James River with 1,500 men and met little resistance. As Arnold was destroying the foundry and other public buildings, Gibson pitched in to save what public stores he could. His work caught the attention of Jefferson, who now saw Gibson as the missing link to a successful campaign.

Jefferson now contacted Washington to suggest that Gibson's regiment go along with Clark and that Gibson serve as Clark's second-in-command. He was somehow convinced that Washington had agreed to do this, and that the two of them were in agreement on the plan. Jefferson then sent Gibson to Philadelphia to take receipt of four tons of gunpowder to be transported to Fort Pitt for the campaign. Gibson, who had no problem serving under a militia officer twelve years younger, was also satisfied with this arrangement. And Clark informed

Jefferson, "Colonel Gibson's regiment is of great worth to us. I am happy in his appointment."[27] But Daniel Brodhead wasn't happy at all.

On December 29, Washington had ordered Brodhead to deliver "all, or as many of the foregoing articles you have it in your power to furnish.... Direct the officers of the company or artillery to be ready to move when Col. Clark should call for them ... and give the enterprise every item which our small force can afford."[28] Washington also told Brodhead to detach a small portion of Gibson's regiment under an officer of the rank of major or lower to serve under Clark. Gibson may not have minded serving under Clark, but Washington was sensitive to military protocol that a federal officer could not serve under a militia officer of equal rank. It was partly to address this that Clark was promoted to brigadier general of Virginia militia on January 22. But Washington had already given Brodhead his orders on the detachment's commanding officer's rank and given him latitude about the size of the detachment, though Brodhead withheld this information until he could use it for maximum effect.

All of Brodhead's overreaching had been done with the goal of taking Detroit in mind, and he was outraged that he was being bypassed in the final glorious assault. He complained to Continental Congress President Joseph Reed,

> I had hitherto been encouraged to flatter myself that I should sooner or later be able to reduce Detroit. It seems that the US cannot furnish either troops or resources for the purpose, but the state of Virginia can.... I have just received instructions from the commander-in-chief to detach my field pieces, howitzers and train, also a part of my small force, under Colonel Clark, who, I am told, is to drive all before him by his supposed unbounded influence in the Western country.[29]

This comment about Clark was intended as sarcastic hyperbole, but it contained much truth. In the spring of 1780, two separate large Indian forces at both Cahokia and Louisville had immediately abandoned plans to attack a smaller force as soon as they heard that Clark might be present. Clark inspired in the Indians the fear and respect that Brodhead could only dream of.

But Brodhead had to comply with his orders, and so he told Clark, "I sincerely wish you may be properly supplied and supported in any operation you undertake and you may rely on every supply I am authorized to afford to facilitate your expedition."[30] But to Washington, he complained, "Brigadier Clark was kind enough to make me a visit and I am sorry to inform your Excellency that he.... Has demanded considerable quantities of our quartermaster store.... I should be happy to know whether it is your intention to permit compliance with any order he may think proper to draw upon the storekeeper."[31]

Brodhead openly speculated that Clark would fail and complained, "it is clear to me that wise men at a great distance view things in the Western country very differently from those who are more intimately acquainted with circumstances and situation."[32] Washington cautioned Brodhead that "the slightest hesitation may have frustrated an enterprise of the highest importance to the peace and safety of the whole western frontier,"[33] but he continued to display passive/aggressive behavior. Brodhead told Jefferson, "I profess to entertain the greatest respect towards your Excellently, but.... I can by no means be justified in suffering the provisions which are designed for the troops under my command to be transported down the river, unless I am instructed to do so by my commander-in-chief."[34]

It would take more than passive/aggressive rhetoric to thwart Clark's theft of Brodhead's glory, but the colonel had a plan for more aggressive action. The Delaware tribe's gradual shift towards the British had been accelerating. Many had followed Captain Pipe to the Sandusky region to live, and even those who remained near Coshocton were less constrained by Gelelemend. Brodhead heard from the Moravians and others of the shift and the Delaware even sent a delegation to Detroit to ask about their friendship. In light of this, Brodhead determined to make a preemptive strike and called for a militia rendezvous. On April 7, 150 Continental troops and 134 militia left Fort Pitt. They managed to approach the principal Delaware town at Coshocton undetected, and launched a successful attack on April 20. The Americans had just one man wounded, while the Delaware had 15 men killed and 20 captured, although it's believed many of the dead were killed after they had been captured.[35]

Afterwards, the Americans declined to press their advantage to other towns, preferring to retire with their booty and pelts. They received a welcome infusion of provisions from the Moravians, who were understandably anxious about also becoming targets. Heckewelder reported that "while the colonel was reassuring me that our Indians had nothing to fear, an officer ... reported that a particular division of militia were preparing to break off for the purpose of destroying the Moravian settlements up the river, and he feared they could not be restrained."[36] It appeared that Brodhead, like Gelelemend, had difficulty controlling his own men. To his credit, Brodhead put an immediate stop to this effort, although, in this case, doing the right thing just made him even more unpopular.

Seven. Brodhead II 1780

This was the only time in the last four years of the war that the American garrison left Fort Pitt, but the small raid had a large impact. The Delaware now abandoned the Muskingum watershed entirely, joining with other hostile tribes in the Sandusky River region closer to Detroit. A small contingent of Delaware under Gelelemend now joined the American forces as scouts, taking up residence on Killbuck Island at the forks of the Ohio. This left the Moravians unprotected as the only Indians in eastern Ohio—a band of pacifists in the middle of No Man's Land. A final result was the raid made problems for Clark. The militia, after turning out for a raid on nearby Indians who they were not at war with, were now much less likely to sign up for an extended foray in to country inhabited by tribes that had always been hostile towards them.

However damaging this development may have been to Clark, Brodhead was unable to take advantage of it. Late in March, a number of local citizens had prepared a remonstrance against Brodhead, and they now sent a voluminous list of complaints to Continental Congress. Written by a man named Alexander Fowler, this document accused Brodhead of corruption and an "enormity of public abuse" that had them "reduced to a contemptible situation.... Colonel Brodhead has not only rendered himself universally obnoxious to the people, but also to many of his officers.... To enumerate to your Excellency all the abuses and grievances here would be an endless task."[37]

Although these charges seemed vague and unfocused, they had to be taken seriously. For one thing, as Continental Congress President Joseph Reed said, "the writer is an auditor of the public accounts and deemed a man of character and intelligence. We are sorry to hear that the information of the inhabitants of that part of the country corresponds in some degree with several particulars in the letter."[38] Another disturbing part of the complaint was that it had been signed by over 400 people—which was more than the entire population of Pittsburgh.

Washington had to address these charges with courts martial. A deputy quartermaster who was also accused of corruption could be tried at Fort Pitt, but, as commander, Brodhead had no local peers to try him. Washington told Fowler to "specify your charges against Colonel Brodhead, deliver him a copy of them and be ready when called upon to make the requisite deposition.... And Colonel Brodhead will be ordered to attend for trial."[39] Washington then told Brodhead:

> You must be sensible that no court could be constituted at Fort Pitt for the trial of an officer of your rank. It must therefore be held at the army: but as it will be impossible to bring down all of the necessary witnesses, the Judge

Advocate Generals sends by this conveyance a deputation to the gentleman usually officiating in that capacity at the post, authorizing him to take depositions.... When the necessary depositions are finished, you will repair to the army and take your trial. You will see the propriety of giving up the command to the officer next in rank while this business is transacting.[40]

Brodhead was gone by the time this letter got to Fort Pitt, and it had to be set aside for him. On May 6, he had informed Gibson, "having obtained leave from his Excellency, the commander-in-chief, to proceed to Philadelphia and represent the affairs of this department, I intend to set out immediately. You will remain in command until is determined that you are otherwise ordered by proper authority."[41] As the Acting Commander of the Western Department, Gibson could hardly abandon his post to serve as a second-in-command to a militia officer. Brodhead also chose this time to reveal that he could not spare a single man from Gibson's regiment to join Clark. After dropping this bombshell, Brodhead left for the east the following day, leaving Colonel John Gibson in command of the Western Department.

Eight

Gibson
1781

Colonel John Gibson seemed like the perfect choice to serve as commander of the Western Department, as among other things, he had served at Fort Pitt longer than any other Continental officer. He had been on the frontier since joining the Forbes expedition as a teenager and helped to build Fort Pitt. The son of an innkeeper in Lancaster, he had learned French and Spanish from his French Huguenot mother and found he had a flair for languages. In the army, he taught himself Delaware, Shawnee, and Seneca, the three most common Indian languages used around Fort Pitt, which made him useful on the frontier for the next 50 years. After serving briefly as a Deputy Indian Commissioner, Gibson became an Indian trader who was respected for both his linguistic skills and his honesty. Captured during Pontiac's Conspiracy, his

There is no portrait of Colonel John Gibson, but his grave is in Pittsburgh's Allegheny Cemetery. He had more experience than any frontier officer, but his fairness to Indians made him suspect (photograph by Brian Williams).

two partners were burned at the stake, while Gibson was adopted into the Delaware tribe. After being repatriated, his liaison with Logan's sister gave him equally strong trade connections with the Mingo tribe.

However, these valuable Indian connections that were his greatest strengths were also his greatest weaknesses in the eyes of local inhabitants. Many on the frontier considered anyone who did business with the Indians as a profiteering enabler of Indian savagery, as one man told Gibson to his face that "the damn traders were worse than the Indians and ought to be killed."[1] The feeling that Gibson was guilty of insufficient hatred of all things Indian was exacerbated by his fathering of a Delaware son that he wound up raising. One officer remarked that Gibson was marked by an "unhappy connection with a certain tribe, which leads people to imagine, for this reason, that he has an attachment to Indians in general."[2] But Gibson was hardly ashamed of his "unhappy connection," as he proudly named the boy John Gibson, Junior, and installed him as an officer in his regiment. While he certainly deserves credit for this, the Indian-hating soldiers at Fort Pitt resented having to salute a teenaged "halfbreed."

Gibson's first priority as commander was to try to keep Clark's campaign from collapsing. He immediately informed Clark of Brodhead's final orders and suggested he appeal directly to General Washington. Clark did this, but was disappointed when Washington replied that he was "sorry to find out your intended expedition against Detroit stands upon so precarious a footing but.... Your present request I cannot think myself at liberty to comply with."[3] Washington also defended Brodhead's decision to Continental Congress' Board of War, saying "If ... Colonel Brodhead saw that the post could not be defended if such a detachment of infantry was made, he was justifiable by the spirit of my order in not sending it."[4]

Another issue facing Gibson was that he was unaware of the nature of his command. He saw himself as a temporary leader until Brodhead returned, as neither he nor Brodhead had seen Washington's orders that would have made it much more apparent that Brodhead might not return at all. Brodhead went on leave to Philadelphia, where the Continental Congress was meeting, but made no effort to report to them. On June 2, Congress President Samuel Huntington informed Washington, "Colonel Brodhead is now in this city. The complaints of the inhabitants in the vicinity of Pittsburgh respecting his conduct are very great.... It seems necessary that the inquiry be speedily made respecting those matters and in such a manner that justice may be done."[5] Accordingly, Washington then sent Brodhead another copy of his May 5 orders:

Eight. Gibson 1781

> I now forward to you a duplicate of my letter of 5 May, lest you should have missed receiving the original on your route from Fort Pitt to Philadelphia. Since that letter was written, many papers have been received tending to criminate your conduct; I have only directed Mr. Fowler who seems principally concerned in the prosecution, to specify the charges and obtain such testimony as he is able and thinks proper to support them: It will be necessary for you to be present at the time when these depositions are taken. I should therefore advise you to return to Fort Pitt for that purpose, as nothing can be done respecting the trial, until all preparations are ... made.[6]

Yet Brodhead remained in Philadelphia for most of the rest of the summer. It seems that the officer who wanted to speed up courts martial in 1780 was in no hurry to expedite his own trial.

Once Clark arrived in western Pennsylvania, he set up his headquarters at Stewart's Crossing (present-day Connellsville, Pennsylvania), but he and Gibson consulted frequently and even celebrated the Fourth of July together. They came up with a new plan, which included Gibson leading his men towards the Sandusky region in a diversionary move, while Clark led the main assault from Vincennes. But Clark was having problems recruiting the nearly 2,000 men he felt he needed. The militia had already been on an earlier expedition, and, as a Virginia military officer, Clark faced hurdles in trying to recruit Pennsylvania residents.

Clark told a colleague, "The inhabitants cry out for an expedition but too few I doubt will turn out, afraid I believe that they will be led on to something too desperate for their delicate stomachs."[7] He tried to draft recruits, which only made things worse. In early August, he expressed his frustration to Governor Jefferson, telling him, "I make it no doubt but it will alarm you to find that I have not left this country. Whoever undertakes to raise an army in this quarter will find himself disappointed.... We have made drafts to no purpose, Governor Reed also wrote them but to no effect.... I could not get Colonel Gibson's regiment."[8]

As it grew increasingly late in the year, Clark feared that if he did not move soon, he would start to lose the 400 recruits he had managed to gather so far. On August 8, he gathered his militia and Major Craig's company of federal artillery, and set off down the Ohio from Wheeling. Five hours later, Colonel Archibald Lochry arrived in town with 100 Pennsylvania militia to augment Clarks force. This group hurried downstream in a desperate attempt to catch up with Clark.

At almost exactly the same time, a large war party under the leadership of the Wyandot chief Half King showed up at Schoenbrunn. This chief had frequently stopped to have his warriors fed by the Moravians before launching their raids on the Americans, but this visit was different, as Half King announced he was there at the request of the British to take the converts into protective custody. Accompanying Half King's 300 warriors were British agent Matthew Elliott and Delaware chiefs Wingenund and Captain Pipe, both of whom had already moved to the Sandusky region. They all tried to convince the missionaries they were safer in British custody, but the Moravians resisted being torn from their homes and farms.

Heckewelder noted, "This speech caused much concern among us, for in the first place none of us had any inclination to ever leave these places, which were so well improved and where we had our support and then we saw that we should be entirely ruined if we were to move away from the towns, especially at this time of year."[9] The Moravians resisted, insisting they at least be permitted to stay until the following spring, but Half King's party remained insistent that the residents of all three mission towns return with him. An increasingly alarmed Zeisberger wrote to Fort Pitt on August 18, warning them of Half King's presence and of their plight. But the garrison of the fort was about to become engulfed in chaos that would prevent them from offering any help to anyone.

The problems began when Brodhead suddenly returned on August 11. He informed Washington, "immediately after my arrival here I informed the officers that from Your Excellency's letter to me I can see myself to be in command as usual, until Mr. Fowler, agreeable to your order had specified the charges against me."[10] He said nothing to his men about turning over command, though all were aware of the pending investigation. But Fowler, the auditor who made the accusations, also served as Judge Advocate. Gibson had recognized this clear conflict of interest and had designated Captain John Finley of the Eighth Pennsylvania to replace Fowler as Judge Advocate.

However, Fowler refused to accept this order and appealed directly to Washington, telling him,

> I have hitherto officiated as Deputy Judge Advocate in this Department, therefore the deputations from the Judge Advocate General came properly directed to me. However the commanding officer here Colonel Gibson, thinks it improper that I should act in the double capacity of Judge Advocate and Prosecutor. For my own part, may it please your Excellency, I should imagine that—by officiating as Deputy Judge Advocate—I naturally became the Prosecutor of a Public Delinquent: but I wish that Colonel Brodhead and Mr. Duncan may have every indulgence and therefore humbly submit this point to your Excellency.[11]

Eight. Gibson 1781

In the absence of a reply, Fowler declared that nothing could be done till he got a definitive answer from the commander-in-chief.

This led Brodhead to conclude "from this refusal of Mr. Fowler's I still consider myself to be in command until the deposition could be taken with propriety."[12] Brodhead told Gibson that "after the depositions were taken relative of the charges exhibited against him, and *it would suit his own conveniency* [italics added] that then he was to repair to headquarters to take his trial."[13] The italicized phrase would seem to indicate that Brodhead had every intention of retaining command by postponing his deposition indefinitely, using his accuser's intransigence to his advantage.

In the absence of specific information, Brodhead resumed command and Gibson briefed him on recent developments. Gibson had scheduled a meeting on August 14 with local militia officers to plan for a proposed September 4 rendezvous where they would leave for the Sandusky expedition. Brodhead thought of going with him, but concluded, "As so many reports have been spread to my disadvantage through the country, my going might possibly retard the people in turning out: besides, I might see a number of the damned rascals who signed the remonstrance and their presence would be disagreeable to me, in particular that rascal Colonel Canon should I meet him I would spit in his face."[14] So Gibson went alone on the overnight trip.

He returned to find a changed situation at Fort Pitt. In his absence, Captain Finley, while searching for papers in his Judge Advocate's capacity, found Washington's original May 5 orders to Brodhead. Upon reading these orders, he concluded that Brodhead was illegally usurping command, and he shared the letter with other officers, who agreed. They then showed these orders to Gibson upon his return, and he also concurred. Some accounts claim that Gibson opposed Brodhead to get revenge for not being allowed to accompany Clark, but Gibson was a reluctant rebel until presented with this evidence. That night, thirteen officers of the Fort Pitt garrison signed this letter to Brodhead:

> We now inform you that from letters of his Excellency the commander-in-chief to you, which have been shown to us by Captain John Finley, that it is our opinion, we cannot with propriety be commanded by you, until you have cleared yourself for the charges which have been exhibited against you, and which are now depending. At the same time we wish to assure you that we entertain the greatest respect for you and was it not for the present situation of affairs there is not one of us but would wish to serve under you.[15]

Brodhead was outraged by this letter. He claimed the signers were from Gibson's regiment, but almost every officer at the post was a signatory. He asked Washington for help, saying "I find myself in the most disagreeable situation I ever experienced. And were it not for the redress I expect from your Excellency's well known justice my situation would be insupportable. I therefore beg to know your Excellency's immediate pleasure and that you will be pleased to instruct me how to treat these seditious proceedings."[16]

The commander-in-chief was a busy man at this time, as he was actively moving his army towards Yorktown. It took approximately eleven days to get a letter between the two forces, so it would be at least three weeks until anyone at Fort Pitt would know Washington's preference. Nothing could be done until then and the situation devolved into chaos quickly, as each commander pursued his own agenda. Brodhead claimed he would try to keep his dispute with Gibson from the troops, but he railed against Fowler. He also announced his intention to lead the Sandusky expedition, even though he wasn't sure if the militia would follow him. Gibson forwarded Zeisberger's letter and worried that "the only thing I dread is that the expedition will fall through which must endanger the loss of General Clark and his army," while noting that "Colonel Brodhead and Mr. Fowler have as yet adopted no method in proceeding to obtain evidence."[17] On August 29, Brodhead informed Washington, "things here are in the utmost confusion, some officers conferring me to be the commanding officer and others Colonel Gibson nor is it likely they will alter until your Excellency's pleasure is expressed."[18]

As the dispute wore on, Brodhead informed Gibson, "I cannot give up my command until I am ordered by the proper authority, and.... I am determined to punish every person concerned who shall either neglect or disobey my orders."[19] Three days later, he made good on this threat by ordering Gibson's arrest, which Gibson dismissed as illegitimate. Brodhead informed Washington of this action very casually in a postscript to a diatribe against Fowler:

Dear General

Colonel Gibson still continues to counteract me, and the officers who favored his claim refuse my orders. Others refuse his, and things are in the utmost confusion.

Mr. Fowler has wrote me repeated insolent letters, denying the right of any person to act as Judge Advocate but himself. I intend to take no notice of him at present; lest he should allege, that I have prevented him from prosecuting his charges against me. But so soon as I can get matters in such a train, as that my trial may be had, I shall punish him as he deserves.

> I'm convinced that a more malicious man does not exist than Mr. Fowler, and I determined so soon as I probably can, to convince the world of his malicious intentions against my reputation....
> Postscript I have arrested Colonel Gibson on 30 August.
> First: for assuming the chief command of this post contrary to the articles of discipline of war, thereby exciting and encouraging mutiny and sedition amongst a number of officers in this department.
> Second: for neglect of duty and disobedience of orders.[20]

The controversy also prevented the garrison from rendering valuable assistance to either Clark or the Moravians, as the September 4 rendezvous scheduled at Fort McIntosh had to be pushed back. Gibson moved the date back to September 12, but Brodhead insisted on a September 15 meeting, so the militia had to choose. Gibson noted, "This threw the country into confusion. However, at the day I had appointed upwards of 100 men assembled but that number was too small to attempt anything: while Colonel Brodhead had the mortification to find that not a single man appeared on the day fixed on for his general rendezvous."[21]

Washington's long-awaited reply finally arrived at Fort Pitt on September 17. When Washington entrusted an officer with a command, he gave him latitude and support: for example, he had defended Brodhead's prerogative to refuse to detach Gibson's regiment to Clark. But the general had no use for any soldier who disobeyed his orders, and from Head of Elk, Maryland, he now sent Brodhead this withering rebuke:

> I have received your letter of 23rd August with its enclosures. Had you adverted to the plain construction of mine of the 5th of May, you would not have been in doubt as to the propriety of your holding the command at Fort Pitt, while your trial was preparing and hearing—as you seem to have misconstrued my meaning in that letter, I have now to request in positive terms, that you do immediately on receipt of this resign your command to Colonel Gibson, who will immediately thereupon assume the same command as had been committed to you. In the meantime I request this unhappy dispute may be brought to a speedy an issue as possible.[22]

At the same time, Washington sent Gibson orders directing him to assume command of the Western Department. He did not write Fowler directly, but instructed Gibson that "You will—from the manifest impropriety in this case—direct that Mr. Fowler do not appear or act as Deputy Advocate in taking the depositions necessary in this trial, nor in any other way in the present case as Judge Advocate ... in this way I hope to have this disagreeable dispute speedily issued."[23]

Washington's ruling was so free of ambiguity that the controversy was settled. Brodhead finally made his deposition on September 29 and went to Philadelphia for his trial. He was acquitted due to a lack of evidence, but he never returned to Fort Pitt. Brodhead's only subsequent contact with Washington came in 1789, when he wrote to congratulate Washington on his election to the presidency and to ask for a federal job. The president replied, "It would be an arduous, if not impracticable task for me to travel over the ground of services rendered by *all* of the officers of the American army.... And do equal justice to merit.... Because ... I have doubts on the propriety of the measure, very few certificates have passed from me."[24] Brodhead got no federal appointment, though he did later secure an appointment as the state surveyor of Pennsylvania.

The men of the Western Department were now free to resume their war efforts, but their embarrassing paralysis had come at a most inopportune time. On September 3, Half King's war party dropped all pretensions of friendship. Accusing the Moravians of working with the Americans, they roughly seized the missionaries and looted their cabins. Their converts were only given a few days to prepare, and on September 8, a total of 317 residents of all three mission towns were forced to abandon their ripening gardens and fields and head for the Sandusky region. While the converts were deposited here, the missionaries were sent on to Detroit to face charges of treason.[25]

However, in Detroit, they were treated well by Major De Peyster, who even returned some of the property that had been taken from them. And Captain Pipe, their political adversary, spoke on their behalf and the missionaries were acquitted. They returned to their brethren along the Sandusky, but still faced grim prospects with no food or shelter and winter coming on. The German speaking missionaries usually named their towns after some uplifting phrase. Schoenbrunn translated as "beautiful spring," and Gnadenhutten meant "huts of grace." But the village they built here would only be referred to as Captives' Town.

The Americans at Fort Pitt were also unable to offer any support to Clark, whose campaign collapsed in failure. After Clark had left Wheeling, Lochry's supplementary force was obliged to build boats before they could try to catch up with them. Clark knew reinforcements were coming, but they were never quite able to catch up to him. Meanwhile, a group of British led Indians under Joseph Brant and George Girty were waiting in ambush for them. Brant had been transferred to the West, there being little left to burn in upstate New York.

Eight. Gibson 1781

This group was supposed to unite with a larger force under Alexander McKee and Simon Girty, when they discovered Clark's force at the mouth of the Great Miami River, where Ohio, Kentucky, and Indiana currently meet. However, they lacked the manpower to attack Clark without McKee's force. Then they learned of Lochry's smaller group following behind, so they waited for them. On August 24, they attacked Lochry and wiped out his force, killing nearly 40 and capturing the rest. The sudden and complete disappearance of his auxiliary force caused Clark to cancel his campaign on September 9.

A few days later, the two British forces united. The educated and world traveling Brant was considered the most civilized of Native Americans, while the illiterate and uncouth Girty was considered the lowest of white men. But both of them shared an affection for alcohol and combat. On this night, the two got drunk and boasted of their exploits so competitively that they drew swords on each other, with disastrous results. Brant got a leg wound that became so badly infected that he barely avoided amputation, while Girty got a slash on his forehead that put him out of action for months. Losing these men even temporarily was a setback for the British.

Captain Henry Bird, who had such a negative first impression of Girty, had changed his tune and wrote General Haldimand, the British military governor at Quebec, "Girty, I assure you, sir, is one of the most useful, disinterested friends in his department that the government has."[26] Girty had been assigned to work with the Mingo tribe originally, but their diminishing numbers and influence led the British to ask him to learn Wyandot, and Girty did so. He would recover from his wounds and return to the fray, with a fresh scar and a story about how he got it from the Americans.

Gibson had waited a long time to command the Western Department, but Washington denied him the chance to show what he could do. Gibson has done nothing wrong during the commander controversy, but he was tainted as being part of an unseemly matter that clearly disgusted Washington, who wanted to bring in an outsider. Washington knew how to handle carping subordinates who had their own agenda like Brodhead, perhaps because he had once been such a creature himself. In his 1758 dealings with Forbes and Bouquet, Washington, had been primarily concerned with the fortunes of himself and Virginia. But he had grown and matured, and was now an American first, and he felt it would look bad if he appointed a Virginia officer to head the department. So he named Brigadier General William Irvine of Pennsylvania to the post. Ironically,

Gibson may have commanded a Virginia regiment, but he was actually a resident of Pennsylvania as were Hand, Brodhead and Irvine.

Irvine was a native of Ireland who graduated from Dublin's prestigious Trinity College and became a naval surgeon during the Seven Years' War. He left the service in 1764 and relocated to Carlisle, Pennsylvania, and started a medical practice there. Siding with the Americans when the revolution began, he was named colonel of a Pennsylvania regiment. He was captured during the 1776 invasion of Canada, and was held for two years before being exchanged. He returned to his regiment and he was promoted to brigadier general in 1779.[27] Irvine also had a connection with Gibson, as his young wife had been raised by a stepmother who was Gibson's sister.

It took a while for the general to arrive at his new posting, so Gibson remained in charge through the fall. He tried again to rendezvous enough militia to mount a campaign, but didn't get the required turnout. The only other event of note that occurred on Gibson's watch was when a handful of Moravian converts returned to Schoenbrunn to harvest grain and were discovered by American troops. They were brought to Fort Pitt, where Gibson treated them well and sent them east to Moravian headquarters. Shortly afterwards, a local family was attacked by Indians. Some accused the pacifist Christian Indians of this attack and faulted Gibson for releasing them.

Irvine had serious reservations about accepting his new job. He had heard rumors of deplorable conditions in the west. One historian sums up the situation at Fort Pitt at this point by saying, "at this juncture Fort Pitt was a little better than a heap of ruins.... The regular forces stationed there wholly incompetent to the exigencies of the service. The controversy about the command of the post has greatly increased the disorder. The garrison was in want of pay, clothing, of even subsistence itself, and, as a consequence was in a mutinous condition."[28]

In addition, there were only 230 men stationed at Fort Pitt, and both of the Virginia and Pennsylvania regiments had been reduced to two companies each, which was too small of a command for a general. Irvine originally wrote to the Board of War, "I must request you will please reconsider the matter," as the job "will be taking on me a command that is no way adequate for an officer of my rank and there is neither money nor materials to put the few troops there in a respectable situation."[29] However, Irvine indicated he might feel differently if Congress could dedicate men and resources to the Western Department. The result was apparently an informal arrangement where Irvine came

Eight. Gibson 1781

out west on a trial basis. Irvine's stated plan was, "to write to Congress for leave to go down the country in January to return in March if they can make it a point I should continue here."[30] So, Irvine's first visit to Fort Pitt was as more of a consultant on a fact-finding tour, and Gibson continued to supervise day-to-day operations at this point.

Irvine arrived at Fort Pitt early in November, and his first impression, as related to his wife, was that "it is truly distressing to see how this country is laid to waste."[31] After a few weeks of closer inspection, he made an even more grim assessment:

> I have been trying to economize, but everything is in so wretched a state that there is very little in my power. I never saw troops cut so deplorable, and at the same time despicable, I figure. Indeed when I arrived, no man I would believe from their appearance that they were soldiers; nay, it would be difficult to determine whether they were *white* men.[32]

Irvine was also critical of the fort itself, claiming it "is in fact nothing but a heap of ruins" and "at best a bad situation for defense."[33] Irvine wasn't completely negative in his assessment. He reported, "as for Colonel Gibson, I think he should continue as long as troops are kept in the district. No man knows this country better, nor any man, I believe, the Indian country so well."[34]

Washington was sympathetic to Irvine's complaints, telling him, "I am not all surprised that you found matters in disorder to the west world.... It is generally the case when a dispute arises respecting command, as the participants make it a point to thwart each other as much as possible."[35] Although he offered sympathy, Washington did not offer any additional men or supplies.

Washington had told Irvine, "I am convinced that the possession and destruction of Detroit is the only means of giving peace and security to the western frontier,"[36] so Irvine focused his study on that goal. After detailed research, he concluded that to take and hold Detroit would require 1,000 Continental troops plus an additional 1,000 militia. He also determined that August or September was the best time to launch the assault, as the ground will be dry, the stream crossings lower, and forage plentiful. In addition, he proposed a new fort be built a few miles downstream on the Ohio, where Chartieres Creek joins the river. This would enable the Americans to reduce Fort Pitt to a blockhouse and eliminate entirely the need for Fort McIntosh.

Shortly after the first of the year, Irvine was summoned to Congress to present his findings. He must have decided to accept his challenge and keep the post, and he left Gibson in command at Fort Pitt for the remainder of the winter. Gibson's biggest problem was the threatened mutiny of the troops, who had not received their pay for months. This was not the same problem it would be for most employees, as the government did promise to provide free food, clothes, and shelter to each soldier. But the government was also failing to provide these basic needs; Gibson reported in late January that the delay of a pork shipment would mean that the troops would be going for over six weeks without meat.[37]

As 1782 began, the American Revolution was basically over on the eastern seaboard. Although there were still armies in the field, almost all combat had ceased. But, in the west, things lagged about a year behind. While the east had seen fighting over Boston, New York, and Philadelphia from 1775 through 1777, in the west at this time both sides were still positioning and bargaining for Indian support. Now the west was the only place where they were still fighting, and 1782 would prove to be one of the bloodiest years of the war on the frontier.

The trouble started unusually early in the year, when, in February, an Indian raiding party attacked the home of a family named Wallace, taking a wife and a young child as captives. A group of about 180 Pennsylvania militia under Colonel David Williamson assembled to pursue the war party. This party was horrified and enraged to find the mutilated remains of Mrs. Wallace and her child along the trail, but they found no Indians until they got to the former town at Gnadenhutten and found several families of Indians working in the fields on March 6.

This group turned out to be 96 Moravian converts who had returned to harvest what grain they could from the previous fall. Early March was starving time for tribes who endured a poor harvest or a harsh winter, and the Moravians had been taken from their fields before harvest time. This group could not possibly be mistaken for a war party, as it was composed of over 70 percent women and children. They seemed happy to see the militia and Williamson's men literally and figuratively disarmed them by promising to take them to Fort Pitt.

But the militia's attitude hardened after they discovered Mrs. Wallace's dress that the raiding party had apparently left in the town. This served to remind them that they had come out in pursuit of Indian scalps, and that this seemed like their best chance to do this. Apologists have tried to excuse the Gnadenhutten Massacre as a crime of passion by men weary of continued Indian depredations. But the way they set out to commit mass murder was far too methodical for people who were supposed to be in the throes of passion.

Williamson was far from a forceful leader. One of the officers at Fort Pitt acknowledged his bravery, but claimed, "he knows too well how high he is in the opinion of the people.... His Oratory is superior to the taste of the people his countrymen, and their bigoted notions stand in lieu of arguments."[38] Seeking to preserve his popularity, Williamson put the captives' fate to a vote. This was the first election ever held on Ohio soil, and the electorate did not acquit itself well, voting by an eight to one margin to commit genocide. With only 18 dissenters, they resolved to kill all the Christian Indians the following day. Then they apparently got a good night's sleep in preparation for the long day ahead. Meanwhile, the captives spent their last night on earth locked in buildings singing hymns and praying.

On the morning of March 8, 1782, the converts were brought out in pairs, hit on the head with a cooper's mallet, and scalped. After 96 men, women, and children had been murdered this way, the militia burned the town and proudly took their scalps back home with them. They were understandably reluctant to share the details of their prowess in combat, but some still yearned to shed more Indian blood.

Although the populace seemed to approve of the militia's conduct, John Gibson was outraged. Calling the perpetrators "the most savage set of miscreants that ever degraded human nature," he said, "had I known of their intentions before it was too late, I should have prevented it by informing the poor sufferers of it."[39] This led to more denouncement of Gibson as an Indian lover.

On Saturday night, March 24, the militia attacked their own side. After the Americans had attacked Coshocton the previous April, a small contingent of about a dozen Delaware under Gelelemend remained loyal to the Americans. These men served as scouts for the Continental Army and took up residence on Killbuck Island, a small sandbar near the confluence of the Ohio. Now, rogue militiamen attacked Killbuck Island, killing some Delaware and taking others prisoner and dispersing regular troops who were present. And, to compound their insubordination, they sent word to Gibson that they intended to scalp him. This was the situation that General William Irvine found when he returned the next day to resume as commander of the Western Department.

Nine

Irvine
1782

General William Irvine was not prepared for the chaos that awaited him when he returned to resume command at Fort Pitt on March 25. On March 8, Washington had ordered, "...you will proceed with all convenient dispatch to Fort Pitt.... And you will take such measures for the security of that post and for the defense of the western frontier as your continental force ... will admit.... I can promise no further addition to your regular force."[1] Irvine left Carlisle on the 18th and arrived a week later to find everything in a state of turmoil.

He reported to Washington, "I arrived here 25 March. At that time things were in greater confusion than can be well conceived. The country people were, to all appearances, in a fit of frenzy.... A party came and attacked a few Delaware Indians who have remained with us, on a small island close by the garrison.... This last outrage was committed the day before I arrived.... A number of wrongheaded men had conceived an opinion that Colonel John Gibson

Brigadier General William Irvine had a successful tenure in command of the Western Department due in part to a willingness to tolerate genocide ("Brig. Gen. William Irvine," The New York Public Library Digital Collections. 1750–1890).

Nine. Irvine 1782

was a friend to the Indians, and that he must be killed also."[2] By a combination of listening to legitimate complaints and punishment, Irvine was now able to report that "things now wear a much more favorable aspect," although "the few remaining Indians ... dare not stir outside the fort.... Civil authority is by no means properly established in this country, which I doubt not proceeds in some degree from inattention of the executives of Virginia and Pennsylvania."[3]

Irvine was hoping this controversy would blow over, but the Gnadenhutten Massacre proved to be too heinous to ignore. A lawyer for the Moravians formally complained that "the tragic scene of erecting two butcher houses or sheds and killing in cold blood 95 brown or tawny sheep of Jesus Christ one by one, is certainly taken notice of by the Shepherd their Creator and Redeemer."[4] On a more earthly level, the Pennsylvania assembly termed the event "an act disgraceful to humanity,"[5] and Governor William Moore wrote to Irvine stating that the council was "desirous of receiving full information on a subject of such importance."[6]

There was no doubt how Irvine felt personally about the massacre, as he had told Washington the Indians were "put to death, it is said, after cool deliberation, and considering the matter for three days. The whole were collected in their churches and tied while singing hymns."[7] But Irvine dreaded the prospect of an investigation. He represented federal authority in a place where no one respected any governmental authority and he knew any scrutiny of the militia would be a setback for the federal war effort. Irvine's paltry continental force was useless without militia support, so he could not afford to alienate anyone. The locals had turned on Brodhead for his corruption earlier and now they raged at Gibson; as Irvine told his wife, "A thousand lies are propagated all across the country against him, poor fellow.... However false this reasoning may be, yet no reasoning will or can convince people to the contrary."[8] Irvine desperately wanted to avoid the fate of his predecessors in terms of popularity with the locals.

Irvine was not alone in his reluctance to investigate. One local citizen told the governor it would be "impossible to ascertain the real truth. No person can give intelligence but those that were along.... Yet they will say nothing."[9] Irvine concurred, telling Moore, "no man can give any account except some of the party themselves, if, therefore, an inquiry should appear serious, they are not obliged nor will they they give evidence. I am of opinion further inquiry into the matter will not only be fruitless, but, in the end, may be attended in disagreeable consequences."[10]

Irvine was even more candid in a letter to his wife, where he almost seemed to boast of his moral cowardice in his desperate attempt to avoid alienating the murderers. After telling her the militia "fell on them while they were singing hymns and killed the whole. Many children were killed in their wretched mothers' arms," he still cautioned her,

> whatever your private opinion of these matters may be, I conjure you by all the ties of affection and as you value my reputation, that you will keep your mind to yourself, and that you will not express any sentiment for or against these deeds;—as it may be alleged, the sentiments you may express may come from me or be mine. No man knows whether I approve or disapprove of killing the Moravians.[11]

This massacre was ultimately considered so horrible that the Americans were shamed into eventually offering land grants as compensation to the Moravians. But none of the killers were ever punished.

While the hostile Indians in the Sandusky region reacted with universal sustained outrage to the Gnadenhutten Massacre, the Moravians themselves could only react in sorrow. Zeisberger lamented in his diary,

> Nowhere is a place to be found where we can retire with our Indians and be secure. The world is already too narrow. From the white people, or so-called Christians, we can hope for no protection, and among the heathen nations also we have no friends left, such outlaws are we! But praise to God, the Lord our God yet lives, who will not forsake us.[12]

Worse yet, the missionaries were again summoned to Detroit at about the same time. Simon Girty was in charge of the travel arrangements, and he ordered a French trader to march the ministers the long way around Lake Erie and to show them no favors. However, the more sympathetic trader offered Zeisberger a horse and arranged for boat passage from Sandusky Bay. According to Heckewelder, when Girty returned and found his instructions had been disregarded, he

> behaved like a madman ... he flew at the Frenchman ... striking him and threatening to split his head in two.... He swore the most horrid oaths respecting us, and continued in that way until after midnight. His oaths were all to the purport that he would never leave the house until he had split our heads in two with a tomahawk and made our brains stick to the wall.... He had somewhere procured liquor and would at every drink renew his oaths, which he repeated until he fell asleep.... Never before did any of us hear ... anybody to rave like him. He appeared like a host of evil spirits. He would sometimes come up to the bolted door between us threatening to chop it to pieces to get at us.[13]

Nine. Irvine 1782

Fortunately, the missionaries left without further incident and Major De Peyster again treated them well at Detroit. The major offered support and encouragement for the Moravians to remain behind British lines. They did so for a few years, and established new missions in both northern Ohio and Canada. They returned to the American fold after a guilty Congress gave them land grants at the original Schoenbrunn and Gnadenhutten sites. After this land was surveyed, they returned to the Tuscarawas Valley, where Zeisberger headed the mission at Goshen, near Schoenbrunn, while Heckewelder led the white support community at Gnadenhutten, where he also served as postmaster and as a county judge. After Zeisberger's death in 1808, Heckewelder retired to Bethlehem, where he wrote two books on Native Americans that were well received.

After their "success" at Gnadenhutten, the local militia now proposed a large scale expedition into the Sandusky region. Irvine could offer encouragement, but neither men nor supplies, as the plan called for a mounted expedition with each militiaman providing his own provisions, horse, and weapon. Irvine believed that a large group of 400 or so men moving quietly and quickly might be able to surprise the Indians. He wrote to Washington on May 21:

> they are accordingly assembling this day in Mingo Bottom, all on horseback with 30 days provisions. As they will elect their officers, I have taken some pains to get Colonel Crawford appointed to command.... He pressed me for some officers. I have sent him Lieutenant Rose, my aide-de-camp, a very vigilant active brave young gentleman, well acquainted with service, and a surgeon. These are all I could venture to spare.[14]

So, an American force was finally leaving Fort Pitt to engage the enemy. But the only members of the Continental Army to go with them were two noncombatants: a surgeon, and an officer acting in an advisory capacity.

Both of these men had interesting stories. The surgeon was Dr. John Knight of the West Augusta Regiment, who would leave behind a vivid account of the campaign's aftermath. And Lieutenant Rose was really Baron Gustavus de Rosenthal, a Russian nobleman who had fled his country after killing a rival in a duel. Coming to America under an assumed name, he joined a Pennsylvania regiment as a surgeon's mate. His education and dignified bearing stood out, and he caught the attention of Irvine, a former military surgeon himself. Irvine made Rose a lieutenant in his regiment, and when he left for Fort Pitt, he brought Rose along as his aide-de-camp.[15] Rose was an acute observer and excellent writer who wrote an account of the expedition.

A total of 468 men gathered along the Ohio River on May 21, more than enough to proceed. But things got off to a slow start, as they had only four canoes with which to ferry all men and supplies across the river. They finally finished this process and gathered at Mingo Bottom (present-day Mingo Junction, Ohio) to elect officers. Some of the militia feared that Rose had been sent to command the mission, but once this was dispelled, their choices were narrowed down to two colonels: Williamson, and Washington's friend and Irvine's choice, William Crawford.

The success of democracy is contingent upon the loser's accepting their defeat, and this looked to be a hotly contested race. However, Rose was able to report to Irvine: "My fears that the present expedition would miscarry have been dispelled this very moment only. Colonels Williamson and Crawford did seem to have numerous and obstinate adherents. The latter carried the election this day but by five votes, and I cannot but give Colonel Williamson the utmost credit ... cheerfully submitted to second in command.... Otherwise ... very likely we should have dispersed."[16]

This large force left the following day, but failed to move either quickly or quietly. The undisciplined militia moved slowly, taking four days to go the 50 miles to the Tuscarawas. Indians who were watching their every move started the sadly plausible rumor that the Americans were coming to murder the rest of the Moravian converts. The British were made aware and sent along over 100 Tories from Butler's Rangers under Captain William Caldwell. After the Americans passed the present-day site of Upper Sandusky, Ohio, on June 4, they were attacked by loyalists and Indians.

Despite being far from their supply lines, the Americans held their own in a day of desultory and sporadic fighting. Casualties were light and the sides evenly matched, but overnight the Indians got reinforcements from other villages in the area. After 150 Shawnee showed up under Alexander McKee, the Americans were tiring and at risk of being surrounded. Crawford tried to organize a quiet retreat at dusk on June 5, but they were discovered and the retreat turned into a rout. Crawford became separated from his men in the confusion, and it was Williamson who led the rest of the retreat back across the Ohio.

After his return, Williamson sent an official report of the retreat to Irvine, and said that he felt, "obliged to Major [sic] Rose for his assistance both in the field of action and in camp. His character, in our camp, is estimable, and his bravery cannot be outdone."[17] But it is the

Nine. Irvine 1782

existence of this report, rather than the content, that is most interesting. Militia leaders almost always filed official reports after expeditions, but Williamson had not done so after Gnadenhutten. He would have been excused for this had he been illiterate, but this report proves he could write, which means that he made a conscious decision to not reveal details of the militia's trip to Gnadenhutten.

The militia feared that Crawford had been killed during the retreat, but he was not so lucky. After Crawford became separated from some family members during the retreat, he stayed to collect them, and this group, which included Dr. Knight, was taken captive. Many of his party were summarily executed, but Crawford and Knight were singled out for special treatment. Crawford thought he might be able to talk his way out of trouble, and asked to speak to Wingenund, a Delaware chief he knew, and Simon Girty, whom he had known since Dunmore's War. These two failed to do anything for him, although Matthew Elliot did apparently try to claim that Crawford might be worth more alive than dead. But the quest for vengeance for the Gnadenhutten Massacre was too great. As John Heckewelder sadly noted, "no man on earth could spare his life—not even the King of England."[18]

Since most of the slain converts had been Delaware, that tribe was given the honor of burning Crawford, although tribesmen from other villages came to watch. On June 10, Crawford and Knight were stripped, painted black as a sign of impending death, and beaten. Crawford was then bound at the wrists and tethered to a post in the ground with firewood around it. At a signal, a crowd rushed up with unloaded rifles and shot powder burns point blank all over Crawford's body and his ears were cut off. As the flames grew, the unfortunate victim was taunted and soon had nothing but hot coals to walk on. Knight reported of Crawford that "in the middle of these extreme tortures, he called to Simon Girty and begged of him to shoot him: but Girty making no answer, he called to him again. Girty then, by way of derision, told the colonel he had no gun at the same time turning to an Indian who was behind him, laughed heartily, and by all his gestures seemed delighted at the horrid scene. Girty then came up to me and bade me prepare for death."[19] After Crawford had been scalped, but was still alive, the scalp was slapped in Knight's face as he was led away.

Dr. Knight was to be sent to a Shawnee village for similar treatment, but he managed to escape. After a three week journey, he showed up at Fort Pitt on July 4, in a state so wretched that "he was weak and scarcely able to articulate.... It was three weeks before he was able to give anything like a continued account of his sufferings."[20] Knight later told his story to writer Hugh Henry Brackenridge, another colorful immigrant to the west. Born in Scotland in 1748, Brackenridge came to America as a child and graduated from Princeton, where he was a classmate of James Madison. He served as a regimental chaplain during the revolution, but turned to a legal career and came to Pittsburgh in 1781. He was also an author who wrote one of the first American novels to have a western setting.

Once he had regained his composure, Knight was able to express to Irvine the state of rage in the Indian camp. Another escapee corroborated Knight's message, as Irvine reported to Washington that "both he and the doctor say they were assured by sundry Indians they formally knew, that not a single soul should in future escape torture, and gave, as a reason for their conduct, the Moravian affair."[21] Lieutenant John Hardin added, "inexperienced men ought not to have their own way in war: that good men must suffer on their account. The murder committed on the Moravians is every day retaliated."[22] Washington responded to Irvine: "For this reason, no person, I think, should, at this time, submit themselves to fall alive into the hands of the Indians."[23] Washington did not fault Irvine for the defeat, telling him, "I am persuaded you did everything in your power to ensure them success. I cannot but regret the misfortunes, and more especially for the loss of Colonel Crawford, for whom I had a very great regard."[24]

Outraged Indians were still pressing the Americans with more frequent and larger attacks. On July 14, the settlement at Hannahstown was destroyed in a raid led by the Mingo chief Guyasuta. The settlers had grown accustomed to raids on individual homes and occasional attacks on forts and more isolated posts. But Hannahstown was a county seat actually located east of Pittsburgh. The raiders killed nine, took twelve captives and destroyed more than 100 cattle, horses, and hogs. They demolished nearly every home in the town, which never recovered.[25]

The leader of this raid, Guyasuta (also spelled Kiashuta and several other ways), offered a good example of shifting Indian loyalties. As a young brave in 1753, Guyasuta had supported the British and Americans and had served as one of Washington's guides to Fort LeBoeuf. A decade later, he joined Pontiac's Conspiracy against the English-speakers, and served as commander of the Indian forces that Bouquet defeated at Bushy Run to lift the siege of Pittsburgh. But by 1770, Guyasuta had switched sides again, and, while on a fall hunt, he ran into Washington

Nine. Irvine 1782

and Crawford on their land hunting expedition and traveled with them briefly. Now, he served the British interests against America in his third switch of sides in as many decades.

Kentucky had not been spared in Indian attacks this year, and Clark was receiving criticism about inadequate defenses. He could hardly afford to build a fort at all of the Ohio River fording places, but he now came up with the idea of a floating fort that could travel between crossings. Clark ordered the construction of the *Miami*, the 73 foot-long galley flagship of the Kentucky navy. This ship carried artillery that was rowed by 110 Kentucky militiamen under Captain Robert George.[26] On their maiden voyage in July, the crew did well going downstream. But they rebelled at the notion of rowing artillery upstream, and the idea was dropped.

But this seeming failure also had an effect on the British. At this time, they had assembled a large force of Butler's Rangers and close to 1,000 Indians from several tribes. The goal of their grand raid was the Wheeling/Pittsburgh area that had been responsible for Gnadenhutten. They had already gotten underway when they were disrupted by rumors that Clark was coming after them with over 4,000 men. The Indians genuinely feared Clark, whether it be for his boldness or his capricious cruelty, and they were truly alarmed. A collection of Shawnee, who would have been the first in Clark's path, was sent to investigate. They discovered that Clark was actually holed up in Louisville with less than 300 men, but someone had seen the *Miami* on the river and ran rampant with rumors. After a delay, the raiding party continued, but they had lost both numbers and momentum.

These changes called for a change of plans, and Caldwell, Elliott, McKee, and both Simon and George Girty now led 70 Rangers and 200 Indians towards Kentucky. Their target was Bryan's Station, near where Bird had his 1780 raid, but this force lacked artillery. They also failed to surprise Bryan's Station or to lure a party out of the fort to be ambushed. After a brief siege, the raiders left as they heard rumors of a large group of a militia heading towards them. But that was part of the plan.

The standard response to an Indian raid was to quickly gather the militia to pursue the raiding party and reclaim captives. The dilemma was that the pursuing party had to be large enough to fight, but if it took too much time to gather a large enough force, the raiders would be long gone. As the militia gathered at Bryan's Station, an officer named Hugh McGary had suggested they wait for reinforcements from other forts, and he had been chided in a way that he felt questioned his manhood.

The militia took up the pursuit, and on August 19, at a place called Blue Licks, caught up with the Indians, who were spotted loitering openly in camp just across the Kentucky River. To experienced hands like Daniel Boone, it looked like a trap, but McGary now took the opportunity to redeem his masculinity. Claiming that anyone who would not follow him was a coward, he demanded they charge the enemy.

The militia then crossed the river into a horrific ambush. The Indians had them trapped in a horseshoe bend in the river, and they proceeded to kill 70 Kentuckians in just fifteen minutes. When the reinforced militia returned to the field a few days later, the bodies of the dead had been mutilated so badly that they were unrecognizable. The Kentuckians had lost two colonels, a major, and four captains, and Daniel Boone had watched his teenaged son Israel die alongside him. McGary escaped without a scratch.

Blue Licks was an utter disaster for the Kentucky settlements. It was a particularly bitter personal defeat for Daniel Boone. Four years earlier, Boone had been captured as part of a group of 28 salt makers here, and now he had to leave his own son on the battlefield at the same place. Boone became so despondent that he questioned why he had ever come to Kentucky. He wrote Virginia Governor (and father and great-grandfather of future U.S. presidents) Benjamin Harrison:

> I have encouraged the people here in this country all that I could, but I can no longer encourage my neighbors nor myself to risk our lives here at such extraordinary hazards.... The number of the enemy lately penetrated into our country, their behavior, adding to this our late unhappy defeat at the Blue Licks, filled us with the deepest concern and anxiety.... We ... deem our situation truly alarming. We can scarcely behold a spot on earth but what reminds us of the fall of some fellow adventurer, massacred by savage hands.... In short, sir, our settlements ... seem to decline and if something is not speedily done we doubt will be wholly depopulated.[27]

This western way of warfare continued, with a counter-raid for every raid, as Clark that fall led an expedition to destroy a trading post that had been supplying raiding parties. Once again, however, he was unable to press on towards Detroit. Clark's greatest success came at age 25, when his daring Vincennes exploits secured lasting fame for himself and a claim to the midwest for his country. Despite repeated efforts, he was never able to achieve his goal of capturing Detroit. Clark's military career after the Revolution was also a disappointment. His patriotism was questioned when he accepted a commission in the French Army, and there were rumors about his drinking problems. Clark had

Nine. Irvine 1782

been awarded large land grants for his service, but lacked the cash to survey the land and pay taxes on it after Virginia denied many of his reimbursement claims. After being injured in a fire, he was cared for by relatives until he died at age 66 in 1818.

This same type of warfare continued after the revolution had officially ended. In 1786, Colonel Benjamin Logan led a militia raid in which Hugh McGary came along as an officer. One of the Shawnee villages they approached was that of Moluntha, an aged chief so pro–American that he flew an American flag above his village. And he was the husband of Nonhelema, also well known for pro–American sympathies. Moluntha was, with the aid of a translator, chatting amiably with military officers when McGary charged up and demanded to know if Moluntha had been at the Blue Licks. The chief, not understanding the question, merely smiled and nodded, whereupon McGary split his head with a tomahawk. An angry McGary claimed he had the right to kill Indians if he wanted, but his crime was too blatant to ignore, and he was arrested. However, his punishment turned out to be merely a one-year suspension from the militia. Nonhelema now had experienced her husband, brother, and nephew all being murdered while in the custody of the Americans she had always supported. She turned to the new country to ask for a pension and reward for services in her old age, but she was only offered a token sum and died soon afterwards.

The British weren't yet finished with their 1782 offensive. A party composed of 50 Rangers under Captain Andrew Bradt, a nephew of John Butler, and 230 assorted warriors under James Girty now headed towards Wheeling. Simon Girty usually got blamed for any ventures involving his brothers, but on this occasion Simon was absent. Wheeling had been worried about such an attack, especially since they had murdered the Moravians who used to warn them. Also, one of their best scouts, Samuel McCullough, who had ridden his horse off a cliff to avoid capture during a previous attack, had recently been killed by Indians. But another scout discovered the attackers' presence and alerted the fort.

When the raiders arrived on the scene on September 11, they found the citizens already "forted up." Bradt tried to parlay to convince the defenders to surrender, but was rebuffed, so the besiegers set out to kill livestock and destroy property outside the gates. As the siege went into a second day, the defenders realized they were dangerously low on gunpowder. They needed a hero to step up, and there were some to choose from. The Wheeling area was already home to Lewis Wetzel, a teen already known for his wilderness acumen. Like Captain Sam Brady, Wetzel's résumé contained several verified cases of rescuing Indian captives as well as dozens of apocryphal versions. But Wetzel was not present at this time, and anyway, the garrison could not spare any marksmen. So it was 16-year-old Betty Zane who stepped up.

Betty, the youngest sister of Colonel Ebeneezer Zane, knew where there was a supply of gunpowder in her brother's cabin just 40 yards outside the fort, and was approved to make a dash to retrieve it. She was able to make it to the cabin by surprising the Indians, but was fired on unsuccessfully on her return trip. Her bravery bolstered the defenders, and Colonel Zane was able to report to Irvine that "the enemy continued at the garrison until the morning of the 13th instant, when they disappeared. Our loss is none.... I believe they have driven the biggest part of our stock away."[28] Neither side knew it yet, but this was the last battle of the American Revolution.

Back at Fort Pitt, Irvine was becoming frustrated with his forced inactivity. His local militia leaders in particular had grown tired of reacting to ever increasing raids, and they pressed him to take his whole force into the field in a proactive strike. But Irvine got little help from Washington. The war in the east was over and treaty negotiations were ongoing, and Washington feared that further stirring up the Indians would retard this process. He did not forbid Irvine from taking action, but limited his support to saying "if attempted, I can only give you my good wishes for success."[29]

Irvine got more support from Clark, with whom he had a considerably better relationship than Brodhead did. Hearing of a proposed campaign, Clark wrote Irvine wanting "to know of the time you march and what is your object,"[30] so he could offer a diversionary offensive. Irvine had some trepidation about the efficacy of the mission, and also had no desire to engage his entire continental force, but he agreed to the expedition. In early September, Colonel Gibson reported, "an expedition is an agitation here against Sandusky, General Irvine to command.... The general takes one thousand militia and one hundred of the regulars from this post which is nearly one half the number here. I am very much afraid it will not be carried into execution, as the people are much divided."[31]

The day for the militia rendezvous was set for September 20. Over 800 troops were expected to join Irvine as he finally got a chance to lead his army outside the gates of Fort Pitt. But, on September 18, Irvine got word from the Board of War that a regiment of continental regulars

Nine. Irvine 1782

currently doing POW camp duty at Lancaster might be free to join him. This welcome piece of news changed everything, as an additional 300 professional soldiers might also spur even more militia to join them. Irvine sent word to send the regiment immediately and moved the rendezvous date back to October 8 to give them time to arrive.

But that date arrived and Irvine still had heard nothing. For the next two weeks, he waited "in a state of the greatest suspense and uncertainty"[32] for word from the east. He finally found out that the orders for the regiment had been mislaid and never delivered. This blunder cost Irvine his only chance to lead his army into battle, as it was now too late in the year to launch a campaign.

This was fine with Washington, who was aware that every time the Americans in the west took the field, they succeeded only in making the Indians angrier. He informed Irvine, "viewing the matter on every side, I think it best the expedition was set aside.... Such excursions only serve to draw the resentment of the savages, and I much fear, that to the conduct of our people may be attributed many of the excesses which have been committed on our frontier."[33]

Although he was denied the opportunity for a military victory, Irvine still used his time well. The war may have been winding down, but he still provided Washington with detailed information about western routes, and he made suggestions about where future fortifications might be located. He also authorized an upgrade of the fort's defenses, as he reported, "The soldiery here have been all summer kept close to duty and extreme hard fatigue in repairs to the fort."[34]

Most frontier stockades were not in use long enough to require much maintenance. For example, of the 33 stockades built by military forces in Ohio between 1750 and 1813, 28 were used for three years or less, and only two lasted longer than five years.[35] But Fort Pitt, the largest and most complex fort built by the British in North America, had a useful period of over 30 years. And no major repairs had been made since the British stopped funding the fort in 1772. A fort, like the roads leading to it, needed regular and expensive repairs to prevent decay.

To facilitate this, Irvine increasingly relied upon the services of Major James Craig. After serving as General Sullivan's head of artillery at the battle of Newtown, Craig had been sent west, where his career flourished, and he stayed in town and later married the daughter of John Neville. It was not unusual for an artillery officer to supervise fort construction and repair, because the engineering skills needed for the science of destruction were similar to those used in construction. As there were no military engineering schools in America until West Point was established in 1804, a foreign trained engineer or a self-taught artilleryman was about the best that could be hoped for as an engineer. After describing the work done on the fort's wood and stone defenses, Irvine was able to report to Washington, "This fort has been much repaired in the course of the summer."[36]

Since peace talks were pending and winter activity was normally light in the west, Irvine requested leave to attend to personal matters in Carlisle. First, he had to supervise the contracting of his small force, as Congress, in anticipation of peace, was disbanding Gibson's Virginia regiment on the first of the year. Irvine stayed through this process and returned east in February of 1783, leaving Lieutenant Colonel Stephen Bayard of the Eighth Pennsylvania in command.

Irvine left no doubt that he found Fort Pitt to be a deplorable posting. When his wife wanted to come west to stay with him, he dissuaded her by saying, "This is the most wretched and miserable vile whole ever man dwelt in."[37] Now that he was back in Carlisle, he hopefully reported, "Since my arrival at this place, the reports and appearance of peace are so flattering I begin to persuade myself there will be little occasion for my returning to Fort Pitt."[38] When it began to look like this may not be the case, Irvine wrote in his next letter to Washington, "If your Excellency should think proper to direct my return to Fort Pitt, I should be greatly obliged by your limiting the time of my stay."[39]

It turned out the war wasn't quite over yet. While delegates were negotiating a treaty in Europe and Americans were waiting for word on this side of the Atlantic, the Indians in the west unexpectedly launched raids on their own. In early April, Bayard wrote Irvine that seventeen settlers had recently been killed or taken captive in separate attacks in the Wheeling area. Washington now ordered Irvine's return, both to counter these raids and to prepare for the transition to peacetime. In his instructions, Washington stated,

> it is probable that a dissolution of the army is not too far distant, but.... I have to desire that you will proceed immediately to Fort Pitt, where your influence and prudence may be much needed. Particular instructions respecting the security and disposition of the stores after disbanding the troops now at the garrison, it is not in my power to give you at this time.[40]

Irvine returned to Fort Pitt in mid–May. The Indian raids soon stopped and conditions became so calm, and provisions so scarce, that Irvine furloughed members of his garrison on a rotating basis all summer. The war in the west wound down with a whimper, not a bang, as

Nine. Irvine 1782

the garrison at Fort Pitt wound up leaving their post just one time in the last four years of the conflict. On September 26, Irvine received word that he could begin releasing his troops and that an officer was en route to relieve him so he could return to Carlisle and civilian life.

In addition to repairing the fort itself, Irvine was also responsible for repairing the army's relationship with the local populace, as apparently his appeasement of the Gnadenhutten murderers proved to be politically expedient. The night before he was to leave, Irvine got a letter signed by a dozen merchants and prominent citizens of the town saying they wished to "Express their thanks to you, and their sense of your merit as an officer."[41]

After Irvine returned home, the first thing he did was free his slaves, saying he couldn't fight a war for liberty and still be a slave holder. He later served one term in the Continental Congress and another in the U.S. Congress and also was a delegate to the Pennsylvania State Constitutional Convention before his death in 1804. Lieutenant John Rose found out in 1784 that he had been pardoned and was free to return to Russia. Before leaving, he told Irvine who he really was and why he had come here. Rose returned to become a baron of the Russian empire, and he continued to correspond with Irvine and then his son until his death in 1829.

Conclusion: 1783–1794

Two months after the Fort Pitt garrison was disbanded, George Washington said goodbye to his officers in New York and the Continental Army was no more. The men who had succeeded in winning independence were now sent back to their homes. But there were a couple of exceptions, and, once again, the Western Department was an outlier. A small guard of troops remained on duty to protect the gunpowder and armaments at Fort Pitt and West Point. At this time, the entire U.S. Army consisted of 55 men at West Point and another 25 at Fort Pitt, and the highest ranking officer was a captain. The entire staff of the War Department consisted of Secretary of War Henry Knox, one clerk, and three messengers.

This was just the way the Founding Fathers wanted it, as they considered a standing army to be a symbol of an oppressive imperial regime typified by the British. Their preference was for citizens to rise up and form an army to defend themselves only when threatened. Their classical model for this was the Roman general Cincinnatus, who retired to his farm, but was recalled when Rome was invaded. After vanquishing the invaders, Cincinnatus did not seek further power or glory, but returned to his plow. When Washington's officers were disbanding to return home to their farms, they formed a fraternal organization called the Society of Cincinnati. Northwest Territory Governor Arthur St. Clair was elected president of this organization and he changed the name of his headquarters city from Losantiville to Cincinnati in honor of this group.

The Americans came by their suspicion of a peacetime army quite honestly, and this deeply held belief showed up in the Bill of Rights that was added to the Constitution in 1791. The well-known First Amendment of this document guarantees freedom of speech, religion, press, assembly, and the equally famous Second Amendment guarantees the

Conclusion: 1783–1794

Fort Pitt was decommissioned in 1792, and all that remains at the original site is this 1764 blockhouse (photograph by the author).

right to bear arms. After addressing these crucial issues, what was the next most important problem the Founding Fathers sought to address? The Third Amendment to the U.S. Constitution prohibits the forced quartering of troops in private homes.

This is never done today, but it had recently happened to the Americans. When the citizens of Boston had in the 1770s thrown taxed tea into the harbor and confronted British troops on the streets, the crown reacted harshly, closing the harbor and sending redcoats to occupy the city. But there was no fort or facility to host that many troops, so they were placed in private homes. Thus, the citizens of Boston were forced to feed and shelter foreign soldiers who were there to protect them from, apparently, themselves. This led to considerable resentment and the ultimate rise up of the minutemen against the redcoats. A lot of the visions of the Founding Fathers have become a reality, but none of them would have predicted, or desired, that the United States would become the world's policeman.

This rejection of a standing army did not last long, however. As Americans continued to stream westward in pursuit of new lands, they

Conclusion: 1783–1794

were opposed by the Indians and the nearby British who supplied and encouraged them. Continental Congress saw that a company of troops wasn't sufficient to win the west, and on June 3, 1784, authorized the creation of the First American Regiment. This federal regiment was composed of 700 men from Pennsylvania, New Jersey, Connecticut, and New York, and they convened at Fort Pitt in December. As Pennsylvania had provided the most troops, their ranking officer, Josiah Hammer, was named commander, and was promoted to become the first general in the new U.S. Army.[1]

The treaty of Paris 1783 had resulted in Great Britain's recognizing the independence of the United States, but not one word in the treaty was said about the Native Americans who had done so much of the fighting. Now, the very land they were living on was being coveted by the new nation. Indians fiercely opposed any settlements across the Ohio River, and were encouraged in this by the British. Great Britain had agreed to vacate Detroit and all of their other Great Lakes forts, but reneged in protest of American loyalists who were forced to flee to Canada without being compensated for property losses. In addition to these foes, the Spanish controlled the mouth of the Mississippi at New Orleans, and expressed their fear of U.S. expansion by charging exorbitant duty fees on all cargo.

A final problem facing the westward expansion of the United States was that the states were not united. Many former colonies that did not specify western boundaries in their original royal charters had staked claims to land in the west. In addition to the Virginia and Pennsylvania controversy over Western Pennsylvania, Connecticut claimed a coast to coast strip of land that corresponded with that state's northern and southern boundaries. A compromise between competing claims was needed before settlement could proceed. The states finally conceded these claims, but specified that certain areas be set aside to give their residents the first opportunity to purchase land there. For example, the northern portion of Ohio was reserved for purchase by Connecticut veterans seeking to buy western lands, which is why Northeast Ohio today is called the Western Reserve.

The new U.S. government hoped to capitalize on settlers' hunger for land by appropriating it from the Indians and selling it to citizens. Continental Congress, a weak body hardly known for bold legislative achievements, passed two noteworthy ordinances to facilitate this.

In 1785 and 1787, Congress addressed the land bordered by the Ohio and Mississippi rivers and the Great Lakes that defined all future

Conclusion: 1783–1794

westward expansion. This new area was approved to produce between three and five states that would be added to the new union as equal members. The new land was to be surveyed and divided up into townships that were comprised of 36 sections of one square mile each, or 640 acres. This system was used in the subsequent settlement of all future states. The proceeds of the sale of one section per township would be used to establish and fund public education, which made Ohio the first place in the world to be settled by people who had a right to public education. The Ordinance of 1787 also made slavery illegal in the newly established Northwest Territory.

Yet all of this talk meant nothing as long as the land they coveted was occupied by Native Americans. The Ohio River had been the border between white and Indian worlds for 20 years, but the Americans now tried to make new claims with some coercive treaties where they tried to force concessions. Fort Pitt was still army headquarters, but the action was gradually shifting downstream. In 1785, the army built Fort Harmar at the mouth of the Muskingum River, and in the next year they constructed Fort Steuben at present-day Steubenville. The purpose of these posts was not just to protect the surveyors working on the first seven ranges of townships, but also to evict squatters already there who had not purchased their land from the government.

In 1788, the first group of legal settlers founded Marietta, along the Ohio just across the Muskingum from Fort Harmar. The U.S. tried to confirm their right to be there with a treaty, but the most notable chiefs did not show up to endorse this. As new settlements propped up on the northern bank of the Ohio over the next few years, the Indians began to coalesce into a formidable union to oppose them.

At this time, there was a large concentration of Indians living between today's Upper Sandusky, Ohio, and Fort Wayne, Indiana. Centered around the Grand Glaize, where the Auglaize River meets the Maumee in present day Defiance, Ohio, this was a conglomeration of several tribes. Led by Little Turtle of the Miami, Blue Jacket of the Shawnee, Buckongahelas of the Delaware, and Tarhe of the Wyandot, these nations came together to launch raids on the newer settlements, as well as the existing settlements already in Kentucky. Harmar's army faced its first test in combating these raids.

Secretary of War Knox's instructions called for the army "to exhibit to the Wabash Indians our power to punish them for their positive depredations by sudden strike, by which their towns and crops may be destroyed."[2] However, Northwest Territorial Governor Arthur St. Clair, not wishing to provoke the British into war, wrote to Detroit to reassure them they were only after Indians. The British shared this information with their Indian allies, of course.

On September 30, 1790, General Harmar left Fort Washington in Cincinnati at the head of 320 regular troops and 1,100 Kentucky militia, about 400 of whom were mounted. Their destination was the principal Miami town of Kekionga at present-day Fort Wayne. This was a key location on the portage between the Maumee and Wabash rivers that connected the Great Lakes to the Mississippi watershed. The American Army destroyed five towns and 20,000 bushels of corn, but were surprised to find no Indians. This was because the Miami under Little Turtle had abandoned their towns, but were lurking nearby, and who now concluded that the American Army was not as large nor formidable as they had heard.

On October 19, they attacked a 150 man reconnaissance party. This force contained a small number of regulars, but was mainly militia under the command of Colonel John Hardin, who had moved west to Kentucky after leaving the Continental Army. This assault demonstrated the main flaws with the militia system, as the militia threw down their weapons and ran, which caused the regular troops who stayed to fight to lose 22 out of their 30 men. Hardin was mortified by this result and yearned for another chance. He convinced Harmar to let him lead an expedition to return to the site of the battlefield three days later. But the result was the same. At these two battles, the Americans lost 183 men including 79 of their full-time regular troops.[3] Harmar tried to claim victory because he inflicted property damage, but the ultimate proof of his defeat was the increase in Indian raids that soon brought immigration to a standstill.

The U.S. government responded by authorizing a larger army to chastise the tribes. George Washington, who was in his second term as president, made the choice to combine civil and military authority and named Governor St. Clair to lead the U.S. Army. St. Clair had been a large landowner in Western Pennsylvania before the war and had served as a major general in the Continental Army. But in his only previous independent command, he evacuated Fort Ticonderoga without a fight during the Saratoga campaign, and the 55-year-old hadn't served in the field for over a decade.

After coming east for a consultation with Washington, who warned him to be prepared for a surprise attack, St. Clair returned to Fort Washington. Here he met setbacks in terms of men and supplies. St. Clair was

Conclusion: 1783–1794

planning on using more regulars than militia, but found he had a poor quality of recruits, and political pressure didn't give him enough time to train them. By the time St. Clair's 2,500 man army finally lumbered out of Cincinnati, it was already late September.

This large force moved slowly, stopping to build forts for a supply line. The weather turned bad, provisions and morale ran low, and the army sometimes only moved five miles a day. Some troops deserted, claiming that their enlistments were up, and St. Clair feared this group might loot supply convoys headed north, so he had to dispatch some of his best troops to guard his supplies from some of his worst troops. At dusk on November 3, 1791, the 1,400 Americans still with St. Clair retired quietly, even though increased Indian activity had been reported in the area.

The next morning, St. Clair received the surprise Washington had warned him about, as a coalition of tribes attacked him furiously. Despite being unprepared, the Americans fought back valiantly, but the Indians shrewdly directed their fire on artillerymen and officers. After a few hours, the surrounded Americans fought their way out, but their retreat quickly became a rout. It had taken the Americans six days to travel the 29 miles from Fort Jefferson, but now, unencumbered by weapons or packs, many of these troops made the return trip in a single day.

The Indians didn't pursue them but celebrated their victory on the field. Simon Girty was alleged to have pointed out officers for his comrades to scalp, and among the dead were George Gibson and Richard Butler, who was St. Clair's second in command. Among the victorious warriors was Butler's son that he had had with Nonhelema. St. Clair's defeat was the worst ever suffered by the United States Army, with two-thirds of the force becoming casualties. Of the 630 dead and 283 wounded, 68 were officers.[4]

Indian confidence was now sky high, which made them less inclined to negotiate. The Americans, however, now realized that they were in a position where they had to talk. They selected a couple of responsible leaders to take messages with peace overtures to Indian strongholds. One of those chosen was John Hardin, who wrote to his wife from Fort Washington on May 19, 1792:

> I expect to start out on Monday next for the Sandusky towns. I am in hopes, if I can be spared, to have the infinite pleasure and happiness of seeing you in two or three months…. Shall I fall sacrifice in this important attempt, the governor has promised me to be your steady friend and that your yearly

supply from the government should not be less than $200.... But, oh, my dear love, As I meditate on myself to think that I have left a peaceable home and so dear a family, and throw my life into the hands of a cruel and savage enemy, I cannot prevent the tears from flowing from my eyes at present, and I do, my love, implore your prayers daily.[5]

Hardin's fears prove to be well founded. He never got to his destination, as he was murdered by his guides, as was another peace messenger. Hardin now joined Cornstalk, White Eyes, and Moluntha as martyred peace advocates. Hardin is not well known today, but the states of Kentucky, Ohio, and Illinois have all named counties for him. The Indian coalition further hardened their position at a large conference held at the Grand Glaize in 1793. More than 3,000 Indians attended this conference. The Americans sent a diplomatic delegation, but they had to pass through British territory, and they never got any closer than Detroit. With firebrands like Simon Girty holding sway, they insisted on the Ohio River as a permanent boundary, and even a warrior like Joseph Brant was marginalized as a moderate for his being willing to move the settlement line to the Muskingum and Tuscarawas Rivers.

This moment proved to be the peak of Girty's career in terms of his influence among the Indians. After the Indians were defeated and Detroit evacuated, Girty was forced to move to Canada where he retired on a British pension with his family. But his wife ultimately left him after too many drunken beatings and Girty died alone in 1818.

The Americans had to do something if they hoped to be able to expand to the west, so they authorized the funding of another army. St. Clair was allowed to remain as governor but resigned his military commission, giving Washington one final opportunity to select a western commander. After much consideration, and some trepidation, he selected General Anthony Wayne to lead what was being called the American Legion. Wayne had earned the nickname "Mad Anthony" for his impetuous behavior during the Revolution, but as an independent commander he proved to be thorough and methodical.

Wayne arrived in Pittsburgh in June 1792, and used the area as his headquarters for recruiting and training. However, Fort Pitt would no longer house the army, as Wayne deemed that the old post had outlived its usefulness. The fort had deteriorated into disrepair since the end of the Revolution, and Wayne decided to replace it. The new fort, called Fort La Fayette, was slightly upstream along the Allegheny from the old fort, at about today's Ninth and Penn Streets. Working on the design was James Craig, who had supervised the previous repairs at Fort Pitt, then stayed in town after marrying John Neville's daughter. After 30 years, Fort Pitt was abandoned.

But this move still wasn't enough to suit Wayne. In trying to turn raw recruits into a fighting force, Wayne hoped to avoid entirely the temptations offered by the city. He had a camp called Legionville constructed about ten miles downstream that he moved the army to in November. At a ceremony to mark the departure of the army from the city, John Gibson commented, "We have sanguine hopes notwithstanding the misfortune of the last two campaigns, that with soldiers in such good health, subordination and discipline, the exultations of a savage enemy might be reduced, and their minds brought to a temper."[6]

Wayne began his response by saying, "The personal respect, and the approbation of my conduct, so very politely and obligingly expressed by the inhabitants of Pittsburgh, have made an indelible impression of esteem and gratitude in my breast, that can only end with life."[7]

Wayne drilled his 2,500 man Legion throughout the winter, and, in April 1793, he took them downstream towards Cincinnati. The only regular troops remaining in Pittsburgh were a handful of men under Major Thomas Butler. But this small garrison would have one more role to play in history.

While these military matters were wrapping up, the town of Pittsburgh was hardly thriving. In 1761, Henry Bouquet took a census that put the population of the infant town around the fort's gates at 332, with 2/3 of them adult males, most of whom were engaged in the Indian fur trade.[8] In 1790, the first U.S. census reported Pittsburgh's population at 376—an increase of just 1.5 people per year over a 29 year span.[9] The borough of Pittsburgh was not officially incorporated yet, though it already had been named the seat of Allegheny County. But growth was still glacial.

This can be contrasted with Philadelphia, the other major Pennsylvania city in the opposite end of the state. In 1790, Philadelphia had a population approximately 90 times larger than Pittsburgh and was the most cosmopolitan city in North America. During the 1790s, when the city served as the national capital, Philadelphia may have contained more talent in one place than any city in U.S. history.

The best example of a collection of this talent came in April of 1793, when a large crowd turned out to watch the first manned flight in the Western Hemisphere. The French balloonists re-created Washington's trip across the Delaware, except they traveled to New Jersey by air rather than by water. Among the crowd watching this event were Washington,

Conclusion: 1783–1794

Adams, Jefferson, Madison, and Monroe—the first five U.S. presidents. Other currency-worthy figures who lived in the city for at least a part of the decade were Hamilton, Jackson, and, of course, Franklin, who died here in 1790.

The scientific world was also well represented in the city during this era. In addition to Franklin was astronomer and mathematician (and first director of the U.S. Mint) David Rittenhouse, the Quaker botanist William Bartram, Dr. Benjamin Rush, and chemist Joseph Priestley. The arts were also well represented, as painter Gilbert Stuart had a studio here, and Francis Hopkinson was a resident. Hopkinson was a Penn grad, lawyer, writer, and signer of the Declaration of Independence who also may have been the nation's first graphic designer and singer/songwriter. He served on the Continental Congress committee that designed the U.S. flag and also designed the official seals for his alma mater, the American Philosophical Association, and the state of New Jersey, and he also composed topical songs about current events.

On the distaff side, Dolly Madison and Betsy Ross were natives, while Martha Washington and Abigail Adams were here during their husbands' presidencies. The city even had an international presence as a haven for refugees. The freethinking Priestley came to America after a British mob had destroyed his laboratory, and Koskiuscsko was exiled here after a failed attempt to prevent foreign powers from dividing up his native Poland. And French foreign minister Talleyrand stayed here until the excesses of the Reign of Terror had passed and then returned to even outlast Napoleon.

Pittsburgh did not suffer only in comparison with towns to the east. When Zeisberger established the mission at Schoenbrunn in 1772, the first thing he did was to build a church and a school. Ten years after this, there was still neither institution in Pittsburgh. Schoenbrunn had a church with a bell and a piano, and Zeisberger self-published a Delaware language grammar textbook for the school, and the streets of the Indian villages were laid out in a grid pattern. Pittsburgh also suffered in comparison to an Indian village 70 miles to the west.

Arthur Lee was among the many who were not impressed with Pittsburgh. Born of a prominent Virginia family, Lee's brothers Richard Henry Lee and Francis Lightfoot Lee both signed the Declaration of Independence. For his education, Arthur was sent to England's Eton College and then to medical school at the University of Edinburgh. He practiced medicine briefly before turning to a law career in London. He traveled in high circles, and in James Boswell's famous biography

Conclusion: 1783–1794

of Samuel Johnson, he was mentioned as being one of the dinner guests the night that Johnson first met his political rival, the pro–American John Wilkes.

When the Revolution began, Lee's international experience led to his doing diplomatic envoy work to Spain and Prussia. He was then sent to join the American delegation in Paris, but here he quarreled with his fellow diplomats. His machinations led to the recall of Silas Deane and caused the normally placid Benjamin Franklin to denounce Lee for "your jealous, suspicious, malignant and quarrelsome temper, which was daily manifesting itself against Mr. Dean, and almost every other person you had any concern with."[10] After being recalled, Lee's next diplomatic assignment involved being sent to Fort McIntosh to help negotiate an Indian treaty. After passing through town, he dismissed it with this assessment:

> Pittsburgh is inhabited almost entirely by Scots-Irish who live in paltry houses and are as dirty as in the nation of Ireland or even Scotland.... There are in the town four attorneys, two doctors, and not a priest of any persuasion, nor church or chapel, so they are likely to be damned without the benefit of clergy. The river encroaches fast on the town. The place, I believe, will never be very considerable.[11]

Some signs of civilization were slowly coming to the area, however. John Gibson helped establish the first church in town. But when the Presbyterian minister refused to let him present his Indian daughter for baptism because the child was not a result of Christian matrimony, Gibson invited the Church of England to establish a second congregation. Hugh Brackenridge was the closest thing to what could pass for an enlightenment figure in town. He, along with Gibson, was a charter trustee for the first school in town that served as the forerunner of the University of Pittsburgh, and he also helped establish the *Pittsburgh Gazette*, the first newspaper west of the Alleghenies.

New settlers were arriving at the same time that national political parties were coalescing. Generally speaking, the residents of Pittsburgh and Allegheny County were more likely to support the Federalist party agenda of Washington and Hamilton, which supported a strong federal government. However, all the surrounding counties contained more support for Jefferson's Democratic-Republican party, which advocated more localized authority. While the state of Pennsylvania skewed Federalist, most of the frontier did not.

In April 1789, a visiting Moravian named Abraham Steiner wrote this description of Pittsburgh:

> The town has not more than 150 houses, most of them poor wooden structures. The location is beyond compare, on a beautiful flats at the junction of the Allegheny and Monongahela.... To the south is the Monongahela. Beyond it is a hill where much coal is being mined. To the west is the Allegheny. Beyond it are rich bottoms and good high land.... To the east is a long hill, where much good sandstone is being quarried. Beautiful though the situation is, the town itself is wretched. Disorder reigns in the streets, and business is only middling because there is no money in circulation.[12]

The lack of hard currency was always a problem on the frontier, and a crude barter economy became the only way to do business. When John Gibson opened a store in 1786, his ad in the *Gazette* promised "the most reasonable terms for cash, country produce, poultry or ginseng"[13] Another item often used as currency in this economy was whiskey. Poor frontier travel conditions made it difficult to ship a corn crop without spoilage, but if farmers could make their corn portable by making it potable, they would have a liquid asset that actually grew in value as it aged. Many Western farmers built their own distilleries, or "stills," to facilitate these transactions.

This way of doing business was threatened by a federal excise tax on whiskey passed in 1791. Washington and his treasury secretary Alexander Hamilton were finding it difficult to launch a new country on the cheap, especially since several of the former colonies already had outstanding debts. Hamilton was able to convince Jefferson and Madison to have the federal government assume these debts in exchange for moving the national capital to the south. The new government hoped to help fund itself partly by taking western lands from Indians and selling it to citizens. But to take this land they needed to raise an army, and to raise an army they needed to raise taxes. A tax on whiskey would hurt Western interests the most, but these same interests would benefit most from the army's presence.

This tax caused universal outrage on the frontier. Since taxes had to be paid in cash, the law meant that a farmer who was charged because he lacked the cash to pay the tax would have to travel during the growing season a great distance at his own expense to defend himself. This sentiment was strongest in western Pennsylvania, where residents had come to expect little from government and therefore had no regard for it. The residents compared themselves to the colonists resisting British taxation and began to organize opposition. Some took the law into their own hands, and tax collectors and supporters were assaulted and some farmers were threatened just for paying their taxes.

Conclusion: 1783–1794

Even the Federalists around Pittsburgh hated the law, but they pointed out that their taxation did come with representation, and the new law passed had to be respected until such time as it could be changed. John Neville became the chief tax collector for the excise. Other leaders appeared in the anti-tax movement. Albert Gallatin, a brilliant Swiss immigrant, opposed the tax, but was careful to not go too far in his statements. Other firebrands, like Washington, Pennsylvania-based lawyer David Bradford, were more dangerously outspoken. The French Revolution was in full swing at this time, and the whiskey rebels were sympathetic to oppressed Frenchmen and often posted French-style liberty poles in their towns. There were a few modifications in the law, but matters were at an uneasy peace until the summer of 1794.

On July 5, U.S. Marshal David Lenox and John Neville were serving writs on scofflaw farmers. Late in the day, they had a heated confrontation with a farmer that drew a crowd, and afterwards they separated, with Lenox returning to town. John Neville, however, in addition to owning a fine home in town, also had a farm called Bower Hill on Chartieres Creek west of town. Here he had a two-story 20' × 40' house and a plantation that was attended by eighteen slaves. Slavery was supposed to be illegal in Pennsylvania, but some who had previously considered themselves Virginians still retained some, with Neville's contingent being the largest in the region.

Neville returned to Bower Hill, but the rumor spread that he and Lenox had abducted the farmer to take to trial. A disgruntled crowd gathered in the night and approached Neville's home around dawn. When Neville heard noises and found a crowd threatening his home, he fired a warning shot that mortally wounded one of the crowd, which inflamed them and started a general fire fight. The outnumbered Neville evened the odds somewhat by arming his slaves and having them return fire, which makes this one of the most unusual battles in American history. In the south, where it was a crime just to teach a slave to read, it would have been unthinkable to give a slave a loaded weapon. But here, a federal tax collector protected his home from an anti-tax mob by arming his slave property. The slaves acquitted themselves well, and were able to save the home.

That afternoon, John Neville and his son Presley came to town to seek help for the attack they anticipated would be coming. Presley Neville was a Penn grad, a former revolutionary war officer who had served as an aide to Lafayette, and the son-in-law of Daniel Morgan, and he had a home near his father. He met with John Gibson, Attorney Hugh Brackenridge, and the county sheriff, but they determined that they lacked the authority for any definitive action other than offering to negotiate. John Neville had better luck approaching Major Thomas Butler at Fort La Fayette, as he was given about a dozen soldiers with which to protect his home.

By 5 p.m. on July 16, a large crowd had gathered around Bower Hill, and John Neville wisely decided to flee before the trouble started. The crowd was informed that Neville was not present, but the house was fired on anyway. As the larger and better organized crowd got close enough to burn some outbuildings, the defenders negotiated a treaty. The family was unharmed, and the troops released, as the mob had no desire to take on the army. But Bower Hill was then burned to the ground, and Neville and Lenox had to flee. The next day John Gibson informed Pennsylvania Governor Thomas Miflin, "I am very sorry to have to inform your Excellency that a civil war has taken place in this country."[14]

Flush with success, the rebels plotted their next move at the funeral of the man killed in the first assault. A mail route had been established between Pittsburgh and Philadelphia in 1788, and they now decided that the best way to find out what was being said about them in town was to rob the mail. On July 26 they did this and took the letters to read. They found five objectionable letters: from Major Butler to Secretary of War Knox, from Presley Neville to his father-in-law Daniel Morgan, from John Gibson to Governor Mifflin, from Clerk of Courts James Brison to Miflin, and from a man named Edward Day to Treasury Secretary Hamilton. Reading what was being said about them enraged the rebels to the point where some proposed burning the town to the ground. The rebels ultimately called for the banishment of the letter writers and determined to rendezvous on August 1 at Braddock's Field just outside of the town.

This announcement obviously threw the townspeople into a panic. On July 31, a dusk meeting was held in a tavern, with "almost the whole of the town convened."[15] The townspeople decided it would be prudent to take the threat seriously, and Day and Brison were exiled. They took no action on Major Butler, who, as a federal officer, was considered outside the purview of the citizenry. They also declined to act on Presley Neville, who was present, and Gibson, who had actually been selected to chair the meeting. But this was not enough to placate the rebels.

The next day, Brackenridge went out to Braddock's Field, where about five to seven thousand rebels had gathered, to make a plea on behalf of the evicted citizens. Brackenridge was a sophisticated and

Conclusion: 1783–1794

urbane wit, but he was no fop. He had earned the rebels' respect as a lawyer defending them previously and he was able to relate well to crude western ways. But he was walking a tightrope in that he had to appeal to the rebels without getting himself in trouble with federal authorities. Brackenridge argued against exile, saying to Bradford, "The sending away of the people is a farce; it will be the best recommendation they can have to the government; they will get into office and be great men by it."[16] But his pleas fell on deaf ears, as Bradford replied, "The people came out to do something, and something they must do."[17]

The rebels offered a safe conduct passport to the exiles, but insisted they had to leave in order for the town to be spared when the troops marched the next day. On August 2, Bradford appeared in a gaudy major general's uniform of his own design suitable for his moment of triumph. As a long line of ragged "troops" entered town, citizens cautiously offered them untaxed whiskey as an appeasement. The rebels entered the town, but re-crossed over the Monongahela rather than risk a confrontation with the federal garrison at Fort La Fayette. This anticlimactic event left an uneasy peace over the town, but the rebels' actions had guaranteed that a strong federal response had to be made.

In 1786, a western Massachusetts farmer named Daniel Shays had led a similar rebellion, but this failed revolt was against the weaker Articles of Confederation. The Whiskey Rebellion was the first domestic challenge to the new Constitutional republic, and President Washington fully realized the seriousness of the threat. The rebels had destroyed the home of the tax collector, fired on federal troops, and robbed the U.S. mail. A federal government that tolerated any of these abuses did not deserve to survive. Supreme Court Justice James Wilson proclaimed the area to be in rebellion, as the laws were "being obstructed by a combination too powerful to be suppressed."[18] Washington called a cabinet meeting on August 2 to discuss this issue, and on the 7th he issued a proclamation to call out a multi-state militia force. Although Washington favored military action, he also agreed to let Governor Mifflin send a delegation west to try and negotiate a peaceful solution.

As this delegation headed west, they were discouraged by the exiles they saw who were fleeing to the east. On August 8, they encountered Lenox and John Neville in Lancaster. This pair had fled down the Ohio to Marietta, then returned east by way of Clarksburg to avoid being recognized. On the ninth, they found Brison in Carlisle, and on the 13th they met Gibson in Bedford. Gibson told them "I am very much afraid ... nothing less than the repeal of the excise law will satisfy them."[19]

Conclusion: 1783–1794

The army that Washington called for was not a true federal army, as it was impossible to collect troops from all states on such short notice. But four different states wound up contributing militia. A total of 5,650 Virginia and Maryland troops came up Braddock's Road, while 7,300 Pennsylvania and New Jersey men followed Forbes' Road. This force of just under 13,000 men was about as large as any army that Washington had ever led at any point in the Revolution. It was twice as large as the Forbes Expedition of 1758. It was ten times larger than General McIntosh's largest concentration of troops during the Revolution. And it was five times larger than the American Legion that General Wayne was leading against the Indians at that very moment. Another army as large would not take the field in Pennsylvania until the Gettysburg Campaign.

And leading it was George Washington, who thus became the first and only sitting president to don a uniform and command troops in the field. His last military campaign was aimed at the same location as his first one had been 40 years previously. His actual performance was mainly ceremonial, as he reviewed the troops from both wings and then returned to Philadelphia. However, his appearance did have an effect. The Whiskey Rebels had gotten some public support when they compared themselves to the colonists protesting the British tea tax. But the idea of taking up arms against George Washington caused that support to shrink considerably. There were also plenty of other wartime heroes who remained in the field with this army, including Alexander Hamilton, Daniel Morgan, and Henry Lee, the future father of Robert E. Lee.

The two wings of the army finally met up on the outskirts of town on October 30. As the huge force became the second army to occupy Pittsburgh in three months, all resistance evaporated. Bradford fled south and didn't stop until he got to Florida. An occupying force remained over the winter while investigations were ongoing. There are often brutal retributions after domestic insurrections, but the Washington administration proved to be magnanimous in victory. Only seventeen men were ever charged, with only two convicted. And they were both pardoned. Far from being punished, the Whiskey Rebels wound up being co-opted. Western Pennsylvania had received little from any government in over 35 years of conflict. Whether it was French versus English, settlers versus Indians, Americans versus British, or Pennsylvania versus Virginia, the pioneers saw government as taking taxes but not offering any protection or even listening to them. But after taking a stand against the whiskey tax, they found the federal government more willing to listen to their needs and include them. The whiskey tax was repealed in 1801 by Jefferson and his treasury secretary, Albert Gallatin.

At almost exactly the same time, Anthony Wayne was leading his American Legion to victory against the tribal coalition. At a stand of fallen timbers along the Maumee River, Wayne turned back an attack in a brief fight on August 20, 1794. This battle had major ramifications, as it was now shown that the Americans were capable of raising an army that could expand and defend its borders. At the Greenville Treaty the following year, the Indians agreed to permit settlement across the Ohio River. This was followed by a treaty with England where they finally agreed to abandon Detroit and other Great Lakes forts, and one with Spain that permitted American commerce on the Mississippi. None of these international developments would have been possible without the military victory in a 45 minute battle that Wayne had spent two years training his army for. After the Battle of Fallen Timbers, there was no more talk of not having a standing army, and over the next century the U.S. Army inflicted a series of defeats on Indians who no longer had any European allies.

Thanks to these triumphs for the Washington Administration, the lawless frontier town of Pittsburgh was no longer lawless or on the frontier. When Washington retired in 1796, the Forks of the Ohio that he was among the first English-speaking white men to see was well on its way to becoming a prominent city that would launch pioneers towards even newer frontiers. By 1795, city businesses included clockmakers, tailors, tanners, weavers, saddlers, wheelwrights, blacksmiths and shoemakers and the town's population quadrupled to 1,565 by 1800.[20]

There would still be controversy and strife to come. The Whiskey Rebellion remained a contentious issue, as Brackenridge's son and John Neville's grandson Neville Craig, the son of James Craig, wrote books defending their families' activities during that affair. Hugh Brackenridge served on the supreme court of Pennsylvania until his death in 1816. John Gibson was named secretary of Indiana territory in 1800. Here he assisted Governor William Henry Harrison by helping negotiate land purchase treaties with the natives. When Harrison left to take command of the army, Gibson succeeded him and led the territory through the chaotic first year of the war of 1812. He returned to Pittsburgh after Indiana achieved statehood and died in 1822. He is buried in Pittsburgh's prestigious Allegheny cemetery, as is John Neville, who died in 1801. Other prominent Americans who are buried in this cemetery include composer Stephen Foster and baseball great Josh Gibson.

Conclusion: 1783–1794

With the frontier moving west and Washington moving to Mount Vernon, there was no longer any need for Washington to have a Western Department. The area around the forks of the Ohio that Washington had been one of the first to see the military significance of was now a launching pad for future westward expansion. The midwestern region to which Fort Pitt was the gateway would be the next one to make the transformation from near-impenetrable forest to modern society. This region is so quintessentially American today that it is hard to imagine that just two and a half centuries ago it was a sparsely populated battleground contested by the U.S., three different European nations, and dozens of separate Indian tribes.

The men of the Continental Army who fought for control of this western land did so under deplorable conditions, facing shortages of manpower, gunpowder, funding, supplies, equipment, support, and even food. And they were engaged in a bitter war with hated Indian foes. These troops were recruited from the ranks of frontier settlers, and were therefore representative of the populace they were trying to protect. They were a hardy lot inured to the harsh conditions, and were willing to do whatever it took to prevail. But they came nowhere close to a military victory, as the only western success came from a single campaign of George Rogers Clark leading Virginia militia.

The Western Department didn't triumph so much as they endured. Nearly every spring, a new commander took charge with high hopes that were soon dashed by cold reality. Considering the disorder that prevailed on this frontier, the real accomplishment of the Continental Army in the west might have been that they kept the area from descending into total chaos. Disorder and distrust of government may have been as large a threat as Indian raids or the British at Detroit, but the American Army tenaciously held on to maintain enough order to transfer to a new nation.

Chapter Notes

Introduction

1. census.gov/history/through the decades/fastfacts/1790.
2. Dale Van Every, Forth to the Wilderness: The First American Frontier 1754–1774 (New York: William Morrow and Co., 1961), p. 64.
3. R.E. Banta, The Ohio (New York: Rinehart and Co., 1949), p. 86.
4. Ted Morgan, Wilderness at Dawn: The Settling of the North American Continent (New York: Simon & Schuster, 1993), p. 324.
5. Gary S. Williams, Gliding to a Better Place: Profiles from Ohio's Territorial Era (Caldwell, OH: Buckeye Book Press, 2000), p. 6.
6. Van Every, Forth to the Wilderness, p. 69.
7. French philosopher Voltaire that it was a cannon fired in the North American wilderness that set the world ablaze. But he did not realize that the man who ordered this would go on to become even more famous than Voltaire.
8. General James Wolfe, who led the British capture of Quebec in 1759, believed that "the Americans are in general the dirtiest, most contemptible cowardly dogs that you can conceive."
9. Leonard W. Labaree, ed., The Papers of Benjamin Franklin, vol. 6, April 1, 1775 through Sept. 30, 1756 (New Haven: Yale University Press, 1963), pp. 13–19.
10. Van Every, Forth to the Wilderness, p. 77.
11. Douglas R. Cubbison, The British Defeat of the French in 1758: A Military History of the Forbes Campaign Against Fort Duquesne (Jefferson, NC: McFarland, 2010), p. 155.
12. Hugh Cleland, George Washington in the Ohio Valley (Pittsburgh: University of Pittsburgh Press, 1955), pp. 183–84.
13. Van Every, Forth to the Wilderness, p. 92.
14. Charles Morse Stotz, Outposts of the War for Empire (Pittsburgh: Historical Society of Western Pennsylvania, 1985), p. 125.
15. Ibid., pp. 134–36.
16. Ibid., pp. 121–24.
17. Ibid., pp. 17–18.
18. Henry Bouquet, Papers of Henry Bouquet (Harrisburg: Pennsylvania Historical Survey, 1941), Series 21646, pp. 103–08.
19. Morgan, Wilderness at Dawn, pp. 344–45.
20. Ibid.
21. Van Every, Forth to the Wilderness, pp. 220–1.
22. Neville B. Craig, The Olden Time, Vol. I (Pittsburgh: Dumas and Co., 1846), p. 420.
23. Cleland, Washington in the Ohio Valley, p. 245.
24. Ibid., p. 261.
25. ibid., p. 259.
26. Ibid., p. 267.
27. Gary S. Williams, Spies, Scoundrels and Rogues of the Ohio Frontier (Caldwell, OH: Buckeye Book Press, 2005), p. 26.
28. Neville Craig, ed., The Olden Time Vol. II (Cincinnati: Robert Clarke and Co., 1876), p. 9.
29. Williams, Spies, Scoundrels and Rogues, p. 27.
30. Ibid., p. 29.

Chapter One

1. John Connolly, "A Narrative of the Transaction, Imprisonment, and Sufferings of John Connolly" (London: self published, 1783), p. 3.
2. Clarence M. Burton, "John Connolly: A Tory of the Revolution," American Antiquarian Society, October 1909, p. 78.
3. Thomas Jefferson, Notes on the State of Virginia (Chapel Hill: University of North Carolina Press, 1982), p. 235.
4. Russell H. Booth, Jr., The Tuscarawas Valley in Indian Days 1750–1797: Original Diaries and Maps (Cambridge, OH: Gomber House Press, 1994), p. 114.
5. Rev. Joseph H. Bausman, History of Beaver County, Pennsylvania, 2 vols. (New York: Knickerbocker Press, 1904), vol. I, p. 28.
6. Founders Online, To Washington from Crawford, May 8, 1774.
7. Reuben Gold Thwaites and Louise Phelps Kellogg, eds., Documentary History of Dunmore's War (Madison: Wisconsin Historical Society, 1905), p. 10.
8. Craig, The Olden Time, vol. II, p. 60.
9. Ibid., vol. I, p. 96.
10. Thwaites and Kellogg, Documentary History, p. 33.
11. Ibid., pp. 19–21.
12. Glenn F. Williams, Dunmore's War: The Last Conflict of America's Colonial Era (Yardley, PA: Westholme, 2017), p. 165.
13. Herman Wellenreuther and Carola Wessel, eds., translated by Julie Weber, The Moravian Mission Diaries of David Zeisberger, 1772–1781 (University Park: Penn State University Press, 2005), p. 220.
14. Ibid., p. 223.
15. Williams, Dunmore's War, p. 240.
16. Ibid., p. 255.
17. Founders Online, To Washington from Crawford, September 20, 1774.
18. Williams, Dunmore's War, p. 291.
19. Thwaites and Kellogg, Documentary History, p. xxi.
20. For a more detailed discussion of the controversy surrounding the events of this day, see Gary S. Williams, No Man Knows This Country Better: The Frontier Life of John Gibson (Akron: University of Akron Press, 2022), pp. 35–39, 121–25.
21. Draper Manuscripts, Series 10E, reel #13, p. 93.
22. Ibid.
23. Jefferson, Notes on Virginia, p. 62.
24. Thwaites and Kellogg, Documentary History, pp. 290–91.
25. American Archives, from the Northern Illinois University Digital Library, vol. 1, p. 963.
26. Ibid.
27. Ibid.
28. Thwaites and Kellogg, Documentary History, p. 307.
29. Ibid., pp. xxiv–xxv.
30. Wellenreuther, Zeisberger Diaries, p. 257.

Chapter Two

1. American Archives, Series 4, vol. 2, p. 1723.
2. Connolly, "Sufferings," p. 5.
3. Clarence Monroe Burton, "John Connolly: A Tory of the Revolution," American Antiquarian Society, October 1895, p. 101.
4. Ibid., pp. 70–71.
5. Cleland, Washington in the Ohio Valley, p. 267.
6. Jon Winkler, Point Pleasant 1774: Prelude to the American Revolution (New York: Osprey, 2014), p. 15.
7. Connolly, "Sufferings," pp. 16–17.
8. Ibid., p. 17.
9. Ibid., p. 16.
10. Rueben Gold Thwaites and Louise Phelps Kellogg, The Revolution on the Upper Ohio, 1775–1777 (Madison: Wisconsin Historical Society, 1908), p. 22.
11. Ibid., p. 41.
12. Ibid.
13. Ibid., p. 64.
14. Ibid., p. 56.
15. Booth, Tuscarawas Valley, p. 119.
16. Van Every, Company of Heroes, p. 62.
17. Thwaites and Kellogg, Revolution on the Upper Ohio, p. 26.
18. Ibid., p. 74.

19. Ibid., p. 87.
20. Ibid., p. 126.
21. American Archives, Series 4, vol. 3, p. 1542.
22. Thwaites and Kellogg, Revolution on the Upper Ohio, pp. 130–31.
23. Founders Online, To Washington from William Cowley, 30 Sept. 1775.
24. Connolly, "Sufferings," p. 24.
25. Ibid., p. 34.
26. Ibid., pp. 36–38.
27. Ibid., p. 53.
28. Ibid., p. 55.
29. Wellenreuther, Zeisberger Diaries, p. 290.
30. Booth, Tuscarawas Valley, p. 113.
31. Ibid., pp. 306–07.
32. Journals of the Continental Congress, vol. 4, p. 304.

Chapter Three

1. Thwaites and Kellogg, Revolution on the Upper Ohio, pp. 31–32.
2. Randolph C. Downes, "George Morgan, Indian Agent Extraordinary, 1776–1779," Western Pennsylvania Historical Survey, 1940, p. 202.
3. Thwaites and Kellogg, Revolution on the Upper Ohio, p. 145.
4. Ibid., p. 185.
5. Louise Phelps Kellogg, Frontier Advance on the Upper Ohio, 1778–9 (Madison: Wisconsin State Historical Society, 1916), p. 411.
6. Michael Nogay, Every Home a Fort: Every Man a Warrior (Weirton, WV: self-published, 2017), p. 52.
7. Van Every, Company of Heroes, p. 81.
8. Thwaites and Kellogg, Revolution on the Upper Ohio, pp. 147–48.
9. Van Every, Company of Heroes, p. 77.
10. Thomas B. Roberts, ed., Memoirs of John Bannister Gibson, Late Chief Justice of Pennsylvania (Pittsburgh: Eichbaum and Co., 1890), pp. 20–23.
11. Thwaites and Kellogg, Revolution on the Upper Ohio, p. 226.
12. Ibid.
13. Wellenreuther, Zeisberger Diaries, p. 335.

14. Thwaites and Kellogg, Revolution on the Upper Ohio, pp. 215–16.
15. Wellenreuther, Zeisberger Diaries, p. 336.
16. Mark M. Boatner, III, Encyclopedia of the American Revolution (New York: Van Rees Press, 1966), p. 927.
17. Thwaites and Kellogg, Revolution on the Upper Ohio, p. 250.
18. Francis B. Heitin, Historical Register of Officers of the Continental Army during the War of the Revolution April 1775 to December 1783 (Washington: Rare Book Publishing Co., 1914), p. 412.
19. Robert K. Wright, The Continental Army: Army Lineage Series (Washington: Center of Military History, U.S. Army, 1986).
20. Thwaites and Kellogg, Revolution on the Upper Ohio, p. 256.

Chapter Four

1. Journals of the Continental Congress, vol. 7, p. 252.
2. Mark M. Boatner, III, Encyclopedia of the American Revolution (New York: Van Rees Press, 1966), p. 484.
3. Ibid.
4. Bob Drury and Tom Clavin, Valley Forge (New York: Simon & Schuster, 2018), p. 17.
5. Ibid., p. 65.
6. Dale Van Every, A Company of Heroes: The American Frontier 1775–1783 (New York: William Morrow and Co., 1962), p. 122.
7. Ibid., p. 113.
8. Ibid., p. 114.
9. Ibid., p. 115.
10. Ibid., p. 110.
11. Rueben Gold Thwaites and Louise Phelps Kellogg, Frontier Defense on the Upper Ohio 1777–1778 (Madison: University of Wisconsin Press, 1912), p. 7.
12. Ibid., p. 2.
13. Ibid., p. 35.
14. Ibid., p. 49.
15. Ibid., p. 62.
16. Gary S. Williams, Spies, Scoundrels, and Rogues of the Ohio Frontier (Caldwell, OH: Buckeye Book Press, 2005), pp. 102–03.

17. Paul Wallace, Thirty Thousand Miles with John Heckewelder (Pittsburgh: University of Pittsburgh Press, 1958), pp. 136–37.
18. Wellenruether, Zeisberger Diaries, p. 401.
19. Thwaites and Kellogg, Frontier Defense, p. 95.
20. Earl Olmstead, Blackcoats Among the Delaware: David Zeisberger on the Ohio Frontier (Kent, OH: Kent State University Press, 1978), p. 27.
21. Thwaites and Kellogg, Frontier Defense, p. 146.
22. Founders Online, To Washington from Hand, 9 November 1777.
23. Thwaites and Kellogg, Frontier Defense, p. 149.
24. Ibid., p. 189.
25. Ibid., p. 177.
26. Founders Online, To Washington from Gibson, 5 December 1777.
27. Heitman, Historical Register of the Officers of the Continental Army, p. 247.
28. Thwaites and Kellogg, Frontier Defense, p. 189.
29. Ibid., p.181.
30. Jeff Dacus, "James Willing and the Mississippi River Expedition," Journal of the American Revolution, April 18, 2019.
31. Edmund C. Burnet, ed., Letters of Members of Continental Congress, Vol. II, July 1, 1776 to December 31, 1777 (Washington, D.C.: Carnegie Institute, 1923), p. 190.
32. Ibid., p. 191.
33. Thwaites and Kellogg, Frontier Defense, p. 201.
34. Ibid., pp. 215–16.
35. Van Every, Company of Heroes, pp. 176–77.
36. Ibid., p. 123.
37. Thwaites and Kellogg, Frontier Defense, p. 144.
38. Ibid., p. 155.
39. Ibid., p. 250.
40. Wallace, Heckewelder, pp. 146–50.
41. Founders Online, From Washington to Laurens, 27 February 1778.
42. Thwaites and Kellogg, Frontier Defense, pp. 293–94.
43. Founders Online, From Washington to Pickering, 23 May 1778.

Chapter Five

1. Founders Online, From George Washington to Lachlan McIntosh, 26 May 1778.
2. Phil Greenwalt, "Lachlan McIntosh," Emerging Revolutionary War Era, emergingrevolutionaywar.org, 3 November 2017.
3. Louise Phelps Kellogg, Frontier Advance on the Upper Ohio (Madison: University of Wisconsin Press, 1914), p. 50.
4. Ibid., p. 55.
5. Founders Online, To Washington from McIntosh, 7 June 1778.
6. Founders Online, To Washington from McIntosh, 10 June 1778.
7. Kellogg, Frontier Advance, pp. 88–89.
8. Williams, Fort Pitt and the Revolution, pp. 89–93.
9. Kellogg, Frontier Advance, p. 121.
10. Ibid., p. 125.
11. Boatner, Encyclopedia of the American Revolution, pp. 618–19.
12. Kellogg, Frontier Advance, p. 127.
13. David Jones, A journal of two visits made to some nations to the west side of the Ohio River in the years 1772, 1773, and 1774 (rpt. Fairfield, WA: Ye Galleon Press, 1973), p. 89.
14. Olmstead, Blackcoats Among the Delaware, p. 14.
15. Wellenruether, Zeisberger Diaries, p. 257.
16. Kellogg, Frontier Advance, p. 433.
17. Ibid., p. 139.
18. Ibid., p. 167.
19. Thomas Pieper and James B. Gidney, Fort Laurens 1778–9: The Revolutionary War in Ohio (Kent: Kent State University Press, 1976), pp. 31–37.
20. John Heckewelder, Narrative of the Missions of the United Brethren among the Delaware and Mohegan Indians (Philadelphia: American Philosophical Association, 1820), p. 152.
21. Kellogg, Frontier Advance, p. 169.
22. Ibid., p. 180.
23. Ibid., p. 144.
24. Ibid., pp. 158–61.
25. Pieper and Gidney, Fort Laurens, p. 41.

26. Alan Fitzpatrick, Wilderness War on the Ohio (Benwood, WV: Fort Henry Publications, 2003), p. 280.
27. Kellogg, Frontier Advance, pp. 188–89.
28. Ibid., p. 200.
29. Ibid., p. 230.
30. Ibid., p. 217.
31. Ibid., p. 216.
32. Ibid., p. 210.
33. Founders Online, To Washington from McIntosh, 12 March 1779.
34. Alan Gintz, The Tuscarawas Navigator (New Philadelphia, OH: Jane's Arts and Letters Shop, 1974).
35. Wellenreuther, Zeisberger Diaries, p. 491.
36. Hiram W. Beckwith, Collections of the Illinois Historical Society, vol. I (Springfield, IL: H.W. Rokker Co., 1903), p. 382.
37. Ibid., p. 386.
38. Consul W. Butterfield, History of the Girtys (Cincinnati: Robert Clarke and Co., 1890), p. 91.
39. Fitzpatrick, Wilderness War, p. 297.
40. Wellenreuther, Zeisberger Diaries, p. 492.
41. Ibid.
42. Kellogg, Frontier Advance, p. 221.
43. Ibid., p. 242.
44. Ibid., p. 226.
45. Van Every, Company of Heroes, p. 179.
46. Pieper and Gidney, Fort Laurens, p. 59.
47. Wellenreuther, Zeisberger Diaries, p. 499.
48. Kellogg, Frontier Advance, p. 257.
49. Ibid., p. 185.
50. Founders Online, To Washington from McIntosh, 3 April 1779.
51. Journals of Continental Congress, vol. XIII, p. 109.
52. Founders Online, From Washington to McIntosh, 3 January 1779.
53. Founders Online, To Washington to McIntosh, 12 March 1779.
54. Ibid.
55. Kellogg, Frontier Advance, p. 251.

Chapter Six

1. Founders Online, From Washington to Brodhead, 5 March 1779.
2. Boatner, Encyclopedia of the American Revolution, pp.115–16.
3. Founders Online, To Washington from Brodhead, 21 March 1779.
4. Ibid., to Washington from Brodhead, 17 April 1779.
5. Ibid.
6. Louise Phelps Kellogg, Frontier Retreat On the Upper Ohio 1779–1781 (Madison: Wisconsin State Historical Society, 1917), p. 42.
7. Kellogg, Advance, pp. 310–11.
8. Founders Online, To Washington from Brodhead, 3 May 1779.
9. Kellogg, Advance, pp. 313–19.
10. Russell H. Booth, Jr., The Tuscarawas Valley in Indian Days 1750–97: Original Journals and Maps (Cambridge, OH: Gomber House Press, 1994), p. 196.
11. Kellogg, Advance, pp. 328–29.
12. Ibid., p. 252.
13. Ibid., p. 345.
14. Founders Online, From Washington to Brodhead, 13 July 1779.
15. Founders Online, letters between Washington and Brodhead.
16. Kellogg, Advance, p. 390.
17. Ibid., p. 237.
18. Ibid., p. 372.
19. Ibid., p. 360.
20. Kellogg, Retreat, pp. 57–61.
21. Van Every, Company of Heroes, pp. 208–11.
22. Founders Online, From Washington to Brodhead, 18 October 1779.
23. Kellogg, Retreat, pp. 81–89.
24. Founders Online, From Washington to Brodhead, 4 January 1780.
25. Founders Online, To Washington from Brodhead, 11 February 1780.
26. Kellogg, Retreat, p. 141.
27. Ibid., p. 159.
28. Founders Online, To Washington from Brodhead, 24 April 1780.
29. Ibid.
30. Founders Online, From Washington to Brodhead, 14 March 1780.
31. Kellogg, Advance, p. 385.
32. Kellogg, Retreat, p. 98.

Chapter Seven

1. George H. Loskiel, History of the Mission of the United Brethren Among the Indians in North America in Three Parts (London: Brethren's Society for the Furtherance of the Gospel, 1794), p. 146.
2. Kellogg, Retreat, p. 176.
3. Van Every, Company of Heroes, pp. 241–45.
4. Larry Nelson, A Man of Distinction Among Them: Alexander McKee and the Ohio Country Frontier, 1754–99 (Kent: Kent State University Press, 1999), p. 115.
5. Van Every, Company of Heroes, p. 244.
6. William Hintzen, The Border Wars of the Upper Ohio Valley, 1769–1794 (Manchester, CT: Precision Shooting, 1999), p. 139.
7. R.E. Banta, The Ohio (New York: Rinehart and Co.,1949), p. 157.
8. Fitzpatrick, Wilderness War, pp. 366–75.
9. Kellogg, Retreat, p. 208.
10. Ibid., pp. 446–57.
11. Founders Online, From Washington to Brodhead, 4 July 1780.
12. Boatner, Encyclopedia of the American Revolution, pp. 748–49.
13. Van Every, Company of Heroes, p. 249.
14. Founders Online, From Washington to Brodhead, 13 October 1780.
15. Kellogg, Retreat, pp. 278–79.
16. Ibid., p. 248.
17. Founders Online, To Washington from Brodhead, 17 October 1780.
18. Kellogg, Retreat, p. 301.
19. Neville B. Craig, The Olden Times, vol. II, p. 327.
20. Kellogg, Retreat, p. 306.
21. Founders Online, From Washington to Brodhead, 18 October 1779.
22. Kellogg, Retreat, p. 165.
23. Van Every, Company of Heroes, p. 245.
24. Kellogg, Retreat, pp. 133–34.
25. Founders Online, From Jefferson to Brodhead, 12 October 1780.
26. Founders Online, From Washington to Jefferson, 28 December 1780.
27. Founders Online, To Jefferson from Clark, 27 March 1781.
28. Founders Online, From Washington to Brodhead, 26 December 1780.
29. Consul W. Butterfield, Washington-Irvine Correspondence (Madison, WI: Daniel Atwood, 1882), p. 54.
30. James Alston James, George Rogers Clark Papers, 1771–1781, VA Series, vol. III (Springfield, IL: Illinois State Historical Society, 1912), p. 509.
31. Founders Online, To Washington from Brodhead, 10 March 1781.
32. Kellogg, Retreat, p. 347.
33. Founders Online, From Washington to Brodhead, 28 February 1781.
34. James, Clark Papers, 1771–1781, pp. 494–95.
35. Kellogg, Retreat, pp. 376–77.
36. Heckewelder, Narrative, p. 214.
37. Kellogg, Retreat, p. 356.
38. Ibid., pp. 387–88.
39. Ibid., p. 34.
40. Founders Online, From Washington to Brodhead, 5 May 1781.
41. Butterfield, Washington-Irvine Correspondence, p. 54.

Chapter Eight

1. Thomas Jefferson, Notes on the State of Virginia (Chapel Hill: University of North Carolina Press, 1982), p. 233.
2. Butterfield, Washington-Irvine Correspondence, p. 344.
3. Founders Online, From Washington to Clark, 30 May 1781.
4. James Alton James, George Rogers Clark Papers, 1781–1784, Virginia Series, vol. IV (Springfield, IL: Illinois State Historical Society, 1926), p. 562.
5. Kellogg, Frontier Retreat, p. 401.
6. Founders Online, From Washington to Brodhead, 12 June 1781.
7. Van Every, A Company of Heroes, p. 259.
8. James, George Rogers Clark Papers, 1771–1781, p. 571.
9. Paul Wallace, Thirty Thousand

(continued with 33. Ibid., p. 99. / 34. Ibid., p. 118. at top)

Miles with John Heckewelder (Pittsburgh: University of Pittsburgh Press, 1958), p. 171.
10. Founders Online, To Washington from Brodhead, 19 August 1781.
11. Kellogg, Frontier Retreat, p. 411.
12. Ibid.
13. Founders Online, To Washington from Gibson, 25 August 1781.
14. Ibid.
15. Founders Online, To Washington from Brodhead (enclosures), 19 August 1781.
16. Ibid.
17. Founders Online, To Washington from Gibson, 25 August 1781.
18. Founders Online, To Washington from Brodhead, 29 August 1781.
19. Craig, The Olden Time, vol. II, p. 397.
20. Founders Online, To Washington from Brodhead, 6 September 1781.
21. Founders Online, To Washington from Gibson, 30 September 1781.
22. Founders Online, From Washington to Brodhead, 6 September 1781.
23. Founders Online, From Washington to Gibson, 6 September1781.
24. Founders Online, From Washington to Brodhead, 12 April 1789.
25. Olmstead, Blackcoats Among the Delaware, pp. 314–15.
26. Butterfield, Girtys, p. 95.
27. Boatner, Encyclopedia of the American Revolution, pp. 545–46.
28. Butterfield, Washington-Irvine Correspondence, pp. 63–64.
29. Ibid., pp. 157–58.
30. Ibid., p. 80.
31. Ibid., p. 341.
32. Ibid., p. 75.
33. Ibid., p. 80.
34. Ibid., pp. 164–65.
35. Ibid., p. 83.
36. Ibid.
37. Ibid., pp. 349–50.
38. Baron de Rosenthal, "Journal of a Volunteer Expedition to Sandusky from May 24 to June 13, 1782," Pennsylvania Magazine of History and Biography 18, no. 2 (1894), p. 294.
39. Butterfield, Washington-Irvine Correspondence, p. 362.

Chapter Nine

1. Butterfield, Washington-Irvine Correspondence, p. 94.
2. Ibid., pp. 99–103.
3. Ibid., pp. 104–08.
4. Ibid., p. 238.
5. Van Every, A Company of Heroes, p. 286.
6. Butterfield, Washington-Irvine Correspondence, pp. 236–37.
7. Ibid., p. 105.
8. Ibid., p. 344.
9. Ibid., p. 341.
10. Ibid., p. 241.
11. Ibid., pp. 344–45.
12. Olmstead, Zeisberger, p. 335.
13. Heckewelder, Narrative, p. 333.
14. Butterfield, Washington-Irvine Correspondence, pp. 113–18.
15. Boatner, Encyclopedia of the American Revolution, pp. 946–47.
16. Butterfield, Washington-Irvine Correspondence, p. 364.
17. Ibid., p. 367.
18. Heckewelder, Narrative, p. 341.
19. Hugh Henry Brackenridge, Indian Atrocities: Narrative of the Perils and Sufferings of Dr. Knight and John Slover (Cincinnati, 1867).
20. Butterfield, Washington-Irvine Correspondence, p. 126.
21. Ibid., p. 127.
22. James, Clark Papers 1781–84, p. 80.
23. Butterfield, Washington-Irvine Correspondence, p. 132.
24. Ibid., p. 125.
25. Ibid., p. 251.
26. Van Every, A Company of Heroes, p. 296.
27. Ibid., p. 301.
28. Butterfield, Washington-Irvine Correspondence, p. 398.
29. Ibid., p. 129.
30. Ibid., p. 392.
31. James, Clark Papers 1781–84, p. 108.
32. Butterfield, Washington-Irvine Correspondence, p. 134.
33. Ibid., p. 141.
34. Ibid., p. 179.
35. Gary S. Williams, The Forts of Ohio (Caldwell, OH: Buckeye Book Press, 2003), pp. 148–49.

36. Butterfield, Washington-Irvine Correspondence, p. 139.
37. Ibid., p. 346.
38. Ibid., p. 144.
39. Ibid., p. 148.
40. Ibid., pp. 149–50.
41. Ibid., p. 151.

Conclusion

1. Hintzen, Border Wars, p. 221.
2. Dale Van Every, Ark of Empire (New York: William Morrow and Co., 1963), p. 221.
3. Ibid., p. 225.
4. Ibid., p. 236.
5. Robert S. Sanders, "Colonel John Hardin and His Letters to his Wife-1792," The Filson Club History Quarterly, vol. 39, Jan. 1965, pp. 5–12.
6. Neville B. Craig, The History of Pittsburgh (Pittsburgh: J.R. Wheldon Co., 1917), p. 208.
7. Ibid., p. 209.
8. Bouquet Papers, Series 21646, pp. 103–08.
9. Stephen Lorant, Pittsburgh: The Story of an American City (New York: Doubleday, 1964), p. 74.
10. Founders Online, From Franklin to Arthur Lee, 4 April 1778.
11. Clarence Busch, "Report of the Committee to Locate the Sites of the Frontier Forts of Pennsylvania," vol. II (Harrisburg: State Printer of Pennsylvania, 1896), p. 150.
12. Wallace, Thirty Thousand Miles, p. 243.
13. Clara Duer, ed., The People and Times of Western Pennsylvania: Pittsburgh Gazette Abstracts, 1786–97, vol. I (Pittsburgh: Western Pennsylvania Genealogical Association, 1988), p .4.
14. Pittsburgh Library, digital.library.pitt.edu.
15. Hugh Henry Brackenridge ed. Daniel Marder, Incidents of the Insurrection (New Haven: College and University Press Service, 1972), p. 96.
16. Ibid., p. 113.
17. Ibid.
18. Leland Baldwin, Whiskey Rebels: The Story of a Frontier Uprising (Pittsburgh: University of Pittsburgh Press, 1939), p. 185.
19. John B. Linn and Dr. William Egle, Papers Relating to What is Known as the Whiskey Insurrection in Western Pennsylvania, 1794, second series, vol. iv (Harrisburg, PA: State Printer, 1890), file S2V4C.
20. Lorant, Pittsburgh, p. 74.

Bibliography

Primary Sources

American Archives. Northern Illinois University Digital Library.
Beckwith, Hiram W. *Collections of the Illinois Historical Society*, vol. I. Springfield, IL: H.W. Rokker Co., 1903.
Booth, Russell H. *The Tuscarawas Valley in Indian Days 1750–1797: Original Journals and Maps*. Cambridge, OH: Gomber House Press, 1994.
Bouquet, Henry. *The Papers of Henry Bouquet*. Harrisburg: Pennsylvania Historical Survey, 1941.
Brackenridge, Hugh Henry. *Incidents of the Insurrection*, edited for the modern reader by Daniel Marder. New Haven: College and University Press Service, 1972.
_____. *Indian Atrocities: Narrative of the Perils and Sufferings of Dr. Knight and John Slover*. Cincinnati, 1867.
Burnett, Edward C., ed. *Letters of Members of Continental Congress, vol. II, July 1, 1776 to Dec. 3, 1777*. Washington, D.C.: Carnegie Institute, 1923.
Butterfield, Consul W. *The Washington-Crawford Letters*. Cincinnati: Robert Clarke and Co., 1877.
_____. *Washington-Irvine Correspondence*. Madison, WI: David Atwood, 1882.
Carter, Clarence, ed. *The Territorial Papers of the United States, Vol. III, Territory Northwest of the River Ohio 1787–1803*. Washington, D.C.: U.S. Govt. Printing Office, 1939.
Connolly, John. "A Narrative of the Transactions, Imprisonment and Suffering of John Connolly." London: self-published, 1783.
Craig, Neville B. *The Olden Time*, 2 vols. Pittsburgh: Dumars and Co., 1846.
Crumrine, Boyd. *Virginia Court Records in Southwestern Pennsylvania 1775–80*. Baltimore: Genealogical Publishing Co., 1981.
Draper, Lyman. The Draper Manuscripts. Wisconsin Historical Society, Madison.
Duer, Clara, ed. *The People and Times of Western Pennsylvania: Pittsburgh Gazette Abstracts, Vol. I, 1786–1797*. Pittsburgh: Western Pennsylvania Genealogical Society, 1988.
_____. *Pittsburgh Gazette Abstracts, Vol. II, 1797–1803*. Apollo, PA: Closson Press, 1986.
Founders Online, https://founders.archives.gov/.
Heckewelder, John. *Narrative of the Mission of the United Brethren Among the Delaware and Mohegan Indians from its Commencement in the Year 1740 to the Close of the Year 1808*. Philadelphia: American Philosophical Society, 1820.
Heitman, Francis B. *Historical Register of Officers of the Continental Army during the War of the Revolution April 1775 to December 1783*. Washington: Rare Book Publishing Co., 1914.
James, James Alton. *George Rogers Clark Papers 1771–1781*: Virginia Series, Vol. III. Springfield: Illinois State Historical Society, 1912.

Bibliography

———. *George Rogers Clark Papers 1781–1784*, Vol IV. Springfield, IL: Illinois State Historical Society, 1926.
Jefferson, Thomas (edited by William Peden). *Notes on the State of Virginia*. Chapel Hill: University of North Carolina Press, 1982.
Jones, David. *A journal of two visits made to some nations of the west side of the Ohio River in the years 1772, 1773 and 1774*. Rpt., Fairfield, WA: Ye Galleon Press, 1973.
Journal of the Convention, May, 1776. Richmond: Ritchie, Trueheart and Duval, 1816.
Journals of the Continental Congress.
Kellogg, Louise Phelps. *Frontier Advance on the Upper Ohio 1778–9*. Madison: Wisconsin State Historical Society, 1916.
———. *Frontier Retreat on the Upper Ohio 1779–1781*. Madison: Wisconsin State Historical Society, 1917.
Linn, John B., and Dr. William Engle. *Papers Relating to What Is Known as the Whiskey Insurrection in Western Pennsylvania 1794*. Pennsylvania Archives, 2nd Series, Vol. IV. Harrisburg, PA: State Printer, 1890.
Loskiel, George. *History of the Mission of the United Brethren Among the Indians in North America in Three Parts*. London: Brethren's Society for Furtherance of the Gospel, 1794.
"Revolutionary Journal and Orderly Book of General Lachlan McIntosh's Expedition, 1778." *Western Pennsylvania Historical Magazine*, Vol. 43, March 1960.
Roberts, Thomas P., ed. *Memoirs of John Bannister Gibson, Late Chief Justice of Pennsylvania*. Pittsburgh: Eichbaum and Co., 1890.
Rosenthal, Baron de (John Rose). "Journal of a Volunteer Expedition to Sandusky from May 24 to June 13, 1782." Rpt. *Pennsylvania Magazine of History and Biography*, July–October 1894.
Sanders, Robert S. "Colonel John Hardin and His Letters to His Wife-1792." *The Filson Club History Quarterly*, vol. 39, January 1965.
Thwaites, Reuben G., and Louise Phelps Kellogg. *Documentary History of Dunmore's War, 1774*. Madison: Wisconsin Historical Society, 1905.
———. *Frontier Defense of the Upper Ohio, 1777–1778*. Madison: Wisconsin Historical Society, 1912.
———. *The Revolution on the Upper Ohio, 1775–1777*. Madison: Wisconsin Historical Society, 1908.
Wallace, Paul. *Thirty Thousand Miles with John Heckewelder*. Pittsburgh: University of Pittsburgh Press, 1958.
Wellenreuther, Herman, and Carola Wessel, eds. *The Moravian Mission Diaries of David Zeisberger 1772–1781* (translated by Julie Weber). University Park: Penn State University Press, 2005.

Secondary Sources

Baldwin, Leland D. *Whiskey Rebels: The Story of a Frontier Uprising*. Pittsburgh: University of Pittsburgh Press, 1939.
Banta, R.E. *The Ohio*. New York: Rinehart and Company, 1949.
Barr, Daniel P. *A Colony Sprung from Hell: Pittsburgh and the Struggle for Authority on the Western Pennsylvania Frontier, 1744–1794*. Kent: Kent State University Press, 2014.
Bausman, Rev. Joseph H. *History of Beaver County, Pennsylvania*, 2 vols. New York: Knickerbocker Press, 1904.
Berg, Fred A. *Encyclopedia of Continental Army Units: Battalions, Regiments and Independent Corps*. Harrisburg: Stackpole Books, 1972.
Boatner, Mark M., III. *Encyclopedia of the American Revolution*. New York: Van Rees Press, 1966.

Bibliography

Bowman, Diana L., ed. *Pennsylvania Herald and York Advertiser, Book I, 1789–1793.* Apollo, PA: Clossen Press, 1996.
Brackenridge, Henry Marie. *History of the Western Insurrection in Western Pennsylvania Commonly called the Whiskey Insurrection, 1794.* Pittsburgh: W.S. Haven, 1859.
Brady, William. "Brodhead's Trail Up the Allegheny 1779." *Western Pennsylvania Historic Magazine* 37 (1954), 19–31.
Buchman, Randall, ed. *The Historic Indian in Ohio.* Columbus: Ohio Historical Society, 1976.
Buck, Solon J., and Elizabeth H. Buck. *The Planting of Civilization in Western Pennsylvania.* Pittsburgh: University of Pittsburgh Press, 1939.
Burton, Clarence M. "John Connolly: A Tory of the Revolution." *American Antiquarian Society*, October 1909, 70–105.
Busch, Clarence. "Report of the Committee to Locate the Sites of the Frontier Forts of Pennsylvania," vol ii. Harrisburg: State Printer of Pennsylvania, 1896.
Butterfield, Consul W. *History of the Girtys.* Cincinnati: Robert Clarke and Co., 1890.
Carter, Henry L. *The Life and Times of Little Turtle: First Sagamore of the Wabash.* Urbana: University of Illinois Press, 1987.
Craig, Neville B. *The History of Pittsburgh.* Pittsburgh: J.R. Weldon Co., 1917.
Crytzer, Brady J. *Fort Pitt: A Frontier History.* Charleston, SC: History Press, 2012.
Cubbison, Douglas R. *The British Defeat of the French in 1758: A Military History of the Forbes Campaign against Fort Duquesne.* Jefferson, NC: McFarland, 2010.
Dacus, Jeff. "James Willing and the Mississippi River Expedition." *Journal of the American Revolution*, April 18, 2019.
De Schweinetz, Edmund. *The Life and Times of David Zeisberger.* Philadelphia: J.B. Lippincott and Co., 1876.
Dowd, Gregory E. *A Spirited Resistance: The North American Indian Struggle for Unity 1745–1815.* Baltimore: Johns Hopkins Press, 1992.
Downes, Randolph. *Council Fires on the Upper Ohio.* Pittsburgh: University of Pittsburgh Press, 1940.
———. "George Morgan, Indian Agent Extraordinary, 1776–1779." *Western Pennsylvania Historical Survey*, 1940.
Drury, Bob, and Tom Clavin. *Valley Forge.* New York: Simon & Schuster, 2018.
Dunn, Walter S., Jr. *Frontier Profit and Loss: The British Army and the Fur Traders 1760–1764.* Westport, CT: Greenwood Press, 1998.
Ferguson, Russell. *Early Western Pennsylvania Politics.* Pittsburgh: University of Pittsburgh Press, 1938.
Find A Grave. https://www.findagrave.com.
Fitzpatrick, Alan. *Wilderness War on the Ohio.* Benwood, WV: Fort Henry Publications, 2003.
Gibson, John Bannister. "General John Gibson." *Western Pennsylvania Historic Magazine*, October 1922, 298–310.
Gintz, Alan F. *The Tuscarawas Navigator.* New Philadelphia, OH: Jane's Art and Letter Shop, 1974.
Gramly, Richard Michael. *Fort Laurens 1778-9: The Archaeological Record.* Richmond: William Byrd Press, 1986.
Green, Karen Mauer. *Index to the Draper Manuscripts, Series NN, The Pittsburgh and Northwest Virginia Papers.* Cooperstown, NY: Frontier Press, 2003.
Greene, George. *History of Old Vincennes and Knox County, Indiana*, v. I. Chicago: S.J. Clarke, 1911.
Hanko, Charles W. *The Life of John Gibson: Soldier, Patriot, Statesman.* Daytona Beach: College Publishing Co., 1955.
Hintzen, William. *The Border Wars of the Upper Ohio Valley 1769–1794.* Manchester, CT: Precision Shooting, 1999.

Bibliography

Horsman Reginald. *Matthew Elliott, British Indian Agent.* Detroit: Wayne State University Press, 1964.
Kappler, Charles J., ed. *Indian Treaties 1778–1883.* Mattilick, NY: Amereon House, 1972.
Leyburn, James G. *The Scotch-Irish: A Social History.* Chapel Hill\: University of North Carolina Press, 1962.
Lorant, Stefan. *Pittsburgh: The Story of an American City.* New York: Doubleday, 1964.
Lossing, Benson J. *The Pictorial Field Book of the Revolution.* New York: Harper and Bros., 1860.
McConnell, Michael M. *A Country Between: The Upper Ohio Valley and its Peoples 1724–1774.* Lincoln: University of Nebraska Press, 1992.
Morgan, Ted. *Wilderness at Dawn: The Settling of the North American Continent.* New York: Simon & Schuster, 1993.
Nelson, Larry. *A Man of Distinction Among Them: Alexander McKee and the Ohio Country Frontier, 1754–1799.* Kent: Kent State University Press, 1999.
Nester, William R. *The Frontier War for American Independence.* Mechanicsburg, PA: Stackpole Books, 2004.
Nogay, Michal Edward. *Every Home a Fort, Every Man a Warrior.* Weirton, WV: self-published, 2017.
O'Donnell, James, III. *Ohio's First Peoples.* Athens: Ohio University Press, 2004.
Olmstead, Earl. *Blackcoats Among the Delaware: David Zeisberger on the Ohio Frontier.* Kent: Kent State University Press, 1991.
_____. *David Zeisberger: A Life Among the Indians.* Kent: Kent State University Press, 1997.
Palmer, John M. *General Von Steuben.* New Haven, CT: Yale University Press, 1937.
Pieper, Thomas I., and James B. Gidney. *Fort Laurens 1778–1779: The Revolutionary War in Ohio.* Kent: Kent State University Press, 1976.
Schaef, Gregory. *Wampum Belts and Peace Trees: George Morgan, Native Americans, and Revolutionary Diplomacy.* Golden, CO: Fulcrum, 1990.
Slaughter, Thomas P. *The Whiskey Rebellion: Frontier Epilogue to the American Revolution.* New York: Oxford University Press, 1986.
Somes, Joseph H.V. *Old Vincennes.* New York: Graphic Books, 1962.
Stapleton, Rev. A. *Memorials of the Huguenots in America with special reference to their emigration to Pennsylvania.* Rpt., Baltimore: Genealogical Publishing Co., 1969.
Stotz, Charles M. *Outposts of the War for Empire.* Pittsburgh: Historical Society of Western Pennsylvania, 1985.
Sugden, John. *Tecumseh: A Life.* New York: Henry Holt, 1998.
Tanner, Helen H. *Atlas of Great Lakes Indian History.* Norman: University of Oklahoma Press, 1987.
Thompson, Robert N. *Disaster on the Sandusky: The Life of Colonel William Crawford.* Staunton, VA: American History Pres, 2017.
Van Every, Dale. *A Company of Heroes: The American Frontier 1775–1783.* New York: William Morrow and Co., 1962.
_____. *Forth to the Wilderness: The First American Frontier, 1754–1774.* New York: William Morrow and Co., 1961.
Van Every, Dale. *Ark of Empire. The American Frontier 1784–1803.* New York: William Morrow and Co., 1963.
Webb, James. *Born Fighting: How the Scots-Irish Shaped America.* New York: Broadway Books, 2004.
Williams, Edward G. *Fort Pitt and the Revolution on the Western Frontier.* Pittsburgh: Historical Society of Western Pennsylvania, 1978.
Williams, Gary S. *The Forts of Ohio.* Caldwell, OH: Buckeye Book Press, 2003.
_____. "George Mason and the Bills of Rights." *The Freeman,* vol. 42, no. 5 (May 1992): 174–177.

Bibliography

_____. *Gliding to a Better Place: Profiles from Ohio's Territorial Era.* Caldwell, OH: Buckeye Book Press, 2000.

_____. *Spies, Scoundrels and Rogues of the Ohio Frontier.* Caldwell, OH: Buckeye Book Press, 2005.

Williams, Glenn F. *Dunmore's War: The Last Conflict of America's Colonial Era.* Yardley, PA: Westholme, 2017.

Winkler, Jon. *Point Pleasant 1774: Prelude to the American Revolution.* New York: Osprey, 2014.

Withers, Alexander S. (edited by R.G. Thwaites). *Chronicles of Border Warfare.* Cincinnati: Stewart and Kidd Co., 1895.

Wright, Robert K. *The Continental Army: Army Lineage Series.* Washington, D.C.: Center of Military History, U.S. Army, 1986.

Index

Numbers in **_bold italics_** indicate pages with illustrations

Adams, Abigail 155
Adams, John 112, 155
Alexandria, VA 42
Allegheny County 154, 156
Allegheny River 9, 10, 80, 91, 96, 157
American Philosophical Society 95, 155
Amherst, Jeffery 16
Anderson 54
Arbuckle, Matthew 49, 50, 65
Arkansas Post 52
Arnold, Benedict 114
Articles of Confederation 160
Athens County, OH 28
Auglaize River 150

Baker's Bottom 23
Bartram, William 155
Bayard, Stephen 144
Baynton and Wharton 47
Beaver, PA 80
Beaver Creek 16, 80
Bedford, PA 160
Bethlehem, PA 71, 104, 135
Bill of Rights 147
Bird, Henry 86, 107, 108, 110, 127, 139
Blue Jacket 112, 150
Blue Licks 140, 141
Bolivar, OH 16, 81
Boone, Daniel 18, 21, 26, 56, 110; Blue Licks defeat 140; captured 65, 107
Boonesborough, KY 61, 107
border dispute between Pennsylvania and Virginia 18–22, 34–35, 55, 73, 100–1, 133
Boston, MA 25, 31, 130, 148; Connolly plot hatched 37, 38, 42
Boswell, James 96, 155
Bouquet, Henry 27, 81, 127, 138, 154; Forbes Campaign and 12–14; Pontiac's Conspiracy and 16–17, 80
Bower Hill 158, 159
Brackenridge, Hugh Henry 138, 156, 159, 162
Braddock, Edward 11, 13
Braddock's Defeat 31 49
Braddock's Field 159
Bradford, David 158, 160, 161
Bradt, Andrew 141
Brady, Sam 97, 111, 142
Brandywine 6, 56, 66
Brant, Joseph 96, 99, 102, 126, 127, 153
Brison, James 159, 160
Brodhead, Daniel 56, 73, 80, ***91***, 93, 100, 101, 104, 105, 112, 133, 142; background 91–92; conflicts with citizens 102, 111; conflicts with troops 83, 102–3, 109, 124; involvement in commander controversy 120–26; later years 126; leads Allegheny campaign 96–99; named to command 90; overreaching 102, 109, 111; popularity 102, 111, 116–17, 125; tries to thwart Clark campaign 113–18, 120
Bryan's Station 139
Buckaloon 98
Buckongahelas 150
Bunker Hill 38
Burr, Aaron 95
Bushy Run 16, 138
Butler, John 95, 99, 141
Butler, Richard 46, 55, 73, 110, 152
Butler, Thomas 154, 159
Butler, Walter 95
Butler's Rangers 136, 139

Cahokia, IL 71, 104, 110, 115; attacked 105–6; captured 76, 77, 83

Index

Caldwell, William 136, 139
Cambray-Digny, Lewis Antoine John Baptiste, Chevalier de 80, 82
Camden 72
Camp Charlotte 35, 36, 40
Canada 6, 44
Canon, Colonel 123
Captain Pipe 25, 28, 78, 81, 116, 122; defends Moravians 126; mother wounded 69
Captina Creek 26
Captive's Town 126
Carleton, Guy 41
Carlisle, PA 76, 128, 132, 144, 160
Catfish Camp *see* Washington, PA
Cave-in-Rock 62
Chapline, Abraham 107
Charleston, SC 56, 75
Charleston, WV 29
Chartieres Creek 129, 158
Cheat River 70
Cherokee Tribe 92
Cherry Valley 95
Cincinnati, OH 99, 147, 152, 154
Cincinnatus 147
Circleville, OH 28
Clark, George Rogers 21, 26, 32, 100, *105*, 110–11, 142; commands all Kentucky forces, 3, 4, 50; Indian fear of 88, 106–8, 115, 139; joint federal/state campaign 113–18, 120–21, 124, 126–27; later years 140–41; popularity 113; Vincennes campaign 71–72, 76–77, 83, 87–88, 95
Clark, John 85
Clarksburg, WV 160
Clay, Henry 95
Clinton, James 96, 98
Columbus, OH 31
Conewego 98
Connecticut 19, 149
Connellsville, PA 18, 66, 121
Connolly, John 24, 25, 26, *35*, 38, 40; background 36; hatches Connolly Plot 37, 42; imprisoned 43; instigates frontier war 19–22; later years 44–45
Continental Army 2, 3, 5, 55, 147, 163; Canadian Dept. 6; coordination between departments 95, 99; Eastern Dept. 6; Highlands Dept. 6; Middle Dept. 5, 56, 66; Northern Dept. 5, 55, 56, 72; Southern Dept. 6, 56, 72
Continental Congress 1, 4, 43, 46, 55, 89, 94, 102; Board of War 69, 72, 74–75, 120, 128, 142; makes plea for Western unity 34–35
Conway Cabal 74
Cornstalk 39, 40, 53, 54; murder 65, 81, 153; Point Pleasant campaign and 27, 29, 30
Cornwallis, Lord 44
Coshocton, OH 17, 54, 93, 131; attacked 116; Heckewelder's ride to 71; principal town of Delaware 27, 84; role in Fort Laurens campaign 86–88
Covington, KY 110
Cowley, William 42
Craig, James 103, 105, 121, 143, 153, 162
Craig, Neville 162
Crawford, William 18, 56, 68, 80, 139; defeat and torture 135–37; during Dunmore's War 23, 26, 28, 31, 32; popularity 66
Cresap, Michael 22, 23, 24, 30
Croghan, George 14, 19, 36
Culloden 25, 26
Cumberland, MD 10
Cumberland Gap 18, 21
Cuyahoga River 68

Day, Edward 159
Deane, Silas 156
Declaration of Independence 32, 34, 40, 54–55, 75, 155
Defiance, OH 150
de Galvez, Bernardo 100, 101, 103
de la Balme, Mottin 109, 112
Delaware, OH 64
Delaware River 19
Delaware Tribe 7, 17, 82, 84; attacked by US 116; contingent travels to Philadelphia 92–94; leadership changes 54, 78, 81; negotiate treaties 40, 77–80
de Leyba, Fernando 106, 112
De Peyster, Arendt 99, 106, 126, 135
Detroit, MI 6, 16, 79, 84, 85, 106, 149, 162; Moravians summoned to 126, 134–35; rejects White Eyes' overtures 53, 79; shortage of troops 51, 60
Dickinson, John 35
Dinwiddie, Governor 10
Draper, Dr. Lyman 1
Dresden, OH 27
Duncan, David 122
Dunmore, Lord 19, 20, *21*, 26, 27, 29, 31, 41, 78–79; background 25; involvement with Connolly plot 35–38, 42; later years 42; popularity 28, 32, 33

180

Index

Easton, PA 96
Eighteenth Irish Foot 58
Eighth Foot 51, 86
Eighth Pennsylvania 55, 56, 73, 76, 79, 92
Ellenipsico 39, 40, 65, 98
Elliott, Matthew 70, 73, 99, 107, 122, 137, 139
Erie, PA 9
Ethiopian Regiment 33
Eton College 155

Fairfax Resolves 32
FallenTimbers 112, 162
Finley, John 122, 123
First American Regiment 148
First Pennsylvania Regiment 58
Flying Crow 40
Forbes, John 12, 13, 16, 119, 127
Foreman, William 62, 63, 64
Forks of the Ohio 7, 9, 10, 14, 162
Fort Bedford 15
Fort Donnelly 76
Fort Dunmore 11, 24, 26, 35; *see also* Fort Pitt
Fort Duquesne 10, 13
Fort Fincastle 26
Fort Frederika 75
Fort Gower 28, 31
Fort Gower Resolves 32
Fort Hand 64, 76, 92
Fort Harmar 150
Fort Henry 59, 61
Fort Jefferson (KY) 100, 106, 110
Fort Jefferson (OH) 152
Fort La Fayette 153, 159, 160
Fort Laurens 84, 85, 86, 92; attacked 87; description 82; siege 88–89
Fort Le Bouef 9, 10, 18, 96, 138
Fort Ligonier 13, 15
Fort Mackinac 15, 99, 105
Fort McIntosh 80, 83, 84, 92, 125, 156
Fort Mercer 34
Fort Necessity 11, 13, 30
Fort Niagara 15, 39, 51, 86, 96, 98–99
"Fort Nonsense" *see* Fort Laurens
Fort Pitt 38, 40, 49, 71, 86, 109, 142, 147, **148**, 149; abandoned 153; constructed 14; decaying condition 24, 128–29, 143; decommissioned by British 19, 24; defined and introduced 3; garrison size 66, 92, 128, 144; under siege 15–16
Fort Presqu'Isle 9

Fort Randolph 59, 65, 76, 92
Fort St. Joseph 112
Fort Stanwix 26
Fort Steuben 150
Fort Ticonderoga 151
Fort Venango 9
Fort Washington 151, 152
Fort Wayne 98, 112, 150, 151
Foster, Stephen 162
Fowler, Alexander 117, 122, 123, 124, 125
Franklin, Benjamin 11, 35, 109, 155, 156
Franklin, PA 98
French Creek 9 98
French Revolution 158
Frontier style of warfare 1–2, 6, 28–29, 59–60, 140–41
Fry, Joshua 10

Gage, Thomas 37, 38, 42
Gallatin, Albert 158, 162
Gates, Horatio 7, 69, 72, 75
Gelelemund 86, 93, 97, 101, 116; becomes principal Delaware chief 78, 81; joins Americans 117, 131
Genesee River 99
Geneva Convention 16
Gentlemen's Magazine 96
George, Robert 139
George Morgan White Eyes 93
Georgia 74, 75
Germantown 56, 59, 66
Gettysburg Campaign 161
Gibson, George 51, 52, 152
Gibson, John 23, 25, 32, 37, 56, 61, 69, 73, 92–94, 97, 102, 104, 109, **119**, 128, 142, 154, 156, 157; background 119–20; commander controversy involvement 122–25; commands at Fort Laurens 82, 84–89; commands at Fort Pitt 65–66, 118, 125–27, 129, 130; diplomatic treaty work 27, 29–31, 33, 39–41, 45–46; Gnadenhutten Massacre reaction 131–33; later years 162; popularity 120, 131, 132–33; proposed Detroit expedition and 114–15, 120–22, 124; Whiskey Rebellion and 159–60
Gibson, John, Jr. 120
Gibson, Josh 162
"Gibson's Lambs" 52
Girty, George 28, 67, 99, 107, 126, 139
Girty, James 28, 71, 107, 141
Girty, Simon 29–30, 38–39, 69–70, 73, 99, 107–8, 137, 139, 141, 152; background 28; deserts to British 69–70;

181

Index

drunken behavior 69, 127, 134, 153; leads Fort Laurens attacks 85–87
Gist, Christopher 10
Gnadenhutten, OH 27, 71, 84, 104, 126; church service at 38; prosperity 63; resettled 135
Gnadenhutten Massacre 130, 133, 137, 139
Goshen, OH 135
Gower, Lord 28
Grand Glaize 150, 153
Grant, James 13
Grave Creek (Moundsville), WV 63
Great Bridge 42
Greathouse, Daniel 23
Greenville Treaty 162
Grenadier Squaw see Nonhelema
Guyasuta 18, 25, 40, 51, 138
Gwinnet, Button 75

Hagerstown, MD 11, 42
Haldimand, General 127
Half King 40, 62, 121, 12, 126
Hamilton, Alexander 94, 95, 155, 157, 159, 161
Hamilton, Henry 53, 60, 68, 79, 99, 102; arrives at Detroit 41, 51; captured by Clark 83, 87, 88
Hand, Edward 65, 70, 72, 75, 77, 96, 128; background 58; disappointments 64, 66, 68–69; named to command 57; planned campaigns 61, 64, 68; popularity 57–58
Hannahstown, PA 19, 20, 34, 138
Hardin, John 50, 97, 98, 138, 151, 152–53
Harmar, Josiah 112, 150, 151
Harpe Brothers 62
Harrison, Benjamin 35, 95, 140
Harrison, William Henry 162
Harrod, James 21
Harrodsburg, KY 61, 107
Head of Elk, MD 125
Heckewelder, John 23, 45, 81, 87, 101, 116, 122, 134, 137; helps American cause 65, 71, 84; later years 135
Henry, Patrick 26, 35, 50, 65, 71, 77, 100
Hesse, Emmanuel 105–6
Hocking River 28
Holliday's Cove (Weirton), WV 50, 92
Hopkinson, Francis 155
Howe, William 59
Humphries, Charles 35
Huntington, Samuel 120

Illinois Country 42, 47, 112
Indiana Company 47
Iroquois Tribe 8–9, 17, 95, 99
Irvine, William 129, 131, *132*, 135, 138, 144; background 128; later years 145; named to command 127; opposes Gnadenhutten investigation 133–34; popularity 145; proposed expedition 142–43
Irwin, Joseph 102

Jackson, Andrew 95, 155
James River 33 114
Jefferson, Thomas 30, 35, 95, 112, 121, 132, 155, 157, 162; plans campaign with Washington 113, 114, 116
Johnson, Samuel 156
Johnson, Sir William 17, 26, 95
Joliet, Father 9
Jones, David 78

Kanawha River 18, 26, 29
Kaskaskia, IL 68, 71, 76, 77, 83, 110
Kellogg, Louise Phelps 1
Kenton, Simon 28, 85, 97, 107, 110
Kentucky 6, 17, 44, 50, 61, 108, 139
"Kentucky Navy" 7, 100, 39
Kentucky River 140
Kiashuta see Guyasuta
Killbuck, John, Jr. see Gelelemund
Killbuck Island 117, 131
King's Mountain 26
Kittanning 49, 59, 64
Knight, Dr. John 135, 137, 138
Knox, Henry 102, 147, 150, 159
Koonay 23, 24

Lafayette, Marquis de 44, 80, 158
Lake Erie 9, 81, 107, 113
Lake Ontario 39
Lancaster, PA 52, 76, 119, 143, 160
Langlade, Charles 105, 106
La Salle, Sieur de 9
Laurens, Henry 72, 75, 82
Lee, Arthur 155–56
Lee, Francis Lightfoot 155
Lee, Henry 161
Lee, Richard Henry 35, 155
Lee, Robert E. 161
Lenox, David 158, 159, 160
Lernoult, Captain 51, 83, 84
Lewis, Andrew 26–29, 31, 38, 77
Lewis, Thomas 77
Lewisburg, WV 26

Index

Lexington and Concord 32, 33, 34, 36
Licking River 100, 108
Linctot, Daniel 104, 110
Linn, William 52, 63
Little Miami River 110
Little Turtle 98, 112, 150
Lochry, Archibald 121, 126, 127
Logan 22–25, 30
Logan, Benjamin 141
Logan's Station (St. Asaph's), KY 61
London 44, 96, 155
Losantiville *see* Cincinnati
Louisville, KY 36, 52, 76, 107, 110, 115, 139
Lynch, Judge 70, 108

Mackey, Aeneas 56
Madison, Dolly 155
Madison, James 138, 155, 157
Mahoning Creek 98
Marietta, OH 150, 160
Marquette, Father 9
Martin's Station, KY 108
Maryland 19
Maryland Journal 57
Mason, George 32
Mason, Samuel 62
Mason-Dixon Line 19
Maumee River 44, 107, 150, 162
Maxwell, William 93, 96
McCauley, Nancy 103
McCullough, Sam 141
McDonald, Angus 26
McGary, Hugh 139, 140, 141
McGuffey's Readers 30
McIntosh, Lachlan 74, 76, 77, 85, 86, 87, 88, 91, 97, 161; background 74–75; feud with Morgan 84, 94; later years 94; leads Fort Laurens expeditions 80–83, 89; named to command 73; popularity 83; requests to be relieved 89–90
McKee, Alexander 36, 70, 73, 107, 110, 127, 136
Mercer, Hugh 14
Miami 139
Miami River 44, 107, 127
Middlebrook, NJ 93
Miflin, Thomas 159, 160
Mingo Bottom 135, 136
Mingo Junction, OH 18, 136
Mingo Tribe 17, 54
Mississippi River 33, 52, 66, 67, 106
Mobile, AL 103
Moluntha 141, 153

Monongahela River 9, 50, 80, 157
Monroe, James 155
Montgomery, John 106
Montreal 14, 45
Moore, William 133
Moravians 27, 79, 104, 130; background 45; church services 38; forcibly removed 126; help American cause 63; need for protection 84, 122; postwar activities 135; success of missions 45, 63
Morgan, Daniel 26, 56, 158, 159, 161
Morgan, George 47, 53, 54, 64, 69, 70, 77–78, 79, 81, 85, 92, 93; background 47–48; distrust of military 48, 83–84, 94; later years 94–95; named as Indian Agent 46, resigns 94
Morganza 95
Morris, Lewis 40
Morris, Robert 67
Mount Vernon 14, 32, 163
Murray, John *see* Dunmore, Lord
Muskingum River 26, 27, 87, 150, 153

Napoleon 155
Natchez, MS 62, 67, 101
Netawatwes 54, 78, 79, 84
Neville, John 24, 56, 143, 154; commands Fort Pitt garrison 38, 40; Whiskey Rebellion activities 158–60, 162
Neville, Presley 158, 159
New Jersey 52
New Madrid, MO 95
New Orleans, LA 32, 52, 67, 78, 99–100, 101
New York City, NY 32, 43, 130
Newcomer *see* Netawatwes
Newcomerstown, OH 54, 84
Newtown 99, 143
Niagara Falls 9
Ninth Virginia Regiment *see* West Augusta Regiment
Nonhelema 30 73, 110, 141, 152
Norfolk, VA 42

Ohio Company of Virginia 9, 12
Ohio River 23, 52, 76, 87, 108, 121, 135; course 17, 80; military boats 67, 76, 100, 126–27, 136
Ohneberg, Sarah 104
Ottawa Tribe 92

Paris 156
Penn, John 20

183

Index

Penn, William 17, 54
Pennsylvania 17, 19, 34–35, 100
Pensacola, FL 103
Philadelphia, PA 13, 33, 48, 93, 120, 130; famous residents 154–55; size 6
Philadelphia Society for the Promotion of Agriculture 95
Pickaway Plains 28
Pickering, Timothy 75
Piqua, OH 106
Pittsburgh, PA 18–19, 24, 34, 36, 45, 67, 162; negative descriptions 144, 154, 156–57; slow growth 154
Pittsburgh Gazette 156, 157
Pluggy's Town 39, 64
Point Pleasant, WV 18, 36, 59, 77, 107, 110; Battle of 29; Cornstalk murdered at 65; fort built 49
Pollock, Oliver 52, 67, 68, 100
Pontiac 15, 16, 40, 47, 78
Pontiac's Conspiracy 27, 73, 93, 119, 138
Poor, Enoch 96
Post, Christian Frederick 78
Potomac River 19
Pourre, Eugenio 112
Priestley, Joseph 155
Princeton, NJ 5, 48, 54, 78, 84, 93
Pulaski, Casimir 109

Quakers 20
Quebec 14, 70, 127

Rappahannock River 42
Rattletrap 67
Rebecca 67
Redbank (Henderson), KY 62
Redstone (Brownsville), PA 71, 112
Reed, Joseph 102, 115, 117
Richmond, VA 114
Rittenhouse, David 155
Rogers, David 99, 100, 107
Rose, John 135, 136, 145
Rosenthal, Gustavus de *see* Rose, John
Ross, Betsy 155
Ross, James 35
Royal American Regiment 15
Ruddell's Station 108
Rush, Benjamin 155
Russell, William 56, 58, 72, 73

St. Clair, Arthur 20, 22, 26, 55, 112, 147; leads failed Indian campaign 150–53
St. Clair's Defeat 11, 152
St. Lawrence River 39, 41, 60
St. Louis, MO 47, 103, 105–6, 112
St. Simons Island, GA 75
Salem (Port Washington), OH 104
Samples, Sam 18, 43, 84, 86 93
Sandusky River 101, 116, 117, 126
Sandy Creek 16, 80
Saratoga 5, 7, 56, 71, 72, 97
Savannah, GA 94
Schoenbrunn, OH 27, 104, 128, 135; forced evacuation 121, 126; prosperity 63, 84, 155
Scioto River 29
Seven Years War 11, 25, 128
Sevier, John 26
Shagamba 40
Shawnee Tribe 17, 40, 41, 54, 73, 92; defeated at Point Pleasant 29–30; turns against Americans 65
Shays, Daniel 160
Shelby, Evan 26
Shepard, David 61
Shippen, Dr. 43
Sinclair, Patrick 105
Sixth Virginia Regiment 66
Smallman, Thomas 25
Society of Cincinnati 147
Springer, Uriah 112
Springfield, OH 110
"Squaw Campaign" 69, 70
Stanwix, John 14
Staunton, VA 20, 55, 66
Steiner, Abraham 156
Stephen, Adam 31, 32, 38
Steuben, Baron von 109
Steubenville, OH 18, 150
Stewart's Crossing 121
Stuart, Gilbert 112, 155
Sullivan, John 95, 98, 143
Surplus, Robert 70
Susquehanna River 9, 98

Talleyrand 155
Tarhe 150
Taylor, Richard 86, 87
Taylor, Zachary 87
Tecumseh 78, 110
Thirteenth Virginia regiment *see* West Augusta Regiment
Thwaites, Rueben Gold 1
Tories on the Frontier 69–70, 108
Treaty of Fort Stanwix 17, 21, 48, 49, 77
Treaty of Paris 15, 76, 149
Trent, William 10, 16
Trenton 5, 54

184

Index

Trinity College 58, 128
Tuscarawas River 16, 27, 80, 81, 136, 153

University of Edinburgh 155
University of Pennsylvania 11, 153, 158
University of Pittsburgh 156
Upper Sandusky 136, 150

Valley Forge 66, 73, 75, 76
Vernon, Frederick 89, 103
Vincennes, IN 95, 105, 107, 121; background 76; Clark's capture 7, 71, 76–77, 83, 87, 88, 140; de la Balme at 110, 112
Virginia 9, 19, 21, 34, 35, 100
Virginia Gazette 32

Wabash River 76, 150
Wakotomica 27
Walker, Thomas 41
Wallace, Mrs. 130
War of Jenkins' Ear 75
Washington, George 2–3, **5**, 6–8, 23, 32, 36, 37, 44, 54, 73, 75, 76, 90, 93, 101, 102, 109, 111, 117, 126, 129, 138, 142–44, 147, 151, 153; background 9–10; commander controversy role 120–25; Conway Cabal threat 72, 74; coordinates army departments in Iroquois campaign 91–92, 95–96, 99; French and Indian War service 9–14; growth 127; immaturity 10, 12–13; plans joint federal state campaign 113–16; popularity 161; Whiskey Rebellion and 157, 160–61, 163
Washington, Martha Custis 14, 155
Washington, PA 23, 24, 158
Wayne, Anthony 112, 153, 154, 161, 162
West Augusta District 19, 55
West Augusta Regiment 58, 59, 72, 79, 92; disbanded 144; organized 55–56; reunited 73, 76

West Point 144, 147
Westmoreland County, PA 19
Wetzel, Lewis 97, 141–42
Wheeling, WV 22, 26, 28, 37, 49, 92, 121, 126; attacked 61–63, 141–42
Whiskey Rebellion 3, 7, 160, 162
White Eyes 37, 61, 71, 79, 80, 93, 98, 153; becomes leader of tribe 54; death 81–82; diplomatic work in Dunmore's War 25, 27, 28, 31, 78; plans with Dunmore 32–33, 38, 53; travels of 33, 78; vision 78
Wilkes, John 156
Wilkes-Barre, PA 76
Wilkinson, James 44
Williamsburg, VA 10, 25, 31–33, 35–36, 38, 100
Williamson, David 130, 131, 136, 137
Willing, James 66–68, 100
Wilson, James 35, 40, 160
Wilson, William 53
Winchester, VA 25, 26, 38, 49
Wingenund 137
Wood, James 38, 39, 45, 53
Worthington, Thomas 95
Wyandot Tribe 92
Wyoming Valley 95

Yellow Creek 22
Yellow Creek Massacre 23, 24
York (Wright's Ferry), PA 36, 43, 75
Yorktown 5, 124
Youghiogheny River 10

Zane, Betty 142
Zane, Ebenezer 22, 142
Zeisberger, David 27, 53, 54, 84, 88, 101, 111, 124, 134, 155; background 45; helps American cause 63, 85, 86, 122; later years 135

www.ingramcontent.com/pod-product-compliance
Lightning Source LLC
Chambersburg PA
CBHW032046300426
44117CB00009B/1211